"This outstanding book is the introduction to happiness many of us have been waiting for: Clear and accessible, engaging, and remarkably comprehensive. It covers not just the philosophy of happiness but also the science, economics, and policy side of happiness, as well as practical issues about how to be happier, and includes non-Western approaches as well. It is the single best overview of research on happiness, and I strongly recommend it both for the classroom and for researchers wanting to learn more about the field, as well as anyone wishing to understand the state of the art in thinking about happiness."

Daniel M. Haybron, *Saint Louis University*

"An engaging and wide-ranging introduction to the study of happiness. The book's perspective is philosophical, and it would be an excellent choice for philosophy courses in ethics or happiness itself. The philosophy here is enriched by well-informed discussions of research in psychology, neuroscience, and economics, which makes it a very fine choice for courses in any field where there is an interest in a philosopher's take on happiness. Indeed, anyone with an interest in happiness—whether or not they are teaching or taking a course—would profit from reading this book. Highly recommended!"

Valerie Tiberius, *University of Minnesota*

THE PHILOSOPHY
OF HAPPINESS

Emerging research on the subject of happiness—in psychology, economics, and public policy—reawakens and breathes new life into long-standing philosophical questions about happiness (e.g., What is it? Can it really be measured or pursued? What is its relationship to morality?). By analyzing this research from a philosophical perspective, Lorraine L. Besser is able to weave together the contributions of other disciplines, and the result is a robust, deeply contoured understanding of happiness made accessible for nonspecialists. This book is the first to thoroughly investigate the fundamental theoretical issues at play in all the major contemporary debates about happiness, and it stands out especially in its critical analysis of empirical research. The book's coverage of the material is comprehensive without being overwhelming. Its structure and pedagogical features will benefit students or anyone studying happiness for the first time: Each chapter opens with an initial overview and ends with a summary and list of suggested readings.

Lorraine L. Besser is Professor of Philosophy at Middlebury College. She has published widely on moral psychology, well-being, and virtue ethics, and is the author of *Eudaimonic Ethics: The Philosophy and Psychology of Living Well* (2014) and coeditor of *The Routledge Companion to Virtue Ethics* (2015).

THE PHILOSOPHY OF HAPPINESS

An Interdisciplinary Introduction

Lorraine L. Besser

Routledge
Taylor & Francis Group

NEW YORK AND LONDON

First published 2021
by Routledge
52 Vanderbilt Avenue, New York, NY 10017

and by Routledge
2 Park Square, Milton Park, Abingdon, Oxon, OX14 4RN

Routledge is an imprint of the Taylor & Francis Group, an informa business

© 2021 Taylor & Francis

Library of Congress Cataloging-in-Publication Data
A catalog record for this title has been requested

ISBN: 978-1-138-24044-5 (hbk)
ISBN: 978-1-138-24045-2 (pbk)
ISBN: 978-1-315-28369-2 (ebk)

Typeset in Bembo
by KnowledgeWorks Global Ltd.

CONTENTS

PREFACE

In writing this interdisciplinary introduction to the philosophy of happiness, I've sought to explore happiness from almost every possible angle, all the while keeping the discussion accessible and focusing on the central themes, research, and theories that have come to define the study of happiness. My approach starts with philosophy and extends to other disciplines—including psychology, economics, neuroscience, and public policy—to deepen and enrich our overall understanding of happiness.

This interdisciplinary approach reflects how happiness is presently studied. While researchers may have a home in one discipline (my home is philosophy), for the most part, we are all interested in the same thing: Understanding what happiness is, what we can learn about it and how, and what we can do with this information. Given this shared interest in a subject that crosses over so many different fields, academic work on happiness is, for the most part, interdisciplinary. Psychologists are talking about Aristotle and Mill, philosophers are talking about biases and introspective capacities, neuroscientists are talking to Buddhist monks, economists are talking about psychological research on behavior, and policy makers are talking about the philosophical positions of paternalism. Interdisciplinary research teams are becoming increasingly common as these conversations evolve. The interdisciplinary nature of this book follows these conversations and tracks the implications they have for the overall study of happiness. Within this book, I examine the central developments happening within these conversations and the research and theories they have given rise to. By analyzing how it is that the particular contributions of each field or line of research informs the contributions of others, we can begin to develop a greater understanding of the whole of happiness.

During the time I've been working on this book, my running joke has been about how writing a book on happiness is a surefire way to become unhappy. This is really only partly true. One thing we'll learn about happiness is that there is a difference between feeling happy and being happy. Writing a book about happiness generates lots of good feelings. And lots of bad feelings. But the project of learning, thinking, and writing about happiness is no doubt one of the most important things I've done.

My efforts to think about happiness have been helped immensely through many conversations with colleagues and students. I'm thankful to my students at Middlebury College for working through much of this material with me and for holding me to high standards of clarity and rigor. I'm thankful to my colleagues across the world whose work on happiness and well-being I've learned so much from, including Anna Alexandrova, Erik Angner, Ben Bramble, Michael Bishop, Dale Dorsey, Dan Haybron, Eden Lin, Shigehiro Oishi, Jason Raibley, and Valerie Tiberius.

Without my friends and family, I'd struggle to even begin to understand what happiness feels like. I'm grateful for the support of my husband, Jody Swearingen, with whom life is never boring and who always encourages me to keep perspective on what counts. And he's almost always right about what counts. I could have saved myself a lot of research by listening to him. While most research shows that children are not a source of happiness, mine really often are, and I could not be more grateful for them, the richness they've brought to my life, and the adventures we've had together. Thank you, Beck and Kagen, Sully and Dylann. Furry children deserve a shout-out in a book on happiness too, and they are indeed a source of happiness. Thank you to Ruby, Luna, and Axel for their companionship and patience while I've been working on this project, and to Roxanne and Rowan for keeping my chair warm.

Some chapters draw on previously published material. Chapters 7 and 8 draw on *Eudaimonic Ethics: The Philosophy and Psychology of Living Well* (Routledge 2014), and Chapter 11 draws on my 2013 work "The Pursuit and Nature of Happiness," *Philosophical Topics, 41*(1), 103–122. I'm grateful for the permission to include this material. Finally, my deepest thanks go out to the team at Routledge Press for their hard work on this project, and especially to my editor, Andrew Beck, for his patience and support.

Introduction

1

INTRODUCTION: THE HISTORY OF HAPPINESS

Happiness is one of the most important things in life. For many of us, it serves as the bottom line: At the end of the day, we just want to be happy. We want this for ourselves, for our family, for our friends. And while we recognize that happiness may not be the only thing that matters, we would be hard-pressed to find someone who genuinely believes happiness to be irrelevant. Indeed, if we ever came across such a person, we'd be deeply confused and likely worried about this person: Who wouldn't think that happiness is a good thing?

Despite widespread agreement that happiness is important, for most of us the concept of "happiness" is a mystery. Sometimes we think about it a lot. We think about it in our deliberations. Will this job make me happy? Will choosing this person as my life partner make me happy? Will eating that chocolate cupcake make me happy? We also think about it in those reflective moments, when we ask, "Am I happy?" The reality is that rarely do we find these deliberations or reflective moments to be fruitful. It is hard to know whether a new job will make you happy; it is even hard to determine whether you are happy in any given moment. There are a range of factors that makes answering these questions challenging, which we will discuss over the course of this book. But one of the most central obstacles seems to be that most of us probably don't know what happiness really is.

Happiness is an important yet fundamentally mysterious concept. It is unsurprising, then, that philosophers have been interested in studying happiness for as long as we have records of philosophy, and that today, what was once fundamentally a philosophical question ("What is happiness?") is one that not only philosophers but also psychologists, economists, even neuroscientists seek to answer. This book will explore the interdisciplinary nature of the study of happiness from within an overarching philosophical perspective. This book will not reveal the one truth about happiness, but it will discuss the variety of ways philosophers have understood happiness and the empirical research regarding the causes and correlates of happiness that has come to inform economic analysis and policy-making. We'll see lines of overlapping thought that help to explain the contours of happiness, and we will see some of the difficulties and challenges involved in studying happiness on both theoretical and empirical levels. We'll also see the potential this work has to inform our decision-making, whether at the individual or policy level.

This introductory chapter briefly covers some of the central historical themes in the study of happiness as a means to set the stage for the contemporary debates and positions that are the focus of this book.

Ancient Greek Philosophy

The works of Plato (381 B.C.E.) and Aristotle (340 B.C.E.) have had a deep and long-lasting influence on Western philosophy, and Aristotle's views on happiness in particular have shaped contemporary research and theories of happiness. Both of these philosophers took happiness to be broad and inclusive. They believed happiness is an all-encompassing feature of our lives; it is that for the sake of which we do all other things. They each offered views of happiness that frame happiness as something that arises when all aspects of oneself are functioning and making the contributions they were designed to make.

Plato frames his view of happiness in terms of "psychic harmony." In the *Republic*, he develops this view by first arguing against the popular opinion that the best way to live is to embrace our appetites and desires. He imagines a character, Glaucon, who seeks to advance his own interests. Like many people, Glaucon believes that happiness arises in proportion to self-interest and that the best way to become happy is to pursue one's desires and appetites at all costs. Plato thinks Glaucon is wrong, and his challenge to this line of thinking has made a lasting impression.

Plato encourages us to consider the kinds of internal conflicts that arise when we prioritize the pursuit of our appetites and desires above other considerations—conflicts that Plato thinks prevent us from being happy. Most of us are familiar with the kind of internal conflict Plato worries about: It arises when we break a friend's trust to satisfy our own ambitions, when we cut corners for our own benefit, and when we break the law to pursue a desire. Even if we don't get "caught" doing any of these things, making the choice to prioritize our own desires and appetites over other things we believe to be important makes us feel bad.

Plato argues that internal conflict arises when the various components of our natures aren't working in harmony. For example, if people fulfill their desires for material goods by breaking the law, they end up ignoring their rational sides, which tell them that laws function as important protective measures to ensure the well-being of all in their jurisdiction. In this case, internal conflict arises because their appetites stifle the directives of reason.

According to Plato, there are three components of our nature (or, as is sometimes interpreted, of our soul): The *appetitive* side, which involves physical-based desires for food, drink, sex, and so on; the *spirited* side, which Plato associates primarily with anger and the desires it gives rise to; and the *rational* side, which involves beliefs and desires that arise from those beliefs. Most important among the beliefs and desires that comprise our rational side are the beliefs we have about what is right and wrong, beliefs that on Plato's account give rise to desires to do what is right and avoid what is wrong.

Plato believes that these parts exist within a natural hierarchy wherein the rational side governs the other. Reason tempers the spirit and directs the appetite, and it does this naturally. While internal conflict arises when people fail to respect the natural hierarchy, psychic harmony arises when the rational side does in fact govern the other sides. Plato describes this state as follows:[1]

> One who is just does not allow any part of himself to do the work of another part or allow the various classes within him to meddle with each other. He regulates well what is really his own and rules himself. He puts himself in order, is his own friend, and harmonizes the three parts of himself like the three limiting notes in a musical scale—high, low, and middle. He brings together these parts and any others there may be in between, and from having been many things he becomes entirely one, moderate and harmonious. (Plato, 381 B.C.E., sec. 443c-e)

We become happy by knowing and respecting our natures and allowing our rationality to bring our spirited and appetitive sides into balance.

Aristotle, a student of Plato, follows the same basic framework as Plato in analyzing happiness. He begins by thinking about human nature and defines happiness broadly in terms of human nature functioning as it should. While Aristotle moves away from Plato's tripartite analysis of human nature, he embraces Plato's prioritization of reason, and our rationality, as the distinctive and authoritative aspect of human nature that shapes what it means for us to be happy.

Why should we prioritize reason? Aristotle's argument is relatively straightforward:[2] Happiness, which he called *eudaimonia*, is the highest good for human beings and so ought to reflect what is distinctive about human beings. Since human beings are distinguished by their capacity to use reason, the highest good for human beings is to use reason in the best possible way. For Aristotle, this means using reason to develop and exercise the virtues, which are dispositions to think, feel, and respond in ways appropriate to the situation. A virtuous person develops the practical wisdom to know what to do and when to do it, and she successfully regulates her emotional states so that she feels the emotions that are appropriate to the situation and conducive to the exercise of virtue. Her development and exercise of virtue allow her to flourish as a human being.

We see that both Plato and Aristotle maintain that there is a fundamental, necessary connection between being virtuous and being happy: One can't be happy without being virtuous and vice versa. This is a bold thesis that has generated lots of debate among contemporary scholars, and it is one that we will return to at several junctures in this book. Is virtue really necessary to happiness? Taken in one light, this is an empirical question. Aristotle and Plato did not have the benefit of contemporary scientific methods, but we do; as we will see in chapters to come, empirical research on happiness and its causes and correlates provides important insight into the nature of happiness and has shaped contemporary discussion of it. Viewed in another light, this is not a purely empirical question but is rather a question of how we *ought* to understand happiness itself. If "happiness" is our highest good, as Plato and Aristotle take it to be, then it makes sense that it ought to involve reason and virtue. But is happiness really our *highest* good, or is it simply a prudential good that most of us value? Many contemporary philosophers think we should understand our highest good in terms of *well-being* rather than *happiness*. We'll sort through these differences in Chapter 2.

Writing shortly after Aristotle, Epicurus (325 B.C.E.) presents a view of happiness that more closely resembles popular usage of the word "happiness." Happiness, for Epicurus, consists in a life of pleasure. This is a view of hedonism, variations of which are prominent in contemporary literature and are the subject of Chapter 3. Hedonistic views of happiness define happiness in terms of pleasure and are differentiated by their particular interpretation of pleasure.

Epicurus takes pleasure to consist in the absence of pain. This leads him to develop a view of hedonism that ends up being more moderate than we might expect. Since pleasure is the absence of pain, the key to happiness is to eliminate sources of pain. We do this by learning as much as we can about the things that give us fear, anxiety, and frustration, and by using this knowledge to moderate our emotional reactions. His four-part "cure" to unhappiness provides a helpful snapshot of this approach:

1. Don't fear the gods.
2. Don't worry about death.
3. What is good is easy to get.
4. What is terrible is easy to endure. (Epicurus, 325 B.C.E., p. vi)

The basic state of happiness that Epicurus describes takes happiness to be a state of mind, and one that does not fundamentally depend on the exercise of reason in the ways in which Aristotle's and Plato's views do. Using reason and being virtuous are important components of the happy life for Epicurus, but rationality and virtue don't define happiness for Epicurus in the ways they do for Aristotle and Plato.

Modern British Philosophy

Philosophical discussion of happiness takes an important turn with the works of British philosophers Jeremy Bentham (1789) and John Stuart Mill (1861). Bentham and Mill follow Epicurus in taking happiness to consist in a state of pleasure, and they develop hedonistic views of happiness differentiated by their specific analyses of pleasure. Yet Bentham and Mill highlight the social and ethical importance of happiness. They recognize that happiness isn't just something we should think about and pursue for ourselves; its importance to each of us entails that we should prioritize the happiness of all. This line of thought motivates the position of utilitarianism, the view according to which we should strive to promote the greatest happiness for all. Bentham argues that utilitarianism ought to drive our legal system, while Mill argues that utilitarianism ought to drive our personal morality. Both defenses of utilitarianism have had a long-lasting influence on moral philosophy and shape contemporary discussions of hedonism.

Bentham (1823) wrote with the aim of reforming the legal system. He argues that laws ought to be gauged by their tendency to promote happiness, which he takes to consist in pleasure and the avoidance of pain. In order to evaluate the laws, then, we need to figure out the extent to which they promote the happiness of all. Bentham advocates doing this by thinking through the expected consequences of any law (or act) and examining the degree of pleasure reasonably expected to follow. To examine the pleasure, Bentham proposes what has come to be called a "hedonic" or "felicific" calculus, which evaluates pleasure by its:

- Intensity,
- Duration,
- Certainty or uncertainty,
- Propinquity,
- Remoteness,
- Fecundity,
- Purity.

Bentham recognizes that the calculus runs differently depending on whether we are considering an individual's happiness or a group of people's happiness, but the basic idea is to give some content into the dimensions of pleasure, which make it better or worse.

Bentham was ambitious both in presenting happiness as the standard for public policy and in making an effort to measure happiness. It is hard to measure happiness. Happiness is a subjective mental state. Even if we follow Bentham in understanding that state exclusively in terms of pleasure, and embrace the hedonic calculus, measuring happiness still requires the daunting task of thinking about how people will respond to the proposed source of pleasure. Bentham does this by thinking through the commonalities that exist between individuals. This approach can go a long way, but it is limited. Contemporary empirical research teaches us that individual differences exist and count, and this is especially the case when thinking about happiness, which is a subjective mental state. This doesn't mean that the task of measuring happiness is pointless but that it is a difficult one. We'll explore the challenges currently facing efforts to measure happiness in Chapter 12, where we will see the importance of looking at long-term data but also the difficulties involved in procuring and analyzing that data.

Perhaps anticipating the challenges of using utilitarianism in the context of public policy, Bentham's follower John Stuart Mill steers the focus of utilitarianism back to the individual level and presents what has come to be regarded as a definitive statement of utilitarianism as a moral theory. Mill argues we should understand "right" and "wrong" solely in terms of an act's tendency to produce happiness, or its opposite, which he took to be pain: "By happiness is intended pleasure and the absence of pain; by unhappiness, pain and the privation of pleasure" (Mill, 1861, Chapter 2).

While Mill endorses hedonism, he also worries that hedonism is misunderstood. Its focus on pleasure misleadingly gives rise to the impression—as is common with contemporary popular usages of the word "hedonism"—that a life devoted to happiness would be one engulfed in sensory pleasures: Eating, drinking, having sex, and so on. Mill thinks these sensory pleasures are important but that there are other kinds of pleasures available to human beings. Human beings have intellectual capacities that open up to them different sources of pleasure, such as the pleasure of reading a novel. These intellectual pleasures, he argues, are of a higher quality than sensory pleasures. Both are still forms of pleasure and so good, but given a choice, we should choose higher-quality, intellectual pleasures—even in less quantities—over sensory pleasures.

Mill's emphasis on considering the quality of pleasures in addition to their quantity presents a broader understanding of pleasure that many have found attractive. His suggestion that pleasure derives from intellectual capacities in addition to physical sources validates the kind of pleasure that we do seem to take in reading a good novel, engaging in intellectual debate, watching films, and so forth. But others worry that this broadening of pleasure ends up diluting the theory: The pleasures that come from sensory sources *feel* different than what comes from intellectual sources. The appeal of hedonism seems to derive from our recognition of the prudential value of *feeling pleasure*; each step we move away from this initial point threatens the appeal of hedonism itself.

This is very much a live debate. Mill's analysis of pleasure has opened the door for many fruitful discussions on the nature of pleasure, and contemporary defenders of hedonism often follow in Mill's footsteps, encouraging us to look beyond physical pleasures and to conceive of pleasure broadly. We'll consider many of these views in Chapter 3.

Asian Philosophy

Happiness is frequently discussed within Asian philosophy, and it finds its historical roots within Hinduism, Buddhism, and Confucianism. These philosophies are deeply informed by metaphysical views regarding the relationship between one's self and the world at large, views that influence significantly their understanding of happiness. Whereas Western philosophers historically have tended to think about happiness in terms of the development of one's self as it is located within the physical world, Asian philosophers tend to advocate releasing oneself from one's individuality and especially from one's bodily presence. Happiness for these philosophers derives from understanding one's connection to others and to the world at large and responding appropriately to this understanding.

Hinduism, for example, prioritizes coming to understand and embrace one's nonmaterial self, described as the "atman." Atman is seen to be one's true, eternal self and is distinguished sharply from one's physical body, which is taken to give rise to a false or egoistic sense of self. Hindus argue that understanding and prioritizing the eternal self puts one on the path toward a state of bliss ("ananda").

In some respects, this de-emphasis of the physical self parallels the ancient Greek philosopher's emphasis on regulating one's bodily desires and dependent emotional states through the use of reason. However, the motivation behind Hinduism's de-emphasis of the physical body is importantly different than it was for the ancient Greek philosophers. Hinduism holds that focusing on the physical body interferes with one's capacity to identify with the spiritual world. Happiness—described here in terms of bliss—depends on freeing the eternal self from the physical self and coming to develop a higher form of consciousness that sees one's eternal self as united with the universal spirit.

We find a similar emphasis on the spiritual aspect of the self within Buddhist philosophy. The physical body gives rise to cravings and aversions that interfere with our capacity to attain enlightenment and to live happily. The more we seek physical pleasures, the more cravings and aversions we generate, establishing patterns that lead us to focus too heavily on the fleeting and impermanent things happening in this world. But we can learn not to react to cravings and aversions, and in time we can come to distance ourselves from bodily needs. This allows us to focus on what *is* important, which is recognizing the truths about the world and our place in it, such as coming to learn that all aspects of the phenomenal world are impermanent and subject to change. They are also interdependent and lacking an essence of intrinsic nature. Learning these features about the world we experience helps us reorient ourselves to it and lessen (or extinguish) the degree of suffering that inevitably arises when we take things to be not as they are.

The central tenets of Buddhist philosophy are often described in terms of "four noble truths":

1. The truth of Suffering: All life is marked by suffering; it is the condition of all sentient beings.
2. The truth of the Causes of Suffering: The primary causes of suffering are attachments and aversions.
3. The truth of the End of Suffering: We can reduce and even eliminate suffering by changing how we think about things so that we don't become attached to phenomena and don't develop cravings with respect to them.
4. The truth of the Path that leads to the End of Suffering. The eightfold path involves developing and leading a virtuous life, marked by the right understanding, right resolve, right speech, right action, right livelihood, right effort, right mindfulness, and right meditation.

We see that essential to enlightenment is recognizing our connections to others and the inevitable suffering that inflicts all sentient beings. Buddhism maintains that reflection on these considerations helps motivate people to reduce the suffering of others and to bring peace and happiness to others and that doing so puts people on the path to enlightenment. The general picture of happiness we see here is one that frames happiness as something that evolves through caring about others, making others happy, and promoting peace and harmony more generally.

Buddhist traditions and meditation practices are often discussed within contemporary Western discussions of happiness. Mindfulness meditation practices, derived from Buddhism, are becoming increasingly well known as powerful tools to enable individuals to reduce stress and to develop a state of equanimity that can help them deal with what life throws at them. While contemporary Western conceptions of happiness have not taken the full route of rejecting the body and its associated individualistic notion of self, much important work is being done to bring the central insights of Buddhism into our discussions of the nature and pursuit of happiness.

Confucian philosophy provides another important historical framework for understanding happiness, and the last we will consider here. Confucianism focuses heavily on understanding the social roles each of us occupy and emphasizes the importance of the rituals surrounding these social roles. Where everyone is appreciative of their roles and the importance of fulfilling them to the larger unit of which they are a part (such as the family unit or humanity itself), they develop a state of harmony with others, and it is within this state of harmony that individuals develop happiness.

In some respects, Confucianism is eudaimonistic insofar as it emphasizes self-cultivation and the development of social virtues that enable individuals to live in harmony. Becoming virtuous is, for Confucius as well as Aristotle, central to the development of happiness. Yet while Aristotle holds that the development of virtues is important insofar as it allows us to function most fully as a rational human being, Confucius emphasizes the development of virtues as a means toward establishing social harmony and promoting the harmonious lives of all.

These are very broad strokes and do not do justice to the complexities of these views nor the differences between subschools within the philosophies themselves, but we do see that each of these Asian philosophies advocates a view of happiness that frames happiness as a kind of peace of mind: A mental state that is nonreactive, especially to bodily inputs, and that is transcendent insofar as it depends on some kind of understanding of the connection between oneself and those around one. As we learn more about the neural bases of happiness, we find increasing evidence that developing this kind of mindset is pivotal to the experience of happiness, and we'll return to this theme in detail in Chapter 9.

Conclusion

The topic of happiness has fascinated philosophers for centuries. Historical discussions of happiness focus on themes and challenges that contemporary researchers continue to struggle with: What is the connection between pleasure and happiness or virtue and happiness? How does satisfying appetites and desires contribute to our happiness? Are there certain ways of thinking about our place in the world that are more conducive to happiness?

As we turn to discuss these questions and others from a contemporary perspective, we'll see the wealth of resources generated through the study of happiness from across disciplines and the ways in which we can use these resources to inform our philosophical understanding of happiness and to develop a richer analysis of the central questions at stake. One of the most important developments in the study of happiness is confidence in our ability to measure and study happiness and its correlates using scientific methods. While by no means a perfect science, researchers already have amassed a lot of data about our experiences of happiness. A central aim of this book is to analyze this data from a philosophical perspective and to explore its implications for how we understand happiness, how we can continue to study and measure happiness, and how we might be able to promote happiness for ourselves and others.

Overview of the Book

This book will cover happiness from a predominantly Western, contemporary perspective. But I hope that through this very preliminary overview of the leading historical views of happiness, we can begin to see just how important and rich a topic we have, one that has long had a legitimate prominent place in historical discourse from around the world. The following chapters of this book explore happiness from many different perspectives. We'll consider the central philosophical questions that arise with respect to understanding happiness, but the book reaches out beyond the philosophy of happiness to consider pressing questions regarding the psychology and economics of happiness, its role in public policy, and some of the challenges that face the interdisciplinary study of happiness.

Part I of the book, "Theory," explores the leading philosophical theories of what happiness is. It begins by considering the difference between happiness and well-being and then considers the philosophical theories of hedonism, the emotional state theory, and satisfaction theories of happiness. Part I will be of particular interest to students of philosophy and to those working in other disciplines who are interested in learning more about how happiness is understood and discussed within a philosophical perspective.

Part II of the book, "What makes us happy?", takes a more interdisciplinary focus and examines the kinds of things that are correlated with happiness. Specific chapters consider the connections between happiness and virtue, wealth, and relationships, taking into account both philosophical arguments and empirical research on these correlations. Other chapters tackle whether (and why) certain emotional states are correlated with happiness, whether or not happiness is something that can be pursued, and finally, whether or not it matters whether happiness arises from a place of authenticity. Part II will be of interest to anyone interested in learning more about how, when, and why happiness arises at the individual level. The interdisciplinary discussions within are suitable for all backgrounds. Those readers who are particularly interested in the scientific study of happiness may find it helpful to read Chapter 12, "The Science of Happiness," which explores challenges that arise in the context of researching happiness on a scientific level, before tackling Part II.

Part III, "The Context of Happiness," explores the influence happiness research has had within the fields of psychology, economics, and public policy as well as the difficulties in conducting empirical research on happiness. We'll see that the impact happiness research has had on these fields is dramatic but that it is also a line of research that is very much still in its nascent stages. Part III will be of particular interest to those working within these fields and more generally to those interested in the potential happiness research has to change how we think about ourselves, our economic decisions, and the priorities we attach to public policies.

By the end of this book, you will have a good feel not only for philosophical views of happiness but also for the central debates that arise from interdisciplinary work on happiness. My hope is that this book will serve not just to help you develop a better understanding of this important topic but also as a stepping-stone to further research and engagement with the topic. We all value and cherish happiness. It is time to get serious in figuring out what happiness is, how to study it, and how to enhance our and others' happiness.

End Notes

1 Plato describes this in terms of "justice," but from a contemporary vantage point, it is clear that the state of psychic harmony he describes is a distinctive form of human happiness.
2 We'll explore the complicating factors of this position in Chapter 2.

References

Aristotle. (340 B.C.E.). *Nicomachean ethics.* (R. Crisp, Ed.). Cambridge, UK: Cambridge University Press.

Bentham, J. (1823). *An introduction to the principles of morals and legislation.* Amherst, NY: Prometheus Books.

Epicurus. (325 B.C.E.). *The Epicurus reader selected writings and testimonia* (L. P. Gerson & B. Inwood, Eds.). Indianapolis, IN: Hackett Publishing.

Mill, J. S. (1861). *Utilitarianism* (G. Sher, Ed.; 2nd ed.). Indianapolis, IN: Hackett Publishing.

Plato. (381 B.C.E.). *Plato: Republic* (C. D. C. Reeve, Ed.). Indianapolis, IN: Hackett Publishing.

PART I
Theory

2

HAPPINESS AND WELL-BEING

Happiness and well-being share much in common. They are both prudential values, which means that they are both states that are valuable to their possessor. They are both states that we want and that we believe will make our lives go better. Perhaps because of these similarities, the terms "happiness" and "well-being" are often treated as synonyms. This is true of everyday discourse and often of academic discussion. Some of the earliest discussions of happiness and well-being took the two to be the same. Aristotle's *Nicomachean Ethics* is premised on the notion that there is one prudential value, our highest end—what he called *eudaimonia*—and whether he meant this highest end to be a form of happiness or well-being is a question still under debate.

Increasingly, though, there is recognition that "happiness" and "well-being" track different states, perhaps even to the extent that one can be happy yet not have well-being or vice versa. This chapter explores the connections between happiness and well-being, primarily as a means to develop a better understanding of our topic—happiness. We'll do this by first considering the most prominent theories of well-being within contemporary discussion and then considering some reasons we might have for thinking happiness is different than these forms of well-being and from well-being in general.

Eudaimonism: Philosophical and Psychological

Aristotle describes the supreme good, that which we all seek, in terms of the Greek word "eudaimonia." For many years, "eudaimonia" was translated as "happiness," although increasingly philosophers take eudaimonia to refer to a form of well-being focused on flourishing.[1]

Aristotle develops his analysis of eudaimonia through reflection on what he took to be the distinctive function of human beings, which is to use our rationality. The best use of our rationality, he argues, is to use reason to regulate our emotional states through the development and exercise of virtues. Virtues, such as temperance, generosity, and courage, are dispositions to think, feel, and respond in ways appropriate to the situation. He thus argues that "the human good turns out to be activity of the soul in accordance with virtue, and if there are several virtues, in accordance with the best and most complete" (Aristotle, 2014, secs. 1098a15-19). We flourish and experience eudaimonia through developing the practical wisdom to know when and how to do our best and by using this wisdom to actively exercise virtue.

Within contemporary philosophy, eudaimonism represents a particular way of thinking about how to live motivated by the Aristotelian notion that living well involves *flourishing as a human being*. Given eudaimonism's emphasis on flourishing, psychologists are becoming increasingly interested in studying eudaimonism. Their approaches are influenced by Aristotle's conception of eudaimonia,[2] but psychological conceptions of eudaimonism differ in significant ways from most philosophical treatments of eudaimonia.

First, while philosophers are in relative agreement that eudaimonia consists in the development of our natures, and that virtue is an important aspect of this, psychologists vary in their basic descriptions of eudaimonia. Some describe eudaimonism in terms of a process of living well, where living well involves satisfying innate psychological needs (Ryan, Huta, & Deci, 2008). Others describe eudaimonia in terms of personal expressiveness (Waterman, 1990a), while others describe it in terms of fulfilling one's potential (Ryff & Singer, 1998), and others describe it in terms of a meaningful life (Steger, 2012).

Second, the emphasis on practical reasoning that has come to define philosophical views of eudaimonia is often missing from psychological conceptions. As the descriptions above suggest, most psychological views of eudaimonia do not mention explicitly the use of reason within their conceptions of eudaimonia.

Third, whereas philosophical accounts of eudaimonia tend to understand eudaimonia in terms of what it means for a *human being* to flourish, psychological accounts show more of a tendency to understand eudaimonia in terms of what it means for an *individual* to flourish. The philosophical focus on flourishing qua human being is one reason why, for the Aristotelian, what is most important is development of the rational capacities we have by virtue of being human.

While these differences between the philosophical and psychological analyses of eudaimonia are significant, there are two unifying threads that help isolate what, in the end, really captures a theory as "eudaimonistic." Both suggest that eudaimonia may be best understood as a theory of well-being rather than happiness. The first theme is that eudaimonism describes an ongoing way of living well—it is a *process* of living well as opposed to the *outcome* of living well. Eudaimonistic views focus on activities and the importance of engaging in them. Mark LeBar makes this point in terms of the difference between being an agent, one who *does* things, and being a patient, one who *receives* things. Eudaimonia is an agentist form of well-being insofar as it "emphasizes that our lives go well for us in virtue of *what we do*, rather than *what happens*" (LeBar, 2013, p. 69; emphasis added).

The second theme is that eudaimonia describes an objective form of well-being. On both philosophical and most psychological views of eudaimonia,[3] whether or not an agent experiences eudaimonia depends on whether or not she engages in activities that make the best use of her capacities, fulfill her needs, demonstrate virtue, and so forth. It does not depend on whether or not she thinks she has well-being, and—counterintuitively—it doesn't depend on whether or not she feels good.[4] This isn't to say that subjective feelings are not important to eudaimonia, or that a eudaimonic life won't generate good feelings, but just that they aren't the goal and so aren't themselves part of eudaimonia.

These two components of eudaimonism—its commitment to seeing living well in terms of an active process that exercises agency and its objectivity—are enough to convince most people that eudaimonism is distinct from happiness—at least from how happiness is ordinarily understood. Everyday conceptions of happiness take happiness to consist in some kind of mental state that feels good; these subjective feelings are constitutive of happiness. We wouldn't call someone happy if he didn't report good feelings. We might, however, describe his life as eudaimonic, provided that his life involved the active use of agency in the manner specified by eudaimonism.

Objective List Theories

A very different way of thinking about well-being is to think not about what it means to function well but rather about what kinds of things comprise a good life. Defenders of objective list theories of well-being argue that well-being consists in a life full of certain objectively valuable goods and that we are better off insofar as we obtain them.

The intuitive appeal of objective list theories is clear: When we think about what we want for ourselves and our loved ones, a range of things comes to mind. We want a life full of friendship, health, achievement, aesthetic pleasure, knowledge, and so on. These things stand out as objectively valuable—that is, as things that make our lives go better regardless of who "we" are. Moreover, these things seem to be disparate. There is no one overarching value that they share. Commonly, items are identified for inclusion on an objective list by their intuitive appeal: Will a life be better with knowledge? If yes, then this warrants including knowledge as an element of well-being.[5]

Most defenders of objective list theories emphasize the importance of achievement, knowledge, friendship, and pleasure to well-being. Some theories emphasize also autonomy, health, aesthetic appreciation or beauty, and happiness. (Notice that happiness is included here as one *element* of well-being.) More controversial is whether or not moral goodness or virtue ought to be included on the list: While, for example, virtue has a place in Guy Fletcher's theory (Fletcher, 2013), Brad Hooker argues that leading a morally good life is not a distinctive element of well-being, although he thinks doing so is an important part of obtaining other elements, such as friendship, achievement, or knowledge (Hooker, 2015). This is a clear point of departure from eudaimonism, which holds that exercising virtue is a necessary component of well-being.

Because the items on the objective list theory are included on the basis of their objective value, its resulting theory of well-being is also objective: We can read off someone's well-being based on the degree to which her life includes the objectively valuable items without further exploring whether or not she desires those things, or whether or not their presence makes her happy, or whether or not she thinks her life is better off in virtue of them.[6] The objectivity inherent to the objective list approach highlights that its conception of well-being differs significantly from most conceptions of happiness. We see this through consideration of two objections some have raised against the objective list theory.

The first objection concerns whether or not the objective list theories present "elitist" conceptions of well-being. As we've seen, central to the development of an objective list theory is to identify certain items that are objectively valuable and so good for someone. This involves making a judgment about what will make someone's life better. Yet, because it is grounded in an account of the objective value of an item, this judgment very well might depart from that person's own judgment about what makes his life better. Given the potential for this kind of disparity, some worry this gives rise to the impression that objective theories are elitist—prescribing "the best life possible" without taking into account the individual's particular situation.

The second objection presses a similar concern regarding the potential for disparity between the theory's assessment of what makes a person's life good and the individual's own assessment. Wherever there is the potential for this disparity, worries of alienation inevitably arise. Within philosophy, "alienation" describes situations in which there is a problematic separation between the subject and something that is or ought to be connected to her, such as her identity, her labor, and her well-being. In this context, the worry is that the ways in which the objective list theory define well-being open up the possibility that an individual might feel alienated from her own well-being. For instance, an objective list theory may specify the importance of aesthetic value or appreciation to one's well-being. Yet, we can imagine an individual who doesn't feel the importance of aesthetic value. If this is the case, he might, upon embracing the objective list theory's account of what makes his life better, feel distanced from his own well-being. He knows that aesthetic appreciation is an important part of well-being, but because he doesn't identify with it as a value, he may feel disconnected and alienated.

These kinds of disparities are indicative of the differences between well-being and happiness. Happiness seems to track an individual's mental state and to be very wrapped up in what an individual desires and how she feels about how her life is going. Objective list theories present an objective account of well-being that seems clearly distinguishable from happiness.

Desire-Fulfillment Theories

In comparison with objective list theories, desire-fulfillment theories take an opposing approach toward understanding well-being. Rather than stipulating well-being in terms of items seen to be objectively valuable, desire-fulfillment theories hold that well-being consists entirely in the fulfillment of one's desires. The content of an individual's well-being is dependent on the particular desires she has and whether or not her desires are fulfilled. What we see here is a reversal of the attitude independence that is essential to an objective list theory's evaluation of valuable aspects of one's life. Whereas objective list theories work from an intuitive conception of what, in general, will make a person's life go well, desire-fulfillment theories hold that a person's life goes well when his specific desires are fulfilled.[7] Desire-fulfillment theories present a more subjective form of well-being that more closely approximates happiness. We'll consider desire fulfillment as a theory of well-being here and then return to the question of how desire fulfillment fits into happiness in Chapter 5.

Desire-fulfillment theories present a theory of well-being that is subjective insofar as an individual's well-being depends on fulfilling her specific desires. Importantly, however, desire-fulfillment theory does not depend on an individual's subjective appraisal of her life or her appreciation that her desires are fulfilled. That is, what matters for these theories is that an individual's desires are fulfilled and not that she experiences a sense of satisfaction in light of the fact that her desires are fulfilled. These kinds of feelings naturally derive from desire fulfillment, but defenders of desire-fulfillment theories maintain they are not necessary for well-being. Well-being is entirely a matter of whether someone's desires are fulfilled.

The appeal of the desire-fulfillment theory is straightforward: We can all agree that our lives tend to go better when our desires are fulfilled rather than frustrated. If Andre desires a healthy, loving relationship and that desire is fulfilled, his life is certainly better off. If he also desires a comfortable level of financial security and that desire is fulfilled, his life is, again, clearly better off. But things get more complicated when we think about some of the messier desires we have, whose fulfillment doesn't clearly make our lives better off. Anthony desires to live in isolation and does so. Is he better off? And what about Jackie, who desires to torture bunnies and does so? Or Sheldon, who desires to count blades of grass all day and does so? Are they better off, and are they experiencing well-being, because their desires are fulfilled?

Some desires just don't seem to be ones whose fulfillment makes us better off. So-called "ill-informed" desires present one of the biggest challenges to desire-fulfillment theories. As their name indicates, these desires are ones that the agent has, yet are based on faulty or incomplete information. Chris Heathwood presents a classic example of ill-informed desires:

> There is a cherry pie before me and I am dying for a slice. Unbeknownst to me, I have recently developed a severe allergy to cherries and so it would in fact not be in my interests to satisfy my desire to eat the slice. (Heathwood, 2015, p. 139)

It isn't clear that fulfilling this desire would make my life better off, and in fact, the opposite seems to be the case.[8]

One way out of this problem is to place some limitations on the desires whose fulfillment counts toward well-being. For example, we might limit the desires that count to ones that we've made on the basis of full information. An idealized version of myself would know that the cherry pie would make me sick so wouldn't have the desire to eat the pie. Appealing to idealization allows us to avoid problematic desires that arise from a lack of information by excluding them: The fulfillment of ill-informed desires doesn't contribute to one's well-being. As L. W. Sumner describes it, whatever the specific requirements instituted through idealization, "only the satisfaction of the surviving subset of desires will count as enhancing our well-being" (Sumner, 1996, pp. 130–131).[9]

Notice what happens in this move to idealization, however: We start to claim that there is more to well-being than simply the fulfillment of desires. At a minimum, it involves claiming that at least some of an individual's desires, when fulfilled, don't contribute to his well-being. This move thereby creates a space in which factors other than the fact that one desires something are potentially introduced to judge one's desires.

What threatens to happen here is that the driving feature of desire-fulfillment theories—which is that one's attitudes ought to dictate the content of one's well-being—becomes lost, and desire-fulfillment theories threaten to look more objective than was initially stipulated. We've seen how this problem can arise in deliberation over what counts as "informed"; the problem becomes more problematic when we look at other kinds of messy desires. How are we to exclude desires such as Jackie's desire to torture bunnies or Sheldon's desire to count blades of grass without appealing to some kind of outside standard to gauge the real value of fulfilling these desires? Defenders of desire-fulfillment theories maintain that the value of desire fulfillment is primary, and they are willing to work out the messiness of these desires to hold on to this insight, yet others worry that the desire fulfillment loses its appeal in some of the efforts made to work out the messiness.

We'll return to talking about desire fulfillment in Chapter 5, where we consider directly its limitations as a theory of happiness as opposed to a theory of well-being. This initial discussion has shown that while desire fulfillment presents an understanding of well-being that is subjective insofar as it is grounded in an individual's specific desires, it doesn't prioritize the mental states experienced by the individual whose desires are fulfilled. If it is possible for an individual to have a fully informed, well-planned desire fulfilled, and for her not to feel happy as a result, then it seems we have a theory of well-being but not happiness.

Hedonism

The view of hedonism has often been taken to be a theory of well-being as opposed to happiness. Hedonism holds that all and only pleasure is valuable, and the classical hedonists (J. S. Mill and Jeremy Bentham) argued that happiness ought to be understood in terms of pleasure. While the classical hedonists present hedonism as a theory of happiness, contemporary philosophers often treat hedonism as a theory of well-being. This is largely because of Derek Parfit's influential classification of philosophical discussions of well-being. His 1984 book *Reasons and Persons* identifies three theories of well-being: Objective list theories, desire-fulfillment theories, and hedonism. While the field of well-being has since proliferated, Parfit's initial classification remains influential.[10] At the time in which Parfit made this classification, philosophical discussions of happiness were almost nonexistent—if philosophers were talking about prudential value, they were talking about well-being. Sometimes they talked about happiness in reference to eudaimonism, but contemporary philosophers prior to the 21st century really didn't focus that much on happiness as it is ordinarily construed.[11] This might be one reason why hedonism was considered, and is still considered by many, to be a theory of well-being rather than happiness. This book treats hedonism as a theory of happiness, which we will explore in much more detail in Chapter 3.

Well-Being versus Happiness

Thus far, we've considered four of the most prominent theories of well-being: Eudaimonism, objective list theories, desire-fulfillment theories, and hedonism. We've seen that there is often overlap between what is considered a theory of "happiness" and what is considered a theory of "well-being." Eudaimonia initially was taken to be a theory of happiness, yet now most consider it as a theory of well-being. Where eudaimonism is embraced as a view of happiness by contemporary philosophers, it is qualified as a form of "human happiness" to avoid confusion with our ordinary usage of the word "happiness." Hedonism is sometimes considered a theory of well-being and sometimes considered a theory of happiness. All of this begets the important question: Are well-being and happiness distinct?

One good place to start answering this question is by considering how people ordinarily use the word "happiness." Consider some examples:

- "I'm so happy that I got a new job!"
- "I can't stop crying all day. I just want to be happy."
- "I don't care what my son chooses for a career; I just want him to be happy."
- "She quit her job. She's broke, but she's finally happy."
- "How can she be so happy when her life is such a mess?"

These quotes are representative of things we say all the time about happiness. And notice what they have in common: They treat happiness as some kind of mental state that is typically but not necessarily associated with aspects of one's life. Consider the first claim: "I'm so happy that I got a new job." This describes one's reaction to an event in one's life that is embraced as a positive one. Likewise, the familiar line "I don't care what my son chooses for a career; I just want him to be happy" suggests that happiness is a state of mind, attainable from within a wide variety of career paths and lifestyles. Finally, the thought "How can she be so happy when her life is such a mess?" reflects the sentiment that happiness can exist even when the objective features that define one's life are suboptimal.

In what follows, we will take happiness to be distinctive from well-being insofar as it describes the mental state of "feeling happy" or "being happy." In contrast, we will take well-being to consist in an evaluation of what benefits a person. To say that Sam is happy is to make a descriptive claim about his mental state. To say that Sam has well-being is to make an evaluation of how his life is going and the extent to which the features of his life make things go better for him. Understood in this way, happiness is a descriptive concept, while well-being is a normative or evaluative concept.[12]

With this distinction in hand, we see that theories of well-being aim to provide an evaluative framework about what makes an individual's life go well, while theories of happiness seek to describe the mental state of feeling or being happy. The difficult work for those studying happiness is to try to move past the descriptions of "being happy" or "feeling happy" and to give more content into this state of mind.

Conclusion

While happiness and well-being are certainly related, there are important differences between them. Well-being describes the value of one's overall life, while happiness describes a mental state. This mental state is of prudential value to the agent, and a good theory of happiness will be able to explain why most people value happiness. As we engage in philosophical reflection about happiness, though, our target is to understand this state as opposed to defend it as a valuable one. In trying to understand happiness, we need to think deeply about the state that we associate with happiness. Is it one primarily marked by good feelings, such as pleasure? Is happiness best understood in terms of moments of happy feelings, or is it something more sustaining and long term? Does it involve reflection on how one's life is going overall? These are just some of the pertinent questions that we will explore in the remaining chapters of Part I.

Chapter Summary

- Theories of well-being and happiness both describe prudential value: Things that are good for the individual. The word "well-being" typically involves an evaluative analysis of what would make someone's life go better, while the word "happiness" involves a description of someone's mental state and is a form of subjective well-being.
- Eudaimonism is a theory of well-being or of "human happiness" that has its roots in Aristotle's philosophy. Eudaimonism states that well-being consists in flourishing as a human being, where this typically involves engaging one's rational faculties and developing virtue.
- Objective list theories are pluralistic theories of well-being insofar as they hold that there are multiple factors that contribute to well-being. The items highlighted by objective list theories as contributing to well-being include knowledge, achievement, friendship, and pleasure. Often, these items are derived from intuitive thinking about what makes a person's life go better.
- Desire-fulfillment theories take well-being to consist in desire fulfillment. They present a theory of well-being that is subjective to the individual but that is also objective insofar as it does not depend on the individual feeling good as a result of desire fulfillment.
- Hedonist theories are sometimes presented as theories of well-being and sometimes as theories of happiness. They hold that pleasure is the only good and that a life of pleasure is the best life. Pleasure is often interpreted broadly to include both physical and mental pleasures.

End Notes

1 Russell (2012) and Badhwar (2014) are notable exceptions; they maintain that eudaimonia is a distinctively human form of happiness—something akin to "true" happiness.
2 See, for example, Waterman (1990b).
3 Some psychological accounts maintain that some subjective feelings are, at least partly, constitutive of eudaimonia. For example, Waterman's most recent formulation of eudaimonism describes it as "a positive subjective state that is the product (or perhaps by-product) of the pursuit of self-realization rather than the objective being sought" (Waterman, 2007).
4 See Tiberius and Hall (2010) for discussion regarding the counterintuitive nature of eudaimonism qua objective theory of well-being.
5 See Hooker (2015, pp. 19–20) for illustration of this approach.
6 Haybron calls this "externalism about well-being" (Haybron, 2008).
7 The form of well-being that derives from desire fulfillment is thus one that is specific to the individual, which, following Haybron, we can classify as being thereby committed to "internalism" about well-being (Haybron, 2008). This kind of internalism holds that well-being ought to be specified in terms of the individual (rather than, say, features about what kinds of experiences are valuable or even features about the species of which the individual is a part).
8 Heathwood defends the desire-fulfillment theory against this objection by appealing to the fact that desire-fulfillment theory is good in itself, even though on occasion it may not be in one's interests all things considered to fulfill a particular desire.
9 See also Rawls (1971) and Griffin (1986).
10 Dorsey (2011) and Fletcher (2013), for example, both begin by noting Parfit's classification as setting the standard, even though they go on to make important arguments against its tenability.
11 As we saw in Chapter 1, happiness was a focus of Bentham and Mill's utilitarianism, and both thought that happiness needed to be understood in terms of hedonism, but contemporary philosophers are more likely to describe their theory as a form of hedonic utilitarianism. Haybron's *The Pursuit of Unhappiness* deserves credit for piquing philosophical interest in happiness considered on its own, independently of its connection to ethical theory (Haybron, 2008).
12 See (Haybron, 2008, p. 29) for further discussion of this distinction.

References

Aristotle. (2014). *Nicomachean ethics* (R. Crisp, Ed.). Cambridge, UK: Cambridge University Press.
Badhwar, N. K. (2014). *Well-being: Happiness in a worthwhile life*. New York: Oxford University Press.
Dorsey, D. (2011). The hedonist's dilemma. *Journal of Moral Philosophy, 8*(2), 173–196.
Fletcher, G. (2013). A fresh start for the objective-list theory of well-being. *Utilitas, 25*(2), 206–220.
Griffin, J. (1986). Well-being: Its Meaning, Measurement, and Moral Importance. Oxford: Clarendon Press.
Haybron, D. M. (2008). *The pursuit of unhappiness*. New York: Oxford University Press.
Heathwood, C. (2015). Desire-fulfillment theory. In G. Fletcher, (Ed.) *Handbook of well-being.* (pp. 135–147). London, UK: Routledge Press.

Hooker, B. (2015). The elements of well-being. *Journal of Practical Philosophy*, *3*(1), 15–35.

LeBar, M. (2013). *The value of living well*. New York: Oxford University Press.

Rawls, J. (1971). *A theory of justice*. Cambridge, MA: Harvard University Press.

Russell, D. C. (2012). *Happiness for humans*. New York: Oxford University Press.

Ryan, R. M., Huta, V., & Deci, E. L. (2008). Living well: A self-determination theory perspective on eudaimonia. *Journal of Happiness Studies*, *9*(1), 139–170.

Ryff, C. D., & Singer, B. H. (1998). The contours of positive human health. *Psychological Inquiry*, *9*(1), 1–28.

Steger, M. F. (2012). Experiencing meaning in life. In P. Wong (Ed.), *Human quest for meaning: Theories, research, and applications* (2nd ed., pp. 165–184). New York: Routledge Press.

Sumner, L. W. (1996). *Welfare, happiness, and ethics*. New York: Clarendon Press.

Tiberius, V., & Hall, A. (2010). Normative theory and psychological research: Hedonism, eudaimonism, and why it matters. *The Journal of Positive Psychology*, *5*(3), 212–225.

Waterman, A. S. (1990a). Personal expressiveness: Philosophical and psychological foundations. *Journal of Mind and Behavior*, *11*(1), 47–74.

Waterman, A. S. (1990b). The relevance of Aristotle's conception of eudaimonia for the psychological study of happiness. *Theoretical and Philosophical Psychology*, *10*(1), 39–44.

Waterman, A. S. (2007). On the importance of distinguishing hedonia and eudaimonia when contemplating the hedonic treadmill. *American Psychologist*, *62*(6), 612–613.

Suggested for Further Reading

On well-being in general:

Fletcher, G. (2016). *The philosophy of well-being: An introduction*. London: Routledge Press.

Fletcher, G. (2016). *The Routledge handbook of well-being*. London: Routledge Press.

Sumner, L. W. (1996). *Welfare, happiness, and ethics*. New York: Oxford Publishing.

On eudaimonism:

Annas, J. (1993). *The morality of happiness*. New York: Oxford University Press.

Besser-Jones, L. (2014). *Eudaimonic ethics: The philosophy and psychology of living well*. (pp. 187-196) New York: Routledge Press.

Besser-Jones, L. (2016). Eudaimonism. In G. Fletcher (Ed.), *The Routledge handbook of well-being*. London: Routledge Press (pp. 187-196).

LeBar, M. (2013). *The value of living well*. New York: Oxford University Press.

Russell, D. C. (2012). *Happiness for humans*. New York: Oxford University Press.

On objective list theories:

Finnis, J. (1980). *Natural law and natural rights*. Oxford: Clarendon Press .

Fletcher, G. (2013). A fresh start for objective list theories. *Utilitas*, *25*(2), 206–220.

Fletcher, G. (2016). Objective list theories. In G. Fletcher (Ed.), *The Routledge handbook of well-being* (pp. 148–160). London: Routledge Press.

On desire-fulfillment theories:

Heathwood, C. (2016). Desire-fulfillment theories. In G. Fletcher (Ed.), *The Routledge handbook of well-being* (pp. 135–147). London: Routledge Press.
Murphy, M. C. (1999). The simple desire-fulfillment theory. *Nous, 33*(2), 247–272.
Rosati, C. S. (1995). Persons, perspectives, and full information accounts of the good. *Ethics, 105*(2), 296–325.

On hedonism:

Bramble, B. (2016). A new defense of hedonism about well-being. *Ergo* 3.
Dorsey, D. (2016). The hedonist's dilemma. *Journal of Moral Philosophy, 8*, 173–196.
Feldman, F. (2004). *Pleasure and the good life: Concerning the nature, varieties and plausibility of hedonism.* Oxford: Clarendon Press.
Gregory, A. (2016). Hedonism. In G. Fletcher (Ed.), *The Routledge handbook of well-being* (pp. 113–123). London: Routledge Press.

3

HEDONISM

If we pull a stranger off the sidewalk and ask him what happiness is, chances are his answer will have something to do with feeling good. Happiness feels good; it is a mental state that feels good. If we push further and ask what "feeling good" involves, chances are he will talk about pleasure. Pleasure feels good. If happiness is about feeling good, it probably involves pleasure.

This line of thought drives hedonism. Hedonistic views about happiness define happiness in terms of pleasure. They therein capture the ordinary view of happiness described above, which we might understand in terms of our pre-theoretic intuitions about happiness. Happiness feels good and consists in lots of pleasurable experiences. Early hedonists, such as Jeremy Bentham and John Stuart Mill, took this view to be obvious and not in need of elaborate defense. Mill, for example, simply states without argument that "by happiness is intended *pleasure*, and the absence of *pain*; by unhappiness, *pain*, and the privation of *pleasure*" (Mill, 2001 p. 7, emphasis in original).

Hedonism as a view about happiness is widely discussed within philosophy and even more so in other disciplines, such as psychology and economics, where it is common to identify happiness with positive feelings. As we will see in this chapter, while the appeal of hedonism as a theory of happiness may be both intuitive and straightforward, in its most straightforward presentation, the theory is open to a number of objections. Much contemporary philosophical work on hedonism involves developing more sophisticated theories that try to capture the intuitive appeal of hedonism while avoiding objections to it.

What Is Hedonism?

The word "hedonism" is used to describe many positions that highlight the importance of pleasure. Used in the context of value theory, hedonism is the position that all and only pleasure is good. This form of "value hedonism" often informs ethical theories: A utilitarian holds that we ought to maximize the good; in combination with value hedonism, a hedonistic utilitarian holds that we ought to maximize pleasure. Similarly, an egoist holds that we ought to maximize our own good; a hedonistic egoist holds that we ought to maximize our own pleasure.

Used in the context of psychology and action theory, hedonism is a theory about what motivates people. This form of "psychological hedonism" holds that people are motivated to pursue pleasure and to avoid pain and that everything we do is, in some shape, for the sake of pleasure. Psychological hedonism can take stronger or weaker forms, and much of the plausibility of psychological hedonism depends on its ability to explain instances where people seem to act freely yet not obviously in promotion of their pleasure.

Our focus will be on hedonism in the context of *prudential value*—something that is good for an individual. As we've seen, in this context, hedonism is sometimes used as a theory of well-being. Taken as a theory of well-being, hedonism maintains that pleasure makes our lives go better. Taken as a theory of happiness, hedonism maintains that pleasure constitutes the mental state of happiness.[1]

This chapter explores hedonism considered as a theory of happiness, according to which happiness consists in feeling pleasure. This is the ordinary view we started with: What does it mean to be happy? To feel pleasure. What should we do to become happy? Engage in pleasurable activities and minimize the painful ones. Things get tricky when we try to analyze pleasure and the sorts of activities that truly generate pleasure, but hedonistic theories of happiness start from this fundamental point.

Classical Hedonism

Classical hedonism is hedonism in its most straightforward form, according to which happiness equals pleasure, and a happy life is a pleasant life—a life that feels good. While classical hedonism has been in the mix of philosophical discussions going back to ancient Greek philosophy, its popularity among contemporary philosophers ebbs and wanes. As L. W. Sumner noted in his 1996 book:

> Time and philosophical fashion have not been kind to hedonism. Although hedonistic theories of various sorts flourished for three centuries or so in their congenial empiricist habitat, they have all but disappeared from the scene. (Sumner, 1996, p. 83)

He goes on to note that hedonism may be "now due for a revival" (Sumner, 1996, p. 83), a point that is coming to fruition. There are new philosophical defenses of hedonism by Feldman (2010) and Bramble (2016), among others, and hedonism comes close to dominating discussions of happiness within psychology and economics.

To appreciate these reinvigorated discussions of hedonism, we must first understand why classical hedonism seems so problematic. The immediate reaction many people have to classical hedonism is likely one of appeal but skepticism. The appeal is clear: Pleasure is a good thing. The skepticism is also clear: Does happiness consist in *only* pleasure? Don't other things count? And don't some pleasures not count?

The following example by Roger Crisp illustrates this line of skepticism:

> *Haydn and the Oyster.* You are a soul in heaven waiting to be allocated a life on Earth. It is late Friday afternoon, and you watch anxiously as the supply of available lives dwindles. When your turn comes, the angel in charge offers you a choice between two lives, that of the composer Joseph Haydn and that of an oyster. Besides composing some wonderful music and influencing the evolution of the symphony, Haydn will meet with success and honour in his own lifetime, be cheerful and popular, travel, and gain much enjoyment from field sports. The oyster's life is far less exciting. Though this is a rather sophisticated oyster, its life will consist only of mild sensual pleasure, rather like that experienced by humans when floating very drunk in a warm bath. When you request the life of Haydn, the angel sighs, "I'll never get rid of this oyster life. It's been hanging around for ages. Look, I'll offer you a special deal. Haydn will die at the age of seventy-seven. But I'll make the oyster life as long as you like." (Crisp, 2002, p. 24)

This example tests the limits of the intuitions that drive hedonism. At a minimum, it suggests that pleasure may not be the only intrinsically valuable thing— at least where pleasure is understood as sensory pleasure, the stuff that feels good. If we want more than the oyster's life, it looks like pleasure is not the only intrinsically valuable thing.

There's a deeper problem at stake in the oyster example, though. This is that it seems *unquestionable* to think that anyone would choose the oyster's life as a happy life. We might settle into an oyster's life, much as the drug addict settles into a life dominated by the hazy pleasures of drugs, but few would choose this life, suggesting that a life full of pleasures may not be the happiest life.

Given the choice between Haydn's life and the oyster's, Haydn's life is the clear choice. And this suggests not only that most think there is more to life than pleasure but also, perhaps, that we also think the kind of life exemplified by Haydn's is the right kind of life for *us*—intelligent, free human beings. What it means to make us happy is something different than what it means to make an oyster happy. To the extent that hedonism seems to equate the two, this is problematic.

This line of thought has become known as "the swine objection," owing to Mill's influential discussion of it. The swine objection accuses hedonism of being a theory fit for swine: "To suppose that life has (as [hedonists] express it) no higher end than pleasure—no better and nobler object of desire and pursuit—they designate as utterly mean and groveling; as a doctrine worthy only of swine" (Mill, 1861, p. 7).

Mill responds to the swine objection by distinguishing between different qualities of pleasures and highlighting the value of pleasures that reflect human capacities. Pleasures can be sensory, and this is what we tend of think of when we talk about pleasure: Foot massages, warm baths, and brownies. But Mill argues that there are many more pleasures available to human beings than sensory ones. Our intellectual capacities open us up to different forms of pleasure, such as reading a book or having a spirited debate. These intellectual pleasures include reading, writing, and engaging, as well as the pleasures of achievement and the aesthetic pleasures that seem to define Haydn's life in the above example. Mill argues that the intellectual pleasures are of a higher quality and that those of us who have experienced both will choose the intellectual pleasures over the physical ones.

If Mill is right, hedonism for humans looks different than it does for bivalves. Humans are capable of higher-quality pleasures than are oysters; this is why we'd choose the life of Haydn over the life of the oyster. In recognizing different qualities of pleasure, and in allowing that human faculties contribute to distinctive kinds of pleasures, Mill's response also helps to relieve—somewhat—the pressure of hedonism's claim that pleasure is the *only* intrinsic good, for it encourages us to think about pleasure more broadly. Pleasure is not just the hazy, feel-good stuff of the oyster; it is also the satisfaction of reading a book, of seeing a good movie, of playing the piano, and of feeling accomplished.

With Mill's distinction between qualities of pleasures in hand, Haydn's life turns out to be a better source of hedonic happiness than the oyster's life. While most of us probably agree that Haydn's life would be happier than the oyster's, we might question whether Mill's analysis delivers the best explanation of it: Is Haydn's life happier insofar as it delivers higher-quality pleasures? Or is there something *beyond pleasure* that explains our preference for Haydn's life? Some worry that Mill's efforts to introduce quality as a dimension of pleasure departs from hedonism and that whatever it is that makes Haydn's life a happier one is not best understood in terms of pleasure.

Pretheoretically, at least, it seems that we can measure pleasure along two variables: Its intensity and its duration. Pleasures are better to the degree that they are more intense for longer periods of time. A 60-minute massage is a better pleasure than eating a chocolate cake because it lasts longer and, in some instances at least, can be more intense.

Mill's suggestion that we add quality as a separate variable from which to measure pleasure is somewhat perplexing, however. Aren't the higher-quality pleasures just ones that are more intense and more lasting than others? T. H. Green (2004) argues that Mill's proposal to consider the quality of pleasure marks a departure from hedonism insofar as it appears to introduce something else of value to the analysis. What makes the so-called higher pleasures a higher quality? It can't be, as Mill suggests, simply that people will choose them, for people could be choosing them for reasons other than the pleasure they offer (and, in any event, we might question whether or not people really would choose the intellectual pleasures over the more physical sensory pleasures). If, as others have argued, Mill seems to be valuing what is noble as its own intrinsic value, then this would be a departure from hedonism's fundamental commitment to seeing pleasure as the only intrinsic value.

This debate tracks an ongoing struggle that defenders of hedonism encounter: On the one hand, defenders of hedonism want to preserve the centrality of pleasure to their theories, but on the other hand, many contemporary defenders of hedonism acknowledge that their accounts of pleasure should accommodate intuitions, as the above, that the oyster's life just doesn't seem preferable to the rich life of a human being.

Reflection on the swine objection, and how to accommodate the different kinds of pleasures that seem to exist, has in contemporary discussion given rise to a further problem: The "heterogeneity" problem. The heterogeneity problem points out that pleasures can *feel* different. Bodily pleasures of massages and orgasms feel different than intellectual pleasures of reading books and writing papers. Compare the pleasure of successfully running a marathon, to the pleasure of watching the first snowfall, to the pleasure of laughing among friends. We call them "pleasures," but are they really the same?

Aaron Smuts describes the basic thrust of the heterogeneity problem as follows:

> We can feel pleasure from eating a juicy peach, smelling clean laundry, emptying a full bladder, seeing the friendly smile of a passing stranger, solving a puzzle, taking a warm bath on a cold day, hearing the laughter of children, watching a cat play with a rubber band, climbing into a soft bed, thinking of someone we love, soaking up the sun, and so on. Undeniably, pleasures come from a wide variety of sources and they also vary radically in size and shape. Although we might not be able to quantify the difference, the pleasure of an orgasm is typically much more intense than the pleasure had from finding our misplaced car keys—that is, they differ in size. In addition, pleasures vary in shape; it seems that the pleasure had

from eating barbeque is of a very different sort than that had from solving a crossword puzzle. The variety of the sources and sizes of the experiences that we call pleasurable has not proved nearly as important in the development of theories of pleasure as that of the variety in shapes. To see why, one merely needs to ask, if pleasures can be as different as circles and squares, why do we call them all by the same name? (Smuts, 2011, pp. 241–242)

The heterogeneity problem is that this vast array of things we call pleasure don't have anything in common; they are too different to be grouped together as the thing that defines our happiness. This problem is a symptom of the fact that defenses of hedonism often lack a well-developed theory of pleasure that sheds light on how these apparently heterogeneous things are the same.

One way to respond to the heterogeneity problem is to acknowledge that there is nothing the diverse sources of pleasure have in common and to maintain instead that the common denominator between them lies within the individual who experiences them as pleasure. This move toward "externalism" about pleasure holds that pleasure derives from the subject's attitudes toward the potential source of pleasure. The first snow may give me pleasure, because I love to ski, but it might elicit dread in Jennifer, insofar as it signals to her the start of a long, gray, cold, and depressing winter. The difference here is explainable wholly in terms of our attitudes and—seemingly—cannot be explained in terms of anything intrinsic to the first snow.

Henry Sidgwick presents a view like this. He argues that the only common quality found in the experience of pleasurable feelings is the relation that holds between desire and volition (or will) and is expressed by the general term "desirable" (Sidgwick, 1981 p. 127). What pleasures have in common, then, is not some kind of shared feelings but that the subject desires them. Within contemporary philosophy, this form of hedonism has become known as "attitudinal hedonism," which we'll explore in the following section.

Another response to the heterogeneity of pleasure, however, is to maintain that it is the "felt quality" of pleasure that counts—its intrinsic phenomenological feel—even in the face of the diverse experiences we have of pleasure. Ben Bramble (2016) pursues this approach. He seeks to explain the heterogeneity problem partly by appeal to our own psychological limitations that prevent us from being able to consistently identify the similar phenomenology of pleasure.[2] Drawing on arguments made by Haybron and Schwitzgebel, Bramble questions whether the heterogeneity problem arises because pleasure is, in fact, heterogeneous or whether it arises because our capacities to introspect and describe our own experiences are limited.

Dan Haybron (2008) argues that we can be unaware of our own mental states to the point where we may not know whether we are in pain or pleasure or whether we are unhappy or happy. Eric Schwitzgebel (2008) argues that we can be mistaken every day about many aspects of our mental life, including what we are seeing, what we are experiencing, and what we are feeling. We might think we hate doing the dishes, but in reality we might derive peace and even pleasure from the ritual.

The problem isn't just that it is difficult to describe those experiences; according to Schwitzgebel, the problem runs deeper: If we aren't reliable introspectors, then we are likely to be mistaken about the basic aspects of our experiences. These concerns lead Bramble to claim that "we should not expect to be able to gain a clear sense of 'the pleasant feeling,' or the way in which all pleasant experiences feel alike" (Bramble, 2016, p. 2012).

If we accept this line of argument, then the heterogeneity problem should not lead us to abandon the intuitive notion, captured by the classical hedonists, that pleasure is important and valuable simply because of its intrinsic felt quality. Pleasures might be experienced differently, and some pleasures might be of a higher quality than others, but binding them together is a uniform felt quality—they feel good.

Attitudinal Hedonism

To many, the problems of classical hedonism are a symptom of a too narrow focus on the experience of pleasure rather than on the ways in which a subject's attitudes and perspective transform that experience. Perhaps it is the case that what makes something pleasant is simply the attitude the subject takes toward it: If I find dishwashing pleasant, it is because I have a positive attitude toward the experience, not because there is anything intrinsic to dishwashing that gives whomever is washing dishes pleasure. So-called attitudinal hedonism takes this approach toward understanding pleasure. Pleasure derives from our attitudes. Attitudinal hedonism offers up an alternative theory of pleasure to anchor hedonism and so moves away from the sensory account of pleasure distinctive to classical hedonism.

When it comes to understanding happiness in terms of hedonism, we might think the move away from sensory pleasure makes an important improvement. Remember that as a theory of happiness, hedonism holds that the mental state of "being happy" is a state of pleasure. It is a descriptive claim, but to be satisfactory as a descriptive claim, the state it identifies as a happy one should be one we recognize as a state of happiness. Because most of us value happiness, recognizing something as a state of happiness also involves seeing that state to be prudentially valuable—something that we would want for ourselves. If you are sympathetic to the swine objection, or would choose Haydn's life over the oyster's life, then it is likely that you think there is something more to the state of happiness then feeling sensory pleasure. What is this "something more"?

Fred Feldman (2010) proposes that we can identify this something more by thinking about cases where sensory pleasures do not track happiness—that is, by thinking of plausible cases in which someone experiences sensory pleasures but isn't happy. Here are two examples Feldman thinks show the divergence between sensory pleasures and happiness and that highlight what is missing from the experience of sensory pleasure on its own: The first example is Dolores, who suffers from long-term serious chronic pain. Dolores learns of a new drug that will reduce significantly yet not completely erase her pain. She feels more sensory pain than pleasure. Yet, she claims to be happy, and this seems convincing. As Feldman writes, "There are many reasons to think that Dolores is happy in the scenario described. She has a smile on her face; she is asserting that she is delighted with the amazing reduction in pain; she is optimistically looking forward to a better future" (Feldman, 2010, p. 33). The second example is of a young woman giving birth without the aid of pain medications. When her husband asks her to describe her emotional state at the time of birth, she reports, "I think the pain was the worst I have ever felt. I didn't realize it would hurt so much. But at the same time I think that was one of the happiest moments of my life" (Feldman, 2010, p. 34).

These examples suggest that we can be happy even when we are in pain and vice versa. If so, then sensory pleasures are neither necessary nor sufficient for happiness—something more is needed to be happy than to feel pleasure. According to Feldman, the above examples show that this something more is an attitude: "How happy you are at a time seems to depend upon your attitude toward things that are happening" (Feldman, 2010, p. 35). Having a positive attitude toward something delivers the subject a particular kind of pleasure—call this "attitudinal pleasure."

Attitudinal pleasure consists in the mental state of being pleased about something, be it about the fact that the sun is shining or that you just got into your first choice of graduate school programs. In each of these instances, there is a particular attitude directed toward a particular object, what we can call a state of affairs (roughly, some aspect of the way the world is). When we are pleased that the sun is shining, we experience a form of attitudinal pleasure. We may or may not *feel* pleasure, but we experience the attitude of taking pleasure in something.

As Feldman is careful to point out, attitudinal pleasure describes an occurrent mental state of being pleased; it is not a disposition to be pleased when the sun shines but is the active state of being pleased that the sun is shining. This doesn't mean that we can only be pleased about things that are actively occurring. We can be pleased about all kinds of things and not just the immediate states of affairs we are presented with. Just as I can be pleased that my children are currently in good places, I can be pleased that I have seen the Great Wall of China or dove the Great Barrier Reef before it suffered the effects of climate change. I can be pleased that the barista got my coffee order right, and I can be pleased that my lecture went well this morning. Big or small, distant or present, as long as I am pleased about it at the present moment, it counts toward my happiness.

As a theory of happiness, attitudinal hedonism holds that an individual is happy to the extent that, in the moment, she is pleased about things more than she is displeased about things: "to be happy is to be on balance attitudinally pleased about things" (Feldman, 2010, p. 110). Because this form of hedonism locates pleasure within one's attitude, it seems less vulnerable to the objection that pleasure doesn't track happiness. As we've seen, when pleasure is described in terms of sensation, we might reasonably question whether or not it maps onto happiness. While my massage this morning felt good, was I really happy, especially as I found myself worrying about an upcoming deadline? The attitudinal hedonistic theory of happiness says that I wasn't really happy unless I found myself pleased about the fact that I was receiving this massage. In making this kind of pro-attitude a necessary condition of happiness, this form of hedonism may avoid this objection.

While attitudinal hedonism may thereby avoid the objection that pleasure doesn't track happiness, its claim that being pleased about a state of affairs is both necessary and sufficient for happiness is one that we might find controversial. Does happiness really always require an object? When we are happy, are we always happy about something? In specifying the attitudinal component as a *propositional attitude*, Feldman's theory maintains that happiness always has an object. A propositional attitude is a mental state that is directed toward a proposition. I am pleased that I am getting a massage; I am displeased that it is cold and gray outside. If attitudinal hedonism is correct, there must always be something I am happy about. I can't just be happy for no reason. Likewise, I can't just be unhappy for no reason. If I am unhappy (or happy), I always have to be unhappy (or happy) about something.

This seems problematic. There do seem to exist what Feldman calls "object-less moods": Mental states that lack specifiable objects but that nonetheless affect our happiness, such as depression and anxiety. Sometimes we are depressed about something: A recent breakup, a rejection, the death of a loved one. But individuals who suffer chronic depression are often just depressed. There is no object of their depression; rather, their depression is generalized and diffuse and prevents them from taking pleasure in otherwise pleasing objects. Can the attitudinal hedonistic theory of happiness explain this? It seems that because there is no attitudinal state of displeasure, the theory can't explain how someone's depression can affect their happiness.

Feldman considers this problem in the context of his example of Ira:

> Let us assume that Ira is anxious, depressed, and irritable. Let us assume that his bad mood has really gotten to him. There is nothing else that counterbalances these bad moods. Ira and all his friends agree: Ira is unhappy.

Let us furthermore assume that when his friends ask Ira to specify the states of affairs in which he is taking intrinsic attitudinal displeasure, he is not able to give a satisfactory response. He just claims to be feeling anxious, depressed, and irritable in general. (Feldman, 2010, p. 138)

Feldman argues that despite Ira's inability to state the object(s) of his unhappiness, there is nonetheless an object. For instance, once we look deeper into Ira's day-to-day life, we see that there are "plenty of states of affairs in which he is taking attitudinal displeasure. He is displeased about the fact that he might lose his job, or that the chances of his losing his job are too great. He is displeased about the fact that his children might get sick. He is displeased about the fact that he is wasting lots of time and energy worrying about things that are probably not going to happen" (Feldman, 2010, p. 139).

This line of thought suggests that those moods we think of as "objectless" might be more properly understood as dispositions to be happy/unhappy. Ira's anxiety disposes him to be displeased about various aspects of his life, while Jack's otherwise positive mental state might dispose him to take pleasure in various aspects of his life. Our moods do seem to function as such: They seem to underwrite and influence the specific attitudes we take toward the things going on in our life. When suffering from depression, I'm more apt to be displeased about a rainy day. When not so suffering, I'm more apt to be pleased by the rainy day and its opportunities for staying in bed and binge-watching my favorite show.

If this is the case, then the pertinent question becomes which of these states we define happiness by: Do we define happiness in terms of the attitudes themselves, as attitudinal hedonism does, or do we define happiness in terms of the underlying mood states that dispose us to form these attitudes? Feldman favors the latter: Happiness is an occurrent state of being pleased. But others, notably Dan Haybron (2008), argue that happiness consists in the underlying mood state. We'll consider his alternative theory of happiness—the "emotional state theory" in the next chapter.

While this objection concerns whether attitudinal hedonism properly accounts for the mental state of happiness, a second objection concerns whether or not attitudinal hedonism is, in the end, really a theory of hedonism. Once we move away from understanding pleasure as a sensation that feels good and instead talk about pleasure in terms of attitudes, are we really talking about the same thing?

In our discussion of classical hedonism, we saw that Mill faced a challenge similar to this in virtue of his position that some pleasures are of a higher quality than others. The worry is that if we claim that some pleasures are better than others, we must be appealing to something else that makes the pleasure better and so departing from hedonism by including something else as a source of value. A parallel objection can be raised with respect to attitudinal hedonism. In claiming that a state of attitudinal pleasure constitutes happiness, as opposed to a state of sensory pleasure, attitudinal hedonism seems to be placing value on the attitudes themselves. This is problematic insofar as the motivating and distinguishing feature of hedonism is the intuitive value of sensory pleasure.

But let us not forget the motivation behind attitudinal hedonism, which is the concern that appeals to sensory pleasure aren't sufficient to explain happiness. While sensory pleasures have an intuitive value, we've seen reason to question *how* valuable they are. We'd choose the life of Haydn over the oyster's, even though the oyster's life promises ongoing, continual sensory pleasure, while Haydn's involves varying circumstances and challenging experiences. This line of thought suggests that while sensory pleasures may be valuable, they aren't *that* valuable and realistically might not anchor well a theory of happiness.

Do attitudes, and specifically the cognitive state of "being pleased about," do a better job in capturing something that is valuable enough to anchor a theory of happiness? We'd all rather be pleased about things going on in our life than not, and it is challenging to think of a state in which we are displeased about our given states of affairs and yet nonetheless happy. Our attitudes do seem to affect our happiness: If I'm displeased about things going on in my life—say, because it is raining, and I've had to postpone a hike with my friends—that attitude certainly seems to affect my happiness. Yet are we comfortable saying that, in light of these attitudes, I am happy?

The starkest problem may be that attitudes don't always feel good: I can be pleased about something without ever feeling good. Reading the newspaper, I can be pleased that they have increased the minimum wage. But unless I've been an advocate, or otherwise personally invested in the issue, it seems weird to think that this kind of attitude is what my happiness rests upon. This attitude, while not disinterested, just doesn't seem to affect me very deeply.[3] While being pleased about something can penetrate deeply—I can be pleased about my son's performance and feel a swell of pride—oftentimes being pleased about something doesn't have this kind of effect. On its own, it seems tangential to my happiness.

The attitudinal hedonism theory of happiness avoids some of the problems facing hedonism in its classical form, but it is not without controversy. Whether one favors attitudinal over sensory hedonism depends in large part on one's intuitions about the nature of pleasure and one's analyses of pleasant experiences.

The Experience Requirement

The debate between attitudinal and sensory hedonism encourages us to think about the nature of pleasure and its role in happiness. Both theories seek to preserve the notion that pleasure is a vital prudential value, but their respective analyses of pleasure diverge in significant ways. Regardless of which theory of hedonism comes out on top, embracing either one of them commits one to the "experience requirement." The experience requirement holds that in order for something to affect your happiness or well-being (or to benefit or harm you more generally), it must affect your experience. If the fact that my son did well on an exam makes me happy, I have to (a) know about it, and (b) experience it as a source of pleasure. If it doesn't affect my experience—say because he keeps it secret—it seems hard to see how it contributes to my happiness.

While the experience requirement may seem intuitive, hedonism's commitment to it gives rise to yet another deeply penetrating objection. The experience requirement maintains that something can be of prudential value only if it is experienced. This places weight on the experience of things rather than the things themselves. It is not my son's performance that makes me happy; it is my experience of it. Yet if all that counts are the experiences of something, then this opens up the possibility that experiences can be valuable even if they are not *real*.

Robert Nozick famously presents this objection in terms of the "experience machine":

> Suppose there were an experience machine that would give you any experience you desired. Superduper neuropsychologists could stimulate your brain so that you would think and feel you were writing a great novel, or making a friend, or reading an interesting book. All the time you would be floating in a tank, with electrodes attached to your brain. Should you plug into this machine for life, preprogramming your life's experiences? If you are worried about missing out on desirable experiences, we can suppose that business enterprises have researched thoroughly the lives of many others. You can pick and choose from their large library or smorgasbord of such experiences, selecting your life's experiences for, say, the next two years. After two years have passed, you will have ten minutes or ten hours out of the tank, to select the experiences of your *next* two years. Of course, while in the tank you won't know that you're there; you'll think that it's all actually happening. Others can also plug into and have the experiences they want, so there's no need to stay unplugged to serve them. (Ignore problems such as who will service the machine if everyone plugs in.) Would you plug in? *What else can matter to us, other than how our lives feel from the inside?* (Nozick, 1974, pp. 42, emphasis in original)

Hedonistic theories about happiness maintain that we should plug in: Nothing else truly matters to our happiness except how it is that our lives feel from the inside. If we are experiencing a life full of pleasure, it doesn't matter whether that pleasure comes from a machine, drugs, or real life.

Psychologists sometimes refer to this kind of theory as one that focuses on the outcome rather than the process. Whereas process-based theories emphasize that what counts is what you do, outcome-based theories emphasize that what counts is the outcome: For hedonism, the outcome is pleasure. But if Nozick is correct, outcome-based theories prioritize the wrong thing: It is what we *do* that counts. Experiences are only important because we want to *do* them and not just to have the experience of them. When we do things, we engage with reality and make actual contact with it. This engagement with reality is also important to our own goals of self-realization: As Nozick puts it, we want to *be* a certain way; we don't want to exist floating in a tank as an "indeterminate blob."

Many philosophers take this line of objection to be decisive against hedonism. Roger Crisp, for example, describes the experience machine as dealing a "near-fatal" blow to hedonism (Crisp, 2006, p. 620). Others are less bothered by the threat of the experience machine and by the experience requirement, seeing the experience requirement to be an important aspect of a theory of well-being. Bramble, for example, offers the following argument in defense of the experience requirement:

1. If something could benefit or harm someone without affecting her experiences (say, fame, success, desire satisfaction, or whatever it may be), then it could do so *even after she is dead.*
2. Nothing can benefit or harm us after we are dead (there can be no posthumous benefits or harms).
   Therefore,
3. Nothing can benefit or harm someone without affecting her experiences (Bramble, 2016, p. 89) "emphasis in original".

I imagine this argument sounds quite plausible: It is counterintuitive to think that we can be *harmed* after our death. If, after Rob's death, his wife throws away his cherished collection of rocks gathered from around the world, there may be a wrong done, but it would be a mistake to say that Rob was harmed. After all, Rob no longer exists.

Hedonism maintains that happiness consists in the mental state of feeling pleasure and so maintains that happiness is, fundamentally, something experienced. While a consequence of this view is that happiness might arise under some unusual circumstances, the claim that we must experience something in order for it to be of prudential value is nonetheless an intuitive and plausible one.

The Empirical Study of Hedonism

As we've seen, philosophers vary widely in their opinions on hedonism. What some take to be decisive objections against hedonism (e.g., the experience machine or the swine objection), others embrace wholeheartedly and see as advantages to the theory. The intuition that pleasure is central to happiness is hard to shake, though, and within other disciplines hedonism enjoys much more popularity than it does within philosophy.

In 1999, psychologists Daniel Kahneman, Ed Diener, and Norbert Schwartz published an anthology titled *Well-Being: The Foundations of Hedonic Psychology*, in which they present hedonic psychology as a new field of psychology. They describe "hedonic psychology" as "the study of what makes experiences and life pleasant or unpleasant. It is concerned with feelings of pleasure and pain, of interest and boredom, of joy and sorry, and of satisfaction and dissatisfaction" (Kahneman, Diener, & Schwarz, 1999, p. ix). While they don't identify happiness solely in terms of pleasure, they and most contemporary psychologists see pleasure as an essential element of happiness, with some using the words "happiness" and "pleasure" interchangeably. As we will discuss in much more detail in our discussion of the science of happiness in Chapter 12, their efforts to stimulate research on pleasure (and happiness more generally) have been vastly successful. Empirical research has revealed some important insight into the causes of pleasure and the ways in which we experience it.

As we have seen, within philosophical discussions of hedonism, there is significant debate about how to understand pleasure. Is pleasure simply the feel-good stuff of orgasms and massages, or is it the less intense but distinctively positive feelings derived from reading a novel or writing a book? While the jury is still out regarding whether or not people prefer the latter to the former, neuroscientific research supports the basic claim that pleasure can be of all sorts. In a series of studies, Kringelbach and colleagues used self-reports of pleasure in conjunction with brain imaging to identify areas in the brain associated with and perhaps responsible for pleasure (Kringelbach, 2010; Kringelbach & Berridge, 2010). They found that the brain mechanisms associated with sensory (physical) pleasures overlap with those associated with the higher-order pleasures:

> From sensory pleasures and drugs of abuse to monetary, aesthetic and musical delights, all pleasures seem to involve the same hedonic brain systems, even when linked to anticipation and memory. Pleasures important to happiness, such as socializing with friends, and related traits of positive hedonic mood are thus all likely to draw upon the same neurobiological roots that evolved for sensory pleasures. The neural overlap may offer a way to generalize from fundamental pleasures that are best understood and so infer larger hedonic brain principles likely to contribute to happiness. (Kringelbach & Berridge, 2010, p. 662)

This research offers a promising way to explain the diversity of pleasures and perhaps a response to the heterogeneity problem. It suggests that Bramble may be right to argue that the heterogeneity problem points only to our limited introspective and descriptive powers. While pleasures might seem disparate, this research suggests that they are nonetheless grounded in the same affective system.

Empirical research on pleasure also turns up some surprises. Perhaps most well known is research regarding adaptation. The human capacity to adapt to changes in our environment is vital to our very survival. But an important consequence of this is that one way in which we adapt is by adapting to changes in our affective states: Faced with an influx of pain, we will gradually adapt to it, effectively negating the effects of the new source of pain. Likewise, faced with an influx of pleasure, we gradually adapt to it. This thereby lessens the impact of particular and potential causes of pleasure.

In a now-classic study on adaptation, Brickman, Coates, and Janoff-Bulman (1978) explored the effects that major "life-changing" events such as winning a lottery or becoming paraplegic have on an individual's levels of happiness, measured hedonically. While the happiness level of both groups changed immediately after the event, within two years their happiness levels rebounded to a position similar to where they were at the outset. For a long time, many took this kind of research to suggest that there is some kind of hedonic setpoint that each of us have, from which we can vary a little bit but can't change dramatically.[4]

That our experiences of positive affect are mitigated by our psychological tendency to adapt to them raises interesting questions for hedonism when considered as a theory of happiness. It raises important concerns regarding the pursuit of happiness, which we discuss in Chapter 11. It may also lend support to Haybron's concern that hedonism's focus on pleasure is too shallow to genuinely capture happiness. If pleasure is so contingent and fleeting, perhaps it is a mistake to think it is so central to happiness. We will consider this line of argument in Chapter 4.

Conclusion

Hedonism works from the plausible intuition that happiness consists in feeling good and defines happiness exclusively in terms of pleasure. Since its earliest formulations, hedonists have struggled to respond to the concern that the human experience of happiness includes more than just physical, sensory pleasures. Some hedonists argue that there is a diversity of pleasures and that they are not all characterized by their felt quality, while others maintain that the felt quality of pleasure is, in fact, the characteristic feature of happiness. Contemporary versions of "attitudinal hedonism" take a different route by arguing that pleasure derives from the attitudes one takes toward one's experiences. While there is much interesting philosophical discussion on the nature of pleasure, hedonism is more widely embraced as a view of happiness within other disciplines, such as psychology and economics, where positive affect is often used as a measure of happiness.

Chapter Summary

- As a theory of happiness, hedonism holds that happiness consists in a life full of pleasures. A happy life is one with more pleasurable experiences overall than painful ones.
- Classical hedonism holds that pleasures are sensory, while attitudinal hedonism holds that pleasures derive from attitudes.
- The swine objection holds that hedonism offers us a life better suited to animals than to humans, because it ignores the higher capabilities of human beings. Mill responds to this objection by introducing the notion of "higher-quality" pleasures.
- The heterogeneity problem holds that what gets called "pleasures" are too diverse and fail to share anything in common. Some respond to the heterogeneity problem by moving to a theory of attitudinal hedonism, while others argue that the heterogeneity problem arises only due to our own inability to introspect and adequately describe our experiences.
- The experience machine is meant to challenge hedonism's commitment to locating happiness within our experience of pleasure. It works on the intuition that we want more out of life than experiences and that if we can get an experience the cheap way—through a machine or through drugs—then the experience itself isn't as valuable as hedonism purports.
- Hedonism enjoys more popularity within psychology than within philosophy, and psychological research on pleasure suggests both that the diverse kinds of things we call pleasure do share the same brain mechanisms and that it is difficult to make changes to our affective states.

End Notes

1 See discussion of happiness and well-being in Chapter 2.
2 In a similar vein, Smuts suggests that the heterogeneity problem arises not because the diverse sources of pleasure share nothing in coming but because of "the paucity of our experiential memory and our inarticulateness when it comes to phenomenal descriptions" (Smuts, 2011, p. 264).
3 Haybron (2008) makes a related charge against (all forms of) hedonism, arguing that pleasure itself is too shallow to comprise the basis of happiness.
4 Recently, though, much of the research supporting the adaptation effect has come under fire, largely due to concerns regarding methodology and to the lack of longer-term, longitudinal studies on it (Diener, Lucas, & Scollon, 2006). We will talk more about this in Chapter 11.

References

Besser-Jones, L. (2013). The pursuit and nature of happiness. *Philosophical Topics, 41*(1), 103–121.

Bramble, B. (2016). A new defense of hedonism about well-being. *Ergo, 3*, 85–112.

Brickman, P., Coates, D., & Janoff-Bulman, R. (1978). Lottery winners and accident victims: Is happiness relative? *Journal of Personality and Social Psychology, 36*(8), 917–927.

Crisp, R. (2002). *Routledge philosophy guidebook to Mill on utilitarianism.* New York: Routledge Press.

Crisp, R. (2006). Hedonism reconsidered. *Philosophy and Phenomenological Research, 73*(3), 619–645.

Diener, E., Lucas, R. E., & Scollon, C. (2006). Beyond the hedonic treadmill: Revising the adaptation theory of well-being. *American Psychologist, 61*(4), 305–314.

Feldman, F. (2010). *What is this thing called happiness?* Oxford: Oxford University Press.

Green, T. H. (2004). *Prolegomena to ethics.* (A. C. Bradley, Ed.). Oxford: Clarendon Press.

Haybron, D. M. (2008). *The pursuit of unhappiness.* New York: Oxford University Press.

Heathwood, C. (2007). The reduction of sensory pleasure to desire. *Philosophical Studies, 133*(1), 23–44.

Kahneman, D., Diener, E., & Schwarz, N. (1999). Preface. In *Well-being: Foundations of hedonic psychology* (pp. ix–xii). New York: Russell Sage Foundation.

Kringelbach, M. L. (2010). The hedonic brain: A functional neuroanatomy of human pleasure. *Pleasures of the Brain*, 202–221.

Kringelbach, M. L., & Berridge, K. C. (2010). The neuroscience of happiness and pleasure. *Social Research*, 77(2), 659–678.

Mason, E. (2007). The nature of pleasure: A critique of Feldman. *Utilitas, 19*(3), 379–387.

Mill, J. S. (2001). *Utilitarianism* (G. Sher, Ed.; 2nd ed.). Indianapolis, IN: Hackett Publishing.

Nozick, R. (1974). *Anarchy, state, and utopia.* New York: Basic Books.

Schwitzgebel, E. (2008). The unreliability of naive introspection. *Philosophical Review, 117*(2), 245–273.

Sidgwick, H. (1981). *The methods of ethics.* Indianapolis, IN: Hackett Publishing.

Smuts, A. (2011). The feels good theory of pleasure. *Philosophical Studies, 155*(2), 241–265.

Sumner, L. W. (1996). *Welfare, happiness, and ethics.* New York: Clarendon Press.

Suggested for Further Reading

On classical hedonism:

Bentham, J. (1972). *An introduction to the principles of morals and legislation.* New York: Wiley.

Crisp, R. (2006). Hedonism reconsidered. *Philosophy and Phenomenological Research, 73*(3), 619–645.

Mill, J. S. (2001). *Utilitarianism.* Indianapolis, IN: Hackett Publishing.

On attitudinal hedonism:

Feldman, F. (2002). The good life: A defense of attitudinal hedonism. *Philosophy and Phenomenological Research, 65*(3), 604–628.

Feldman, F. (2010). *What is this thing called happiness?* Oxford: Oxford University Press.

Heathwood, C. (2007). The reduction of sensory pleasure to desire. *Philosophical Studies,* *133*(1), 23–44.

On the swine objection:

Dorsey, D. (2013). The authority of competence and quality as extrinsic. *British Journal for the History of Philosophy, 21*(1), 78–99.
Mill, J. S. (2001). *Utilitarianism.* Indianapolis, IN: Hackett Publishing.
Saunders, B. (2010). J. S. Mill's conception of utility. *Utilitas, 22*(1), 52–69.

On the heterogeneity problem:

Bramble, B. (2016). A new defense of hedonism about well-being. *Ergo, 3*(4), 85–112.
Smuts, A. (2011). The feels good theory of pleasure. *Philosophical Studies, 155*(2), 241–265.

On the experience machine and the experience requirement:

Hawkins, J. (2016). The experience machine and requirement. In G. Fletcher (Ed.), *The Routledge companion to well-being* (pp. 355–365). London: Routledge Press.
Hewitt, S. (2010). What do our intuitions about the experience machine really tell us about hedonism? *Philosophical Studies, 151*(3), 331–349.
Lin, E. (2016). How to use the experience machine. *Utilitas, 28*(3) 314–332.

On the psychology of pleasure:

Deiner, E., Lucas, R. E., & Scollon, C. (2006). Beyond the hedonic treadmill: Revising the adaptation theory of well-being. *American Psychologist, 61*(4), 305–314.
Frederick, S., & Loewenstein, G. (1999). Hedonic adaptation. In D. Kahneman, E. Diener, & N. Schwarz (Eds.), *Well-being: Foundations of hedonic psychology,* (pp. 302–339). New York: Russell Sage Foundation.
Frijda, N. H. (1999). Emotions and hedonic experience. In D. Kahneman, E. Diener, & N. Schwarz (Eds.), *Well-being: Foundations of hedonic psychology,* (pp. 302–339). New York: Russell Sage Foundation.
Lucas, R. E. (2007). Adaptation and the set-point model of well-being: Does happiness change after major life events? *Current Directions in Psychological Science, 16*(2), 75–79.

4

EMOTIONAL STATE THEORY
OF HAPPINESS

The discussion of hedonism in Chapter 3 shows the intuitive plausibility of the notion that happiness consists in feeling positive, warm, subjective states—in feeling *good*. Yet it also introduced reasons for thinking there may be more to happiness than feeling good. Feeling good is great, but it is also sometimes fleeting, unstable, and somewhat shallow.

Consider the examples of pleasures raised in discussion of hedonism. These included the pleasures of eating a juicy peach, the pleasures of floating very drunk in a warm bath like an oyster, the pleasures of experiencing the first snow, and the pleasures of emptying a very full bladder. Hedonists also talk about the pleasures of reading a book, solving a crossword puzzle, and taking pride in one's accomplishments. These latter pleasures seem to be different than the former. One clear difference seems to be that the latter pleasures affect us differently than do the former. Chances are the pleasure of eating a juicy peach doesn't have much of an impact on how your day is going, nor does emptying a full bladder. These experiences are great in the moment, but they quickly pass and leave the subject in relatively the same place she was. It seems possible that one can be deeply unhappy while simultaneously taking pleasure in eating the chocolate cake. In contrast, the pleasure that arises from taking pride in one's accomplishments delivers a sense of satisfaction that infiltrates oneself, and the pleasure that arises from reading a book can vibrate with the subject for days. It seems harder (although perhaps not impossible) to find a case where someone experiences these sorts of pleasures without those pleasures affecting her happiness.

This line of thought suggests that some pleasures are deeper than others. They don't simply enter into our phenomenological experience and then fly out the door; they linger and affect the subject on a psychological level. And if we are tempted to think that these pleasures are more important insofar as they have this penetrating effect, then we are on the first step toward entertaining the central idea of the "emotional state theory of happiness," which highlights the importance of central, rather than peripheral, affective states and takes a person's overall emotional condition to comprise happiness.

The emotional state theory of happiness is a relative newcomer to the philosophy of happiness. Developed by Dan Haybron (2008), the emotional state theory presents an alternative to hedonism and raises important questions regarding the overall nature and phenomenology of happiness. Its central features are twofold: First, it takes happiness to consist in an overall emotional condition. Second, it describes the content of this condition as one characterized by attunement, engagement, and endorsement. Let's take a look at each of these central features.

An Overall Emotional Condition

The emotional state theory takes happiness to consist in a psychological state; yet rather than define this state in terms of one particular state, such as feeling good, the emotional state theorist takes the state of happiness to consist in one's overall emotional condition, which consists in the aggregate of one's emotions and moods. The emotional state theorist thus from the start takes happiness to include more than just moments of feeling good and encourages us to reflect on "the long-term psychological sense of the term" (Haybron, 2008, p. 30). This is the sense of happiness we invoke when we think about *being a happy person*. A happy person doesn't always feel an acute state of happiness; she may not always *feel* happy, but there is nonetheless the real sense in which she is happy overall.

When we think about what it feels like to be happy overall (as opposed to being happy in a particular moment), it becomes important to look for affective states that seem to have a longer-lasting effect than, say, the pleasure of eating the juicy peach; we want to look for affective states that are happiness-constituting. Haybron is skeptical that hedonism can explain happiness-constituting states. He worries that the pleasurable states that are the focus of hedonism are often shallow and irrelevant to our happiness considered from the long-term perspective and so are not always happiness-constituting.

So, what are happiness-constituting states? The short answer is that they are affective states that make a difference to your overall emotional condition. Compare, again, the difference between the pleasure that comes from emptying a full bladder to the satisfaction that arises from feeling pride in one's accomplishments. Both pleasurable states, but the latter hits deeper. It contributes to and even helps to define one's overall emotional condition. It reverberates and is a reliable source of positivity; it helps one to define oneself and gives rise to new desires and motivations.

One way to understand the difference between shallow affective states, which might feel good but lack any sustaining impact on one's happiness, and deeper affective states, which Haybron takes to be happiness-constituting, is in terms of the difference between *central* and *peripheral* affective states. Central affective states are central insofar as they penetrate our inner core, whereas peripheral affective states come and go without any lasting impact on us. Because of their depth, "central affective states seem to constitute changes in us, and are not merely things that happen to us, mainly because they concern an individual's dispositions" (Haybron, 2008, p. 130).

We can distinguish central states from peripheral affective states along the following dimensions[1]:

1. Central affective states influence the subject's dispositions and make it more likely that she experiences other affective states. Just as being depressed makes it less likely that a person will experience pleasure, being elated makes it more likely that a person will experience pleasure. Being depressed and elated are central affective states insofar as they have this dispositional quality; if a state lacks this dispositional quality, it is peripheral.

2. Central affective states are often described in terms of their physiological presentations. We use words like "gut-wrenching," "heart-rending," and "lifting you up" to describe central affective states, while peripheral states tend to be those that "bounce right off you" (Haybron, 2008, p. 129).

3. Central affective states penetrate the self—they create a change in the subject, and, in contrast to peripheral affective states, are not merely things that happen to a subject and leave her unchanged.

4. Central affective states are productive, not just insofar as they dispose a subject toward other affective modes but also insofar as they generate "various physiological changes, biasing cognition and behavior, etc." (Haybron, 2008, p. 130). As such, central affective states generate a variety of these kinds of causal consequences to central affective states that peripheral affective states lack. Peripheral affective states occur but, again, leave the subject relatively unchanged.

5. Central affective states are persistent and so pervasive. They linger, infiltrating the subject and making an ongoing impact. They thereby become pervasive: "They are frequently diffuse and nonspecific in character, tending to permeate the whole of consciousness and seeing the tone thereof" (Haybron, 2008, p. 131). Consider again the states of depression and elatedness. Depression shapes one's psyche, making the depressed person see colors less vibrantly and feel pain more sharply, and making him less able to pick up on the positive aspects of his experience. Elatedness makes one laugh more, appreciate the warm breeze, and think more sharply.

6. Finally, central affective states are profound in virtue of their depth and come to be states we define ourselves in terms of. They "seem to run all the way through us, in some sense, feeling like states of *us* rather than impingements from without" (Haybron, 2008, p. 131, emphasis in original). Consider, again, the differences between feeling pleasure at emptying a full bladder and feeling satisfaction at one's accomplishments.

These dimensions of central affective states make it such that they define one's overall emotional condition.

With the distinction between central and peripheral affective states in place, we can begin to develop a better understanding of what the emotional state theory takes happiness to consist in. In this view, happiness is a feature of one's overall emotional condition, which is constituted by moods arising from (or perhaps, equivalent to) central affective states.[2] Peripheral affective states do not affect one's happiness, simply because they are too fleeting and fragile to contribute to a person's overall mood condition. This means that some pleasures do not contribute to a person's happiness, but some do.

In focusing on one's overall emotional condition rather than exclusively on the particular affective states one is experiencing, Haybron's conception of happiness makes an important shift away from thinking about happiness as an occurrent, potentially fleeting state. To wrap our heads around this shift, it is helpful to think about what Haybron takes to be the emotional state that stands as the opposite to happiness: Depression. While, for the hedonist, happiness is pleasure and pain is the opposite, for the emotional state theorist, depression is the opposite of happiness. Depression serves as a prototypical emotional state for Haybron: It has the depth and dispositionality, it penetrates the self, it has a pervasive and lasting impact, and so on. And it is a negative emotional state that transforms our experiences in negative ways. When one is depressed, one's emotional condition prevents one from enjoying daily life; even the massage can feel bad. Yet when one is happy, one's emotional condition lifts one up and colors one's experiences in a positive direction.

The Content of a Happy Emotional State

If happiness is an emotional state whose opposite is depression, what does it consist in? Haybron suggests there are three dimensions to the emotional state of happiness: *attunement*, *engagement*, and *endorsement*. Each of these dimensions concerns how it is that a given person relates to and experiences his activities. Say, for example, you enroll in an economics course. Whether or not you find the course to be enjoyable, and a source of happiness, depends largely on how it is that you are able to embrace the course. Does it click with you? Does it spark interest and contribute to other interests you might have? Can you find yourself engaging in it wholeheartedly or is it always with reserve and resentment? According to the emotional state theory, these are the kinds of dimensions within which happiness lies.

Haybron believes the most central aspect of happiness is attunement. Attunement involves a kind of inner peace and confidence that has the effect of opening and expanding one's mood. Within a state of attunement there is no separation between the subject and her experiences; she is completely attuned to their environment and activities. Nothing holds her back, and she experiences no struggles. She is comfortable not just in her own skin but in her world.

Part of being so attuned is to allow oneself to experience one's emotions fully and to let them thrive. There is, as Haybron describes, an "openness or expansiveness of mood or spirit, or a sense of freedom" (2008, p. 117) that derives from attunement, the lack of which can be understood in terms of emotional compression. Someone who is emotionally compressed has emotions that are stifled and inhibited by his activities and interactions. The very things that make him an individual, and that which he needs to realize his self, are blocked from him. Compression is "effectively the sleep of individuality" (2008, p. 120), Haybron writes, while attunement is the path toward self-realization and expression.

Engagement is also important to the emotional state of happiness and takes the form of exuberance or enthusiasm. We are engaged when we enthusiastically take up what life has to offer, as opposed to listlessly going through the motions and letting life happen to us. Indeed, lack of engagement is one of the hallmarks of a state of depression. Depression prevents someone from being able to engage; even though a depressed person may be able to function well, she lacks the enthusiasm toward life that comes through engaging in it.

Engaging in activities is importantly different than doing the activity: A student engaged in her economics class has a completely different experience than the student who lacks such engagement, even if their activities (reading, doing homework, etc.) are exactly the same. While the engaged student embraces the challenges of the course with an open attitude and throws herself into the material, the withdrawn student reads the material with annoyance and shows up in class only to watch the clock and count the minutes until it is over. According to Haybron, the engaged student is clearly the happier one.

Endorsement rounds out this analysis of happiness as an emotional state. Happy people tend to endorse their life. This is the "smiley-face" aspect of happiness: Smiles are taken to reflect the subject's judgment that her life is good. As Haybron notes, this is the "prototypically American version of happiness" (2008, p. 113), and, as we'll discuss in the following chapter, variations of "life satisfaction" theories come close (along with hedonism) to dominating research on happiness. The emotional state theory maintains this intuition, describing it in terms of endorsement, yet also stresses it is only one of the three features (attunement, engagement, and endorsement) of a state of happiness.

The resulting picture of happiness is as follows: Happiness consists in an overall emotional state, constituted by moods and emotions. Being happy disposes one to have positive moods and emotions in the same sense in which being depressed disposes one to have negative moods and emotions. The state of happiness itself is one that involves being attuned to one's surroundings and activities and engaging with them, often with exuberance and joy, as well as positively endorsing one's life.

Is This Happiness?

The emotional state theory presents a rich, nuanced, and intriguing account of happiness. And the emotional state that it presents is undoubtedly an important one, of significant prudential value to its bearer. Without questioning the value of the emotional state described here, though, some have questioned whether or not it is, in fact, happiness itself.

As a way into this line of criticism, it will be helpful to think again about the state of depression against which this view of happiness is juxtaposed. Depression is a mental condition that shapes and colors one's experiences in a negative manner, preventing one from taking joy or pleasure in one's activities and often preventing one from engaging in activities in the first place. Is it the opposite of happiness? Many people, as well as ordinary discourse, seem to take "sadness," rather than depression, to be the opposite of happiness. Sadness consists in the active experience of unpleasant emotions that hit deeply and generate physiological changes in the subject. I'm sad when thinking about my missing cat but happy when playing with my dog; I'm sad when I wake up in the morning and just feel like crying but happy when I wake up energized and excited for the morning run. Depression might *make* me sad, but there seems to be a real difference between being sad and being depressed. Haybron denies this: "One is unhappy by virtue of being *depressed*, not by virtue of experiencing the unpleasantness of depression" (2008, p. 108, original emphasis), and several have criticized his emotional state theory for presenting something more like the *conditions* of being happy. On this line of criticism, the emotional state serves as the mental state that enables us to be happy, parallel to the ways in which the emotional state of depression serves as a condition for being sad, but is not itself a state of happiness.

Hill (2009) traces this concern to Haybron's focus on mood propensities and the primary role he assigns them. We saw this aspect of the emotional state theory in the distinction between the central affective states that comprise happiness and the peripheral affective states that are excluded from happiness. Central affective states are deep, profound, persistent, and pervasive. They are also productive, insofar as they prompt new affective states and physiological changes within the subject. This productivity ties into what Haybron describes as their dispositional quality and takes to be the essential feature of central affective states:

> What primarily distinguishes central affective states, I would suggest, is that they *dispose* agents to experience certain affects rather than others. This, indeed, appears to be their essential characteristic: insofar as one's emotional disposition is altered by virtue of being in an affective state, that state is central. If it makes no difference, it is peripheral. While in a depressed mood, for instance, an individual will likely find little pleasure in what happens, will tend to look on the dark side of things, and may more likely be saddened by negative events. An elated person will exhibit the opposite tendencies. And someone afflicted by anxiety will tend to multiply and exaggerate potential threats, experience greater upset at setbacks, and be more prone to experience fear and perhaps anger. Whereas a more serene individual will tend to take things in stride, see fewer causes for anxiety, worry less about peripheral threats, etc. Contrast these states with the clearly peripheral ones: neither the mild irritation expressed at dropping a pencil nor the trivial pleasure of driving past a pretty house appear to have any direct impact on what other emotions one is likely to experience. (Haybron, 2008, p. 130)

One reason why Haybron places such importance upon the dispositional quality of central affective states is to highlight the ways in which such states contribute to and form constitutive parts of one's self. This contrast is particularly important to his criticism of hedonism and efforts to develop an alternative to it; but understanding happiness in terms of dispositional qualities, and mood propensities, is controversial.

Hill (2009) argues that mood propensities ought not to be considered constitutive of happiness. His strategy is to explore cases where a subject has a negative mood propensity (so ought to count as unhappy on Haybron's analysis) yet nonetheless seems happy. His own example explores a man who is averse to rodeos, and so has a negative mood propensity toward it, but for a variety of reasons ended up at a rodeo and "happy" (where this is based on experiencing positive central affective states). His standing aversion to rodeos has not changed.[3] If there are cases where mood propensities and happiness/unhappiness come apart, such as in the rodeo example, or in the case of a gloomy teenager who finds herself having fun at the theme park her parents dragged her to against her will, then this calls into question the emotional states theorist's commitment to understanding happiness in terms of mood propensities.

Klausen (2016) raises a related concern. He worries that the emotional state theory confuses things that are instrumental to happiness (or serve as the conditions for happiness) with happiness itself:

Mood propensities are obviously an extremely important *means* to happiness. They are the closest one can come to a universal tool for producing and maintaining this much-desired mood. This accounts for Haybron's observations, without compelling us to build mood propensities into the notion of happiness itself. (Klausen, 2016, p. 1003)

Happiness, Klausen goes on to argue, is itself a "categorical psychological state." Categorical psychological states are occurrent rather than dispositional; they are the states that we experience on a conscious level. We feel them or are aware of them. To say that happiness is a categorical psychological state is to say that we are happy when we feel happy, or when we experience whatever positive feelings and emotions that we take to comprise happiness.[4]

Many people do seem to think of happiness in terms of categorical psychological states, but at least one difficulty this view faces is how to make sense of the long-term sense of happiness, or what we mean when we say that "Heidi is a happy person." This is the sense invoked by the emotional state theorist, and taking happiness to include mood propensities and dispositions is a helpful way to understand what it means to be a happy person. It is unrealistic to think anyone could experience the positive psychological states distinctive to happiness at all times: We all feel stressed out at times, experience disruptive changes in life, lose people we love, and so on. A plausible view of happiness ought to account for these periods while nonetheless accounting for the fact that we do think people can live happy lives even with the inevitable gaps in positive psychological states. Haybron's account explains this in terms of mood propensities: Heidi is happy even when stressed out about a deadline because of her overall mood propensities. Because Klausen rejects that happiness is even partly constituted by mood propensities, his burden is to explain how Heidi can be happy when she is stressed out. He does this by invoking John Stuart Mill's appeal to the importance of the overall balance of happy states: "A happy person may be temporarily depressed, have only experiences that are indifferent to her happiness, or even have no conscious experiences at all, for example during a period of dreamless sleep. If she has enough happiness-constitutive experiences over a broader span of time, she can still be said to be happy in the long-term sense" (Klausen, 2016, p. 997).

Happiness and Well-Being, Again

Our discussion of the emotional state theory of happiness raises important questions regarding the nature of the state that we call "happiness." Whereas hedonism holds that happiness consists in the experience of pleasurable states, the emotional state theory holds that there is much more to happiness than pleasurable states and that some pleasurable states don't even contribute to happiness.

Central to Haybron's motivation for developing the emotional state theory is his commitment to seeing happiness as something that hits deeper than does pleasure. He is concerned that hedonism focuses too much on states that can be both shallow (the pleasure of eating a juicy peach) and irrelevant to happiness (the pleasure of emptying a full bladder). According to Haybron, "happiness has a depth that the pleasure theory misses" (Haybron, 2008, p. 108). This explains why Haybron focuses so much on mood propensities and on central affective states that hit deeply and penetrate in a way peripheral affective states do not.

Does happiness really have this kind of depth, however? Klausen worries that Haybron overestimates the depth and stability associated with happiness, making it out to be something more robust and important than it is. Happiness, according to Klausen, can be "relatively superficial, transient, fragile or dependent on pure luck and fortunate circumstances" (Klausen, 2016, p. 996). Relatedly, I've suggested that happiness is simply a reflection of how well our mind is functioning and is not necessarily something that we can control or set out to pursue (Besser-Jones, 2013). Both of these views take happiness to be less reflective of something deep and essentially connected to the self and to be more akin to an enjoyable state that might be fragile, and might be superficial, but regardless is something that is of prudential value to its bearer.

At this point one might reasonably question whether or not we are talking about the same thing, and with this in mind it is helpful to think back to our initial discussion of the difference between happiness and well-being. Here, we saw that while there are a variety of ways to distinguish between the two, one common way is to view well-being as involving an evaluative claim about what makes someone's life go well and to view happiness as a form of subjective well-being that describes a person's mental state. While Haybron would maintain that the emotional state theory is a theory of happiness as opposed to well-being, someone like Klausen might argue that the depth and robustness Haybron takes to be a criterion of happiness pushes the emotional state closer to that of one of well-being.

This isn't the first time we've hit a disagreement that largely boils down to intuitions, and it won't be the last. Philosophical theorizing makes a variety of uses of intuitions, and sometimes we hit points of juncture, like the one here, where we seem forced to decide: Does happiness have to have depth and make contributions to the self? If not, then we might find ourselves back to hedonism. But if so, then the emotional state theory presents an attractive and compelling view.

Conclusion

By framing happiness as an emotional condition, the emotional state theory seeks to capture a deeper, long-lasting form of happiness than a theory like hedonism is able to provide. Happiness isn't just moments of feeling pleasure, for these moments are likely too shallow and fleeting to affect a subject's mental state. Being happy is a state that disposes us to have these moments of happiness, but more importantly it is one in which we are attuned to our circumstances, in which we are fully engaged in our activities, and in which we endorse how our life is going. The emotional state theory presents a unique framework for thinking about happiness, yet in downplaying the importance of moments of feeling happy, and in prioritizing the long-term sense of happiness, it begets questions about whether or not it has gotten its target correct.

Chapter Summary

- The emotional state theory holds that happiness is a feature of one's overall emotional condition and is constituted by central affective states and mood propensities.
- Central affective states differ from peripheral affective states insofar as central affective states are dispositional, often described in physiological terms like "get to us," penetrate the self, and in general are profound, persistent, and pervasive.
- The actual states constitutive of happiness are attunement, engagement, and endorsement. These states describe ideal ways in which a person interacts with her environment and views her experiences.
- The inclusion of dispositions and mood propensities into the state of happiness is largely distinctive to the emotional state theory and raises questions about the depth associated with happiness.

End Notes

1 Haybron (2008, pp. 128–133). Here, I follow Hill's (2009) analysis.
2 Haybron maintains that central affective states present as similar to moods and may very well be moods or mood-like states as opposed to mere emotions or affective states.
3 Haybron (2010) questions whether or not this case invokes the sense of "negative mood propensity" that is relevant to happiness.
4 For the hedonist, this would be pleasant feelings, but we don't have to limit the feelings to hedonic ones; as we will see in the next chapter, it is possible to maintain that happiness is a categorical psychological state while describing that state in terms other than pleasure.

References

Besser-Jones, L. (2013). The pursuit and nature of happiness. *Philosophical Topics, 41*(1), 103–121.

Haybron, D. M. (2008). *The pursuit of unhappiness*. New York: Oxford University Press.

Haybron, D. M. (2010). Mood propensity as a constituent of happiness: A rejoinder to Hill. *Journal of Happiness Studies, 11*(1), 19–31.

Hill, S. (2009). Haybron on mood propensity and happiness. *Journal of Happiness Studies,* *10*(2), 215–228. https://doi.org/10.1007/s10902-007-9076-z

Klausen, S. H. (2016). Happiness, dispositions and the self. *Journal of Happiness Studies,* *17*(3), 995–1013. https://doi.org/10.1007/s10902-015-9628-6

Suggested for Further Reading

On the emotional state theory of happiness:

Haybron, D. M. (2008). *The pursuit of unhappiness.* New York: Oxford University Press.

On the debate between emotional state theory and hedonism:

Haybron, D. M. (2001). Happiness and pleasure. *Philosophy and Phenomenological Research,* *62*(3), 501–528.

Haybron, D. M. (2016). Mental state approaches to well-being. In M. D. Adler & M. Fleurbaey (Eds.), *The Oxford handbook of well-being and public policy* (Vol. 1), pp. 347–378. New York: Oxford University Press.

Morris, S. (2011). In defense of the hedonistic account of happiness. *Philosophical Psychology,* *24*(2), 261–281.

On the inclusion of mood propensities:

Haybron, D. M. (2010). Mood propensity as a constituent to happiness: A rejoinder to Hill. *Journal of Happiness Studies,* *11*, 19–31.

Hill, S. (2009). Haybron on mood propensity and happiness. *Journal of Happiness Studies,* *10*, 215–228.

Klausen, S. H. (2016). Happiness, dispositions, and the self. *Journal of Happiness Studies,* *17*, 995–1013.

5

HAPPINESS AS SATISFACTION

Most of us probably think that there is a deep connection between being satisfied and being happy. Being satisfied is often taken to indicate happiness, just as being dissatisfied is often taken to be a marker of unhappiness. It is hard to imagine a scenario in which being dissatisfied doesn't inhibit your happiness. Justin works from home doing online marketing. Yet he finds little satisfaction from it, instead wishing he could take the risk and open up his own bar. It would be unreasonable to deny that his dissatisfaction and wish to change things does not affect his happiness. But does this mean that happiness itself is a state of satisfaction? And if so, what kind of satisfaction?

The final philosophical approach to theorizing about happiness we will consider takes happiness to consist in some form of satisfaction—be it a state of desire satisfaction, in which one's desires are fulfilled, or a state of life satisfaction, in which one is satisfied overall with how one's life is going. Within philosophical discussion, desire fulfillment theories are most often discussed in the context of well-being as opposed to happiness.[1] Yet it is certainly worth considering the plausibility and limitations of thinking about happiness in terms of desire fulfillment, and doing so will help us appreciate the motivation and nature of the life satisfaction theories of happiness that enjoy much popularity.

Desire Fulfillment

Theories of desire fulfillment are relatively straightforward, maintaining the intuitively plausible view that one is better off to the extent that one's desires are fulfilled. The plausibility of this view derives largely from its focus on the individual: Whether or not something benefits an individual depends exclusively here on whether or not she desires it. If she desires it, and her desire is fulfilled, then she is better off as a result. Desire fulfillment seems to be a clear illustration of a prudential value insofar as the value is premised on the connection between the individual's desire and that desire being fulfilled.

Are All Desires Good for You?

As we saw in Chapter 2, many worry that the initial plausibility of this view becomes threatened by the nature of some of our desires. Not all our desires are for things that actually make us better off. We can desire to do drugs, to eat ice cream even though we are allergic to it, to hurt another person, to sleep all day, and so on. These kinds of desires call into question whether or not it is the *fulfillment* of desires that makes one better off, or the fulfillment of *desires that are good for you* that makes one better off.

Heathwood (2006) describes desires whose satisfaction is not good for us in terms of "defective desires." Defective desires include *ill-informed desires*, such as the desire to eat the ice cream cone you think is nondairy but is not, and *irrational desires*, such as the desire to do drugs. Ill-informed desires arise when an individual desires something yet lacks important information about that thing, the knowledge of which would likely prevent him from desiring it. For example, if Susie desires the ice cream cone that she thinks is nondairy yet in fact is full of dairy, it would be bad for her to fulfill that desire. Her desire is ill informed and so defective. Irrational desires arise when an individual desires something that conflicts with other things he desires or conflicts with his welfare. Examples of irrational desires include desires to smoke or do drugs, desires to avoid doctors or exercise, and so on.

Some versions of desire fulfillment theories work to exclude defective desires by focusing on those desires one has or would have only when one is fully informed and acting rationally, thereby ensuring that only those desires whose fulfillment is good for us count as prudentially valuable.[2] Yet others worry that this move doesn't go far enough and that there are troubling features of desires in general that call into question whether or not we are better off to the extent that we fulfill desires, even when those desires are fully informed and rational.

The first of these features is that desires often change. Kaif may have had a long-standing, deeply rooted desire to study paleontology, but as soon as he stepped foot into his first philosophy class, that desire went out the window. Jenny desires to shave her head every time the humidity index hits 90%; but this desire fades away as soon as the index drops. The changing nature of desires suggests that desires are unstable—even fickle. If desires are so unstable, it is difficult to see how they can be the things whose fulfillment makes us better off and structures our happiness.

A second concerning feature of desires is that they often concern things that are remote. Raphael desires a reduction in greenhouse gasses, Sarah desires peace in the Middle East, and Rachel desires a woman to become U.S. president. According to the desire fulfillment theory, the fulfillment of these desires benefits the individual who desires them, and she is happier by virtue of those desires being fulfilled. Yet the sense in which remote desires benefit the individual who desires them is unclear, making it challenging to see how the fulfillment of remote desires can be part of her happiness.

The desire fulfillment theory maintains that desire fulfillment benefits the individual by virtue of satisfying her desire, yet the above lines of argument call into question the connection between desire fulfillment and benefit. If not all desires are such that their fulfillment is of prudential value to the person who desires them, then we might reasonably question whether happiness can consist in desire fulfillment.

In the next two sections we will dig deeper into this question by exploring first the relationship between desire fulfillment and happiness. Here we consider L. W. Sumner's (1996) argument that desire fulfillment is a *source* of happiness rather than a *state* of happiness. We will then explore the possibility that what counts with respect to happiness is not fulfillment of desires but a state of satisfaction. Here, we consider a line of argument put forward by John Kekes (1982) that questions the impact desire fulfillment has on one's overall satisfaction with life.

The Relationship between Desire Fulfillment and Happiness

Our goal in analyzing the different philosophical accounts of happiness is, at root, to explore a particular theory's capacity to explain the nature of happiness itself. What is this state we call happiness? As we try to answer this question, it pays to keep in mind the difference between things that *contribute* to happiness and things that are *constitutive* of happiness. Constitutive aspects of something are components of the thing in itself and are inseparable from it. Sumner (1996) questions whether or not desire fulfillment is truly constitutive of happiness as opposed to being one source of happiness. He argues that desire fulfillment is something that tends to make us happy, and so is a reliable source of happiness, but that it shouldn't be taken to be happiness itself, which is what the desire fulfillment theory maintains.

What is the relationship between desire fulfillment and happiness? Certainly most of us agree that, in general, whether or not our desires are fulfilled matters to our happiness. When we think about how to be happy, we often start by thinking about what we want. We take our desires to inform the content of our happiness. We also tend to assume that when we get what we want, we'll be happy.[3] If I want to sell my house, and my house is sold, then I ought to be satisfied by virtue of my desire being fulfilled, and I ought to be happy.

These kinds of thoughts may lead us to assume that desire fulfillment is more tightly connected to happiness than it may, in fact, be. Already we have seen that many of these connections do not always hold. There isn't always a tight connection between having one's desires fulfilled and feeling happy as a result. I could feel empty once I sold my house, or perhaps feel remorse and regret over so doing, even though it is what I desired. Experiencing this kind of emptiness in the face of having an important desire fulfilled is commonplace and is borne out by empirical research regarding the short-lived impact changes to our situations have, even when those changes are greatly desired, such as winning a lottery or getting tenure.[4] If these gaps are likely, then desire fulfillment can't be constitutive of happiness.

Sumner (1996) analyzes this in terms of a problem of level.[5] Desire fulfillment theories pick out one aspect of what makes our lives go well, which is "getting what we want," and identify that aspect as happiness itself. Getting what we want may be an important source of happiness, but it can't be happiness itself for it is neither necessary nor sufficient for happiness. We can be happy when we don't get what we want, just as we can get what we want and not be happy.

Rather than identify desire fulfillment with happiness, Sumner encourages us to think about why desire fulfillment is an important source of happiness. Why is desire fulfillment an important source of happiness? Perhaps it is because we tend to be satisfied when our desires are fulfilled, and so perhaps what is most important to happiness is this sense of satisfaction rather than the fact that desires are fulfilled.

Desire Fulfillment or Life Satisfaction?

Those sympathetic to the above line of argument may also find the next line of argument compelling. Fulfilling one's desires is important and typically delivers a sense of satisfaction. When Simon gets into his dream school, the satisfaction of having that desire fulfilled is important and seems clearly associated with happiness. But imagine that Simon's stress levels about his schoolwork are off the charts, that Simon's parents are going through an ugly divorce, and that the sun hasn't been out in weeks. These aspects of Simon's life seem to affect his happiness and the effect his desire fulfillment has on his happiness, yet their impact is not naturally explained in terms of other desires he has. Sometimes things affect us independently of whether or not we desire them. The desire fulfillment theory struggles to explain this.

John Kekes suggests that desire fulfillment may be a better track of momentary feelings of happiness as opposed to a state of happiness. Simon may *feel* happy due to his desire fulfillment, but the circumstances of his life inhibit him from *being* happy. More formally, Kekes argues that having one's desires fulfilled delivers a "first-order" satisfaction, which makes one feel happy. But happiness overall is a "second-order" satisfaction, which arises from reflecting on one's life overall and does not depend on the fulfillment of any one desire. He argues that "a man cannot be lastingly happy unless he frequently feels happy. But one can feel happy and yet not be lastingly happy, for the transitory satisfaction may not amount to overall satisfaction with one's life" (Kekes, 1982, p. 361).

This line of argument directs us toward understanding happiness in terms of life satisfaction rather than desire fulfillment. It suggests that more than desire fulfillment influences happiness and that the reason why desire fulfillment is important is because it is an important source of happiness. We tend to be more satisfied with our lives to the extent that we have our desires fulfilled. But desire fulfillment itself isn't constitutive of happiness—rather, what is constitutive of happiness is a state of being satisfied with one's life overall.

Life Satisfaction

Life satisfaction views of happiness hold that happiness consists in being satisfied with one's life overall. This state of life satisfaction offers a deeper and more comprehensive approach to understanding happiness than we find within desire fulfillment theories and hedonistic theories of happiness. While these theories may provide plausible analyses of *feeling happy* (by virtue of fulfilling one's desires or feeling pleasure), defenders of life satisfaction theory argue that happiness is a lasting state not reducible to feeling happy. Like the emotional state theory, the life satisfaction theory seeks to explain what it means for someone to *be* happy, allowing that someone can be happy without necessarily feeling happy in the moment and conversely that someone can feel happy without being happy, as in the example of Simon discussed above. Simon might feel happy because his desire is fulfilled, but he might otherwise be very unsatisfied with his life and may not be happy.

Several lines of thought motivate the life satisfaction theory, which are prominent within philosophy and psychology. The first we've seen already, which is a concern that while desires and sensations are important sources of feeling happy, they aren't constitutive of happiness, for we can imagine a number of cases in which people may feel happy as a result of their desires and sensations but are not actually happy. The life satisfaction theory preserves the importance of desires and sensations as sources of happiness without collapsing them into happiness itself.

The second line of argument motivating life satisfaction theories of happiness appeals to their capacity to explain happiness in terms of the subject's own assessment of her mental state. For the life satisfaction theorist, what is most important is that the subject is satisfied with her life, and this state of satisfaction constitutes happiness. By locating happiness within the subject's own assessment of her life, life satisfaction theories preserve the subjectivity we typically associate with happiness. Doing so is particularly important for the project of understanding happiness, where the task is to describe the mental state of happiness as opposed to prescribing a particular kind of life as a good one. While the latter involves making an evaluation of what is best for the individual (and so is best construed as an analysis of well-being), the former involves developing a descriptive account of the state of happiness as individuals experience it.[6] Many have argued that respecting the subjectivity of happiness is essential to this project insofar as it preserves the efforts to describe. This is particularly important within the scientific study of happiness, where life satisfaction theories are increasingly popular.

Ed Diener, a psychologist whose work on happiness has stimulated much current scientific research, motivates the life satisfaction theory by appeal to its reliance on the individual as the ultimate judge of whether or not she is happy. He argues that

> it is a hallmark of the subjective well-being area [happiness] that it centers on the person's own judgments, not upon some criterion which is judged to be important by the researcher. For example, although health, energy, and so forth may be desirable, particular individuals may place different values on them. It is for this reason that we need to ask the person for their overall evaluation of their life, rather than summing across their satisfaction with specific domains, to obtain a measure of overall life satisfaction. (Diener, Emmons, Larsen, & Griffin, 1985, p. 71)

Life satisfaction theories are defined by this kind of commitment to defining happiness in terms of an individual's judgment about how their life is going.

Challenges for Life Satisfaction Theories

Life satisfaction theories take happiness to depend heavily on an individual's perception of how his life is going. Over the course of judging their life satisfaction, it will most often be the case that subjects think about the objective features of their life, such as whether or not they are in a good relationship or successful in their career. An individual experiences life satisfaction when his life is going how he wants it to, when there is a fit between how his life is going and how he wants his life to be going. We see these themes clearly illustrated in Jussi Suikkanen's formulation of the life satisfaction theory. He argues that a person, S, is happy to degree n at time t if and only if:

1. There is a certain life that S has lived up to t,
2. at t, S has an ideal life plan for her life,
3. at t, S has a moderately detailed conception of how her life has transpired so far, and
4. at t, S judges that her actual life so far matches her ideal life-plan to degree n. (Suikkanen, 2011, p. 151)

The driving point here is that happiness exists insofar as the circumstances of one's life match one's expectations of it.

Life satisfaction theories present a form of happiness that takes into direct consideration the impact states of affairs have on a subject's mental state, and many take this to be a key advantage of this approach. Diener, for example, argues that it is essential that the subject judge her degree of satisfaction herself, based on her own standards:

> Life satisfaction refers to a cognitive, judgmental process... Judgments of satisfaction are dependent upon a comparison of one's circumstances with what is thought to be an appropriate standard. It is important to point out that the judgment of how satisfied people are with their present state of affairs is based on a comparison with a standard which each individual sets for him or herself; it is not externally imposed. (Diener et al., 1985, p. 71)

If happiness is a matter of how the *subject* feels about the objective conditions of her life, then the subject must be the judge of her own satisfaction.

We see that happiness for the life satisfaction theorist consists in the mental state of being satisfied by the states of affairs that comprise one's life. Yet what if the subject errs in the process of evaluating the objective circumstances of life? While the life satisfaction theorist's efforts to prioritize the subject's perspective is well motivated, the messy realities of what is involved in actual life satisfaction judgments reveal what many take to be deep problems with the life satisfaction approach.

Deception[7]

The 1998 movie *The Truman Show* depicts the small-town life of Truman Burbank, who, unbeknownst to him, is the subject of a reality TV show and has been since he was adopted as a young child by the TV corporation. Every person he engages with—his wife, his employer, his neighbor, and his friends—are paid actors following a script geared toward giving Truman an ideal life. When Truman reflects on his life, his life (unsurprisingly) lives up to his expectations of it. He has a kind and loving wife, a great job, plenty of friends to spend time with, and no financial stress. On a straightforward interpretation of the life satisfaction theory, Truman should count as happy. And he is happy—at least until he finds out the reality behind his life. When he finds out the reality of his life, his satisfaction fades rapidly. He questions his wife's love and commitment, looks differently at his friends and coworkers, and finds himself unable to take satisfaction in, or to enjoy, his life given the knowledge that it is a farce.

Scenarios such as Truman's are not as far off as we might think. Spouses have affairs and even families that they keep secret from their partners. It is commonplace to laud one's coworker in person all the while talking behind his back. That person thinks he is well respected, but his perception couldn't be further from the truth. It isn't hard to imagine that there is at least one aspect of all of our lives where our perception of it fails to track reality. Putting this in the terminology described above, the concern is that our mental states do not always reflect accurately the states of affairs of which they are about. Given that judgments of life satisfaction are dependent on our perceptions of reality, the bridge they provide between our states of mind and states of affairs is tenuous. This limitation forces us to make some tough calls about whether or not a given person counts as happy. Is that much-maligned coworker happy insofar as he thinks people respect him? Is Truman happy before he finds out the truth about his life?

There are a number of moves one can take to respond to this threat of deception. The first is to understand the judgment invoked in life satisfaction to be a hypothetical judgment rather than an actual judgment. In this interpretation, what is most important is that a subject would judge herself satisfied with her life were she to do so with full information. While Truman actually might judge himself as satisfied, if he were fully informed about the conditions of his life, he would not be satisfied. A hypothetical judgment preserves an emphasis on the states of affairs: What counts most are the objective conditions of the individual's life and not she actual judgment of it.

A second move is to bite the bullet and accept that Truman is happy when he judges that his life meets his expectations for it, even if his judgment fails to track reality. This move defaults to the actual judgment a subject makes: If the subject deems herself satisfied with her life, that judgment is what counts with respect to her happiness. This approach highlights as most important the subject's own experience of her life and takes happiness to consist simply in the satisfaction one experiences with one's life. Sumner (1996) thinks this is the right way to think about happiness and one that follows from happiness's status as a mental state: "Happiness (or unhappiness) is a response by a subject to her life considerations *as she sees them*. It is a matter of whether she is finding the *perceived* conditions of her life satisfying or fulfilling" (Sumner, 1996, p. 156, emphasis in original).[8] This move places more weight on the individual's subjective judgment of satisfaction, taking her mental states to weigh more heavily than the states of affairs they are directed toward.

Subjective Limitations

The problem of deception is that is that an individual's perceptions of her reality are liable to be ill informed, making it the case that the information on which her judgment is predicated is false. A separate problem concerns whether or not, even when an individual's perceptions of her reality are well informed, her *judgment* that her life is ideal (or not) tracks her actual satisfaction with life.

The judgment of life satisfaction is based on either a cognitive appraisal of the extent to which one's life lives up to one's expectations or an affect-based sense of satisfaction with one's life, or some combination of both. Some, notably Haybron (2008), have argued that an individual's psychological tendencies and limitations threaten the weight life satisfaction theories place on these judgments, whether those judgments are taken to be cognitive or affective.

The first concern regards the standard one might realistically use to gauge one's satisfaction in the context of making a cognitive judgment. Most of us likely have rough ideas of what we think will constitute an ideal life. We may want to have a family, a personally and financially rewarding job, and to make contributions to our communities. These are the things we likely think about when asked to judge how satisfied we are with our life. But should these rough ideas be granted as much weight as the life satisfaction theorist grants them? The life satisfaction theorist grants them an authoritative status, but the reality is that these rough ideas are likely just that: Rough approximations of an ideal life. Very rarely do we work out a full account of what our ideal life looks like. If so, then it seems a mistake to hold that happiness consists in positive life evaluations of how one's life meets one's ideal.

Haybron describes this problem in terms of "attitude scarcity." He argues that we have good grounds to doubt that, "as a matter of empirical fact, people actually have attitudes toward their lives that are both robust enough and well-enough grounded in the facts of their lives to have the kind of significance happiness is thought to possess" (Haybron, 2008, p. 80). The problem here is twofold. First, most of us simply do not reflect on our lives to the extent necessary to deliver well-grounded judgments of life satisfaction that genuinely reflect the ways in which our lives approximate what we value. Second, even were we to engage in such reflection, that reflection is apt to be subject to a number of distorting influences.

Consider the rough ideals listed off above: A family, a good job, and community engagement. It is easy to assert these ideals because they are well engrained within society. And when someone is presented with the task of ranking how much he agrees with statements such as "In most ways, my life is close to ideal," chances are these are the things he invokes. But if these ideals are societal rather than individual, the individual's judgment of life satisfaction may fail to track his happiness. The reality is that even when we engage in reflection regarding our ideal life, such reflection likely will be subject to norms that implicitly press individuals toward embracing the ideals of their society. Put this tendency together with our tendency to report increased satisfaction when we think we are doing better than others (and correspondingly, decreased satisfaction when we think we are doing worse),[9] and questions arise regarding what it is we are actually tracking when we judge life satisfaction.

Consider also the wide body of psychological research exploring the ways in which the specific circumstances we experience in the moment of judgment influence those judgments. Whether or not we are in a good mood, for example, influences whether we rank our satisfaction at a 4 or a 5, making the difference between the two negligible at best, especially when we consider the little things that can prompt good moods, such as finding a dime or smelling freshly baked cookies.[10] These little things can distort our judgments.

Finally, it is becoming increasingly documented that some cultures are more optimistic than others and that these discrepancies in levels of optimism (as well as positive affect) show themselves in discrepancies in reported life satisfaction. Latin America, for example, regularly ranks high on the life satisfaction scale, while Japan ranks much lower. But these may be explainable by factors other than that they are happy, such as whether or not being optimistic is encouraged in one's culture. Diener et al., for example, explain Latin American countries' high levels of subjective well-being (SWB) as "a propensity to view life experiences in a rosy light because they value affect and a positive view of life. By the same token, Japan's relatively low SWB suggests a relative absence of the propensity to evaluate aspects of life positively" (Diener, Napa-Scollon, Oishi, Dzokoto, & Suh, 2000, pp. 160–161). These influences show the ways in which our judgments of life satisfaction may be distorted. This calls into question whether or not these judgments are reflective of happiness in the sense required by the life satisfaction theorist.[11]

Similar problems arise with respect to our capacity to make affective judgments. An affective judgment of life satisfaction invokes an emotional response to one's life—a sense of satisfaction or being pleased with one's life. Unlike cognitive judgments, affective judgments don't require standards of appraisal. Rather, in making an affective judgment, a subject reports her sense of satisfaction, or how she *feels* about her life. Sumner describes this in terms of *experiencing* satisfaction and takes it to be an important component of happiness: "More is involved in being happy than the bare positive evaluation: you must also experience your life as satisfying or fulfilling" (Sumner, 1996, p. 146).

Affective judgments are less cognitively demanding on a subject but nonetheless depend on a subject's ability to introspect and describe her emotional states. And this is something that proves to be more difficult than we might first think. Haybron (2008) argues that we don't have this kind of awareness and access to our affective states and that incidences of "affective ignorance" are quite common. Our ability to access and accurately describe our affective states is inhibited by a range of phenomena: Sometimes, for example, our preconceived beliefs about how we ought to be living our lives obscure how we are actually feeling. We might think that we should be satisfied with life because we've checked off all the right boxes (marriage, family, stable job). This might lead us to think that we feel satisfied when in fact we are deeply troubled and unsatisfied with life. Other times we've become so accustomed to our affective states that we find it difficult to gauge whether or not we are feeling positive affect or painful affect. We are also forgetful, and our memories are liable to leave out things that may have affected our levels of satisfaction. Even the things we do remember are liable to be blurred, as we tend to focus on the peak effects (e.g., losing the game) and to overlook the events leading up to them. All these considerations translate into difficulties in gauging our affective states. If we can't gauge our affective states, then even if the judgment involved in life satisfaction is affective rather than cognitive, it is still vulnerable to distortion.

Conclusion

The life satisfaction view maintains that happiness consists in being satisfied with one's life overall. We've seen many reasons why both philosophers and psychologists have found this approach to be appealing. Taking happiness to consist in life satisfaction preserves the subjectivity associated with happiness by taking the subject to be the authority of her own happiness; it delivers an understanding of happiness as lasting and covering the shape of one's life rather than an independent aspect of it; moreover, life satisfaction itself seems to capture a deep form of happiness. We've also seen that judgments of life satisfaction can be problematic and may not always reflect the degrees to which subjects genuinely feel or even judge themselves to be satisfied. This subjective limitation doesn't necessarily mean that we are wrong to think happiness consists in life satisfaction, for it doesn't extinguish the appeal of so doing. It may only threaten whether or not we can know when we are happy, or whether or not we are the best judges of our own happiness.

Life satisfaction theories are widely embraced within psychology and have informed much empirical research on happiness. As we move away from philosophical analysis of what happiness is and toward discussion of interdisciplinary research on happiness, we'll see more discussion of life satisfaction as well as hedonism. Most interdisciplinary research on happiness currently tends to see happiness as a combination of life satisfaction and hedonism, setting aside the philosophical differences and limitations of each theory—theoretical differences that may not translate to differences within the empirical presentation and study of happiness. When it comes to understanding the kinds of things that make us happy, and how happiness is studied within different disciplines, we'll see that much can be learned about happiness even absent a precise, shared specification of it.

Chapter Summary

- Theories of desire fulfillment face challenges because not all desires seem relevant to one's prudential value, and the fulfillment of some desires may even be harmful to the individual.
- While desire fulfillment theories define prudential value in terms of the fulfillment of desires, life satisfaction theories track an individual's overall satisfaction with her life and leave it up to the individual to determine what aspects of her life affect her life satisfaction and the degree to which they do so.
- Life satisfaction theories prioritize an individual's judgment that he is satisfied with his life. Depending on the particular theory, this judgment may be cognitive, affective, or both; and it may be hypothetical or actual.
- Life satisfaction judgments are often subject to various subjective limitations, including the possibility of being deceived, the influence of societal norms and biases, and situational influences that distort our judgments.

End Notes

1 See discussion of this in Chapter 2.
2 See Chapter 2 for fuller discussion of this move and its limitations.
3 We'll discuss some of the difficulties of this assumption in Chapter 10.
4 See Chapter 10 for further discussion.
5 He also thinks it arises with respect to hedonism and objective list theories.
6 Recently there have been efforts to develop a philosophical theory of well-being in terms of life satisfaction. Tiberius (2018) and Raibley (2013) develop versions of life satisfaction theory that frame well-being in terms of living a life that respects what one values. In introducing a standard to gauge how one's life is going and make an evaluative claim about how one should live, this theory sits as a theory of well-being. Because this standard is derived from the subject's values, it is a theory of well-being in which well-being is defined in terms of the subject's value and so presents a theory of well-being that is subjective.
7 See Chapter 11 for an extended discussion of this problem.
8 Sumner goes on to maintain that well-being or welfare requires more than happiness; it requires that one's perceptions of her conditions are informed and autonomous, so that one's perceptions of her conditions are accurate. He calls this "authentic happiness."
9 See, for example, Campbell, Converse, and Rodgers (1976).
10 Schwarz and Strack (1999) pursue this line of argument.
11 They also pose problems for the study and measurement of happiness, which we will discuss in Chapter 12.

References

Campbell, A., Converse, P. E., & Rodgers, W. L. (1976). *The quality of American life: Perceptions, evaluations, and satisfactions.* New York: Russell Sage Foundation.

Diener, E., Emmons, R. A., Larsen, R. J., & Griffin, S. (1985). The satisfaction with life scale. *Journal of Personality Assessment, 49*(1), 71–75.

Diener, E., Napa-Scollon, C. K., Oishi, S., Dzokoto, V., & Suh, E. M. (2000). Positivity and the construction of life satisfaction judgments: Global happiness is not the sum of its parts. *Journal of Happiness Studies, 1*(2), 159–176.

Feldman, F. (2008). Whole life satisfaction concepts of happiness. *Theoria, 74*(3), 219–238.

Haybron, D. M. (2008). *The pursuit of unhappiness.* New York: Oxford University Press.

Heathwood, C. (2006). Desire satisfaction and hedonism. *Philosophical Studies, 128*(3), 539–563.

Kekes, J. (1982). Happiness. *Mind, 91*(363), 358–376.

Raibley, J. (2013). Values, Agency, and Welfare. *Philosophical Topics, 41*(1), 187–214.

Schwarz, N., & Strack, F. (1999). Reports of subjective well-being: Judgmental processes and their methodological implications. *Well-Being: The Foundations of Hedonic Psychology, 7,* 61–84.

Suikkanen, J. (2011). An improved whole life satisfaction theory of happiness. *International Journal of Wellbeing, 1*(1), 149–166.

Sumner, L. W. (1996). *Welfare, happiness, and ethics.* New York: Clarendon Press.

Tiberius, V. (2018). *Well-Being as Value Fulfillment: How We Can Help Each Other to Live Well.* New York: Oxford University Press.

Suggested for Further Reading

On desire satisfaction and its limitations:

Heathwood, C. (2005). The problem of defective desires. *Australian Journal of Philosophy, 83*(4), 487–504.

Heathwood, C. (2015). Desire fulfillment theory. In G. Fletcher (Ed.), *Handbook of well-being* (pp. 135–147). London: Routledge Press.

Sumner, L. W. (1996). *Welfare, happiness, and ethics.* New York: Clarendon Press, chapter 5.

On general defenses of life satisfaction:

Diener, E. O., & Lucas, R. E. (2009). Subjective well-being: The science of happiness and life satisfaction. In S. J. Lopez & C. R. Snyder (Eds.), *Oxford handbook of positive psychology.* (pp. 63–73). New York: Oxford University Press.

Kekes, J. (1982). Happiness. *Mind, 91*(363), 358–376.

Suikkanen, J. (2011). An improved whole life satisfaction theory of happiness. *International Journal of Well-Being, 1*(1), 149–166.

Tatarkiewicz, W. (1976). *Analysis of happiness.* The Hague: Martinus Nijhoff.

On criticisms of life satisfaction:

Feldman, F. (2008). Whole life satisfaction concepts of happiness. *Theoria, 74*(3), 219–238.

Haybron, D. (2008). *The pursuit of unhappiness.* New York: Oxford University Press, chapter 5.

Schwarz, N., & Strack, F. (1999). Reports of subjective well-being: Judgmental processes and their methodological implications. *Well-Being: The Foundations of Hedonic Psychology, 7,* 61–84.

PART II

What Makes Us Happy?

6

HAPPINESS AND MATERIAL WEALTH

Wealth is often on our minds when we think about happiness. The rich seem happy, the poor seem sad, and those in between always seem to be striving for more. For many, building wealth serves as the ultimate goal: While recognizing that other things are important, we often make our most important decisions on the basis of their impact on our wealth. We think about wealth when we decide which careers to pursue and which partners to spend our lives with, when we pursue higher-paying jobs and uproot our families to take them.

While, if asked, we might hesitate to *equate* happiness with wealth, the reality is that many of our decisions reflect the belief that wealth comprises an important part of happiness. And it is clear why—wealth represents access to the things we need and want. Lack of wealth threatens our capacity to satisfy our needs and desires; this certainly seems to affect our happiness. By and large, research affirms that wealth is important to our happiness. But it also reveals some surprising results that demand interpretation and further reflection on just how wealth influences happiness.

As we think about the sources and correlates of happiness, it will be helpful to distinguish between those that are "internal" and those that are "external." Internal conditions of happiness describe components such as our attitudes, our motivations, and our emotions. It is generally thought that the internal factors are up to us: We can choose to see the world as half full or half empty, we can choose whether or not to respond to a lost opportunity with lament, and so forth. External conditions, in contrast, are those things we have less direct control over. External conditions of happiness describe the circumstances of our lives, the state of affairs ranging the gamut from where we live and whom we engage with to our standard of living and access to health care. To the extent that our happiness depends on external conditions, it seems that we are in less direct control of it. While these platitudes—"we can control the internal but not the external"—don't pan out exactly as we tend to think, the distinction between external and internal conditions of happiness is itself an important one, with particularly interesting implications for understanding how wealth contributes to happiness.

Wealth tracks part of the external conditions of happiness. But how much wealth is needed? And if wealth is important to happiness, is more wealth always preferable? This chapter explores these questions. Much of our discussion will revolve around three influential findings regarding the relationship between wealth and happiness. The first is the Easterlin paradox, which observes that wealth tracks reported life satisfaction but only up to a certain point. The second is the adaptation hypothesis, which maintains that our levels of affect adapt to changes in our environment. Adaptation threatens to mitigate the lasting impact external conditions have on our happiness. The third finding concerns the negative impact associated with *valuing* wealth and materialism more generally. These findings significantly influence discussion of and research regarding the complex relationship between wealth and happiness.

As we move away from Part I's analysis of philosophical theories of happiness and toward consideration of the causes and conditions of happiness (in Part II) and the study of happiness (in Part III), we will begin to talk more about "subjective well-being" than any particular theory of happiness. This language is somewhat misleading given the important philosophical differences between well-being and happiness, yet it has become the norm within interdisciplinary discourse on happiness. As we discussed in Chapter 2, strictly speaking, well-being invokes an evaluation of what makes a good life, whereas happiness describes a mental state. Theories of well-being can be either subjective or objective, depending on how they describe what makes a good life. The language of "subjective well-being," however, is treated as synonymous with happiness in virtue of capturing the notion that the mental state of happiness is one that is *subjectively experienced.*

Subjective well-being has come to represent a generic form of happiness, and it is most often taken to be some combination of life satisfaction and positive (hedonic) affect. At certain points, it will become important whether we are talking exactly about life satisfaction or affect or some other aspect of subjective well-being, but unless specified, I will treat "subjective well-being" as synonymous to this generic sense of happiness.

When Is Wealth Important and Why?

Within contemporary societies, wealth serves as a bridge between our needs, wants, and desires and their satisfaction. We need things, and things cost money;

wealth allows us access to the things we need. This bridge is essential to the satisfaction of our basic needs for food, clean water, and shelter.

Does happiness depend on the satisfaction of these needs? It is indeed challenging to imagine how any level of happiness is possible when our basic needs go unfulfilled. In theory, a view of happiness that takes it to consist in purely an internal state of mind might maintain that happiness is independent of *all* need satisfaction. This kind of view, familiar to Stoic and Buddhist traditions, maintains that happiness involves the development of a mental state that is void of attachments to the external material world. Premised on the importance of recognizing the limited extent to which we can control things external to us, these theories advocate developing a state of mind that is not contingent to conditions of our daily lives.

The task of obtaining a positive mental state in the face of severely limited resources, however, is daunting. Where one is hungry and lacking a warm, safe space to sleep, one's failure to meet one's basic needs creates a constant source of stress that negatively affects one's physical and psychological well-being. There is abundant research establishing positive correlations between subjective well-being and one's capacity for meeting one's subsistence needs.

Research by Kahneman and Deaton (2010), for example, finds that within the United States, increases in income correlate with increases in positive affect until one's income reaches approximately $75,000. Subjects earning below $75,000 tend to experience more stress and pain from life's events. They report more experiences of worry, stress, and headaches; and the emotional pain that results from physical illnesses, divorces, and loneliness is "significantly exacerbated by poverty," leading Kahneman and Deaton to "conclude that a lack of money brings both emotional misery and low life evaluation" (2010, p. 16491).

Results like this are not surprising. Anyone who has ever experienced financial stress knows that it infiltrates all aspects of one's life. The pressures created when you can't pay your bills or buy food or are forced to go without health care don't go away. Their threat is pervasive and difficult to compartmentalize.

In contrast, people who are wealthy tend to have greater levels of physical and mental health and experience fewer stressful life events. They are less likely to be the victims of violent crimes, and they survive better and live longer. They have children who are less likely to drop out of school or to become pregnant at a young age.

These advantages do seem to translate to greater levels of happiness, but perhaps not to the degree we might expect. There are clearly some reasons for thinking that money comes into play with respect to our subjective well-being. It seems particularly true that a lack of money negatively affects our happiness. Awareness of the negative effects that come with financial struggles leads many people to value and prioritize material goods. Because a lack of money hampers our happiness so significantly, many tend to think that money—and material goods more generally—are the key to happiness, and they structure their lives in the pursuit of it. But just because a lack of wealth negatively affects our subjective well-being, does it really hold that the converse is true and that the more wealth we have, the happier we will be?

Relatively early work on this subject challenges this perspective. Economist Richard Easterlin's research (1974) investigates whether or not increases in income track increases in happiness at the societal level, where happiness is understood primarily in terms of life satisfaction. Among his findings is that despite the fact that GDP and incomes within the United States increased significantly between post World War II and the 1970s, the average reported happiness of individuals did not. Subsequent data on the GDP and income levels within the United States between the 1970s and the 2000s corroborate this finding. GDP has increased a whopping 73% during this period, and family income has increased by 37%, yet average happiness levels have remained flat (perhaps even decreasing slightly) (Angeles, 2011, p. 68).

The Easterlin paradox, as it is often called, challenges what was, and continues to be, a widespread assumption that income tracks happiness. This assumption seems particularly live within the field of economics, for reasons Frey and Stutzer describe as follows:

> A higher income expands individuals' and countries' opportunity set; that is, more goods and services can be consumed. The few people not interested in more commodities need not consume them; they have the freedom to dispose of any unwanted surplus free of charge. It therefore seems obvious that income and happiness go together (provided, of course that the two are correctly measured). Consequently, economics textbooks do not even make an effort to come up with a reason, but simply state that utility U is raised by income Y. (Frey & Stutzer, 2010, p. 73)[1]

It isn't just economists who make this assumption: Something like this assumption is rampant in society and in our everyday reflections and deliberations. We assume that the more we make, the happier we will be. If the Easterlin paradox holds, then the very perspective from which we view wealth might be wrong. We need wealth, but *more* might not always be better.

A certain level of material comfort is necessary to provide for one's needs and to buffer against the threats we face daily. This explains why wealthier countries on the whole consistently rank higher on subjective well-being than poorer countries. And while there is some evidence that within a country, wealthier tend to be happier than poorer and fare much better than the poorer in avoiding extreme levels of unhappiness,[2] there is also evidence suggesting that this effect is constrained. Once we have a level of material comfort, the impact of more money on our subjective well-being is questionable. Multiple lines of research show that once income levels hit a certain point, correlations between wealth and happiness fall apart. A 2018 analysis shows a global satiation point for life satisfaction at $95,000 (Jebb, Tay, Diener, & Oishi, 2018). The satiation point does seem to vary depending on whether we are tracking life satisfaction or positive affect, but satiation points have been identified for each of these dimensions as well as for emotional well-being.[3]

Adaptation and Expectations

The above analysis of the effect wealth has on happiness shows that there seems to be a satiation point at which point increases in income no longer track increases in life satisfaction. Anyone who has ever gotten a raise and then wondered three months later where the extra money went probably won't find this surprising. We quickly get used to increases in income. While higher income levels offer more opportunities for acquiring material goods, the acquisition of these goods doesn't seem to have positive effects on our subjective well-being. Psychological analysis of this cycle suggests a twofold explanation. First, there is a psychological process of adaptation that affects our experiences of happiness. Second, material goods themselves are not a reliable source of happiness.

Our needs and wants are largely reflective of what we expect is feasible for us. As a broke college student, Rory has pretty low expectations when it comes to resources and material goods. He knows he doesn't have enough money to eat out every night and that he'd rather spend his money on pitcher nights at the bar. So it doesn't bother him when he eats ramen on most nights and cereal on the other nights. When Rory graduates and obtains his first full-time job, however, his attitude shifts. He expects not to rely on ramen and cereal for dinners. He expects to be able to eat out on a regular basis and to have after-work drinks with his friends even when there are no specials. The first month of being able to do so is great: He enjoys the freedom of going out for a drink whenever he feels like it, the variety of eating different kinds of foods, and the experiences of being out with friends. But soon these opportunities become his norm. The novelty of eating out wears off, yet the expectation of being able to do so stands. Ramen and cereal no longer suffice.

This is a familiar phenomenon. Rory experiences an increase in income. This increase affords him more opportunities, and his expectations raise in proportion to the increase. What he takes himself to need and to want evolves accordingly. When in college, Rory needed—and wanted—only cheap, filling food. When gainfully employed, Rory finds that he now needs and wants variety in his diet, tasty food that doesn't weigh him down, and not to cook for himself. He is able to provide for his needs, but overall he finds himself in a similar standing with respect to his income: Just as his small stipend in college provided only enough for his needs, his new income provides only enough for his needs. The change in needs and wants tracks the change in income, stabilizing the impact his extra income has on his happiness. Rory has adapted.

Adaptation is part of our neurological response system. This system is designed to alert us to *changes* in our environment. Presentation of new stimuli triggers a new reaction: This is why finding a $20 bill abandoned on the sidewalk is so exciting and makes one feel good—because it is out of the ordinary. Yet presentation of stable conditions triggers little to no reaction: After a few months, even a $100-per-week raise in one's income likely generates no reaction. It feels good to look at one's bank account in the beginning and to see the *change* the raise delivers. But once the income is stabilized and no longer presents change, these positive attitudes are no longer triggered. We have adapted to the change. Because we have adapted and effectively neutralized our levels of stimulation, when asked whether or not we are especially happy in light of our income, we'll likely say no. Adaptation theory maintains, correspondingly, that people judge themselves to be happy based on their current level of stimulation and whether that current level is higher or lower than what they are used to.

This system of adaptation has proved advantageous from an evolutionary perspective. We can't function at high levels of alertness at all times; rather, it is to our advantage to have a neurological response system that alerts us to changes but that adapts to steady states and so is not in a constant state of activation. Yet, while evolutionarily advantageous, the adaptive process functions to minimize the impact changes to our situations have on our subjective well-being.

A well-known study by Brickman, Coates, and Janoff-Bulman (1978) investigates the long-term impact significant life changes have on our affective states. Their research looks at individuals experiencing positive life changes (winning the lottery) or negative life changes (becoming paraplegic) with the aim of understanding the impact these major life changes have upon their experiences of positive affect. Their initial studies found that while both groups experienced changes in happiness levels immediately following the events, after two years their levels had returned to baseline, where they stabilized.

Focusing in particular on the limited effect winning the lottery has on their subjects' happiness levels, Brickman et al. offer two primary reasons for this effect. The first is that winning the lottery changes one's point of contrast, making it the case that subjects fail to take pleasure in the things they used to:

> Winning a million dollars is both a distinctive event and an event that is relevant to many other life occurrences. Since it constitutes an extremely positive comparison point, however, the thrill of winning the lottery should result in an upward shift in adaptation level. Consequently, many ordinary events may seem less pleasurable, since they now compare less favorably with past experience. Thus, while winning $1 million can make

new pleasures available, it may also make old pleasures seem less enjoyable. That new pleasures are offset by compensatory loss of old ones should in turn militate against any general gain in happiness by lottery winners. (Brickman et al., 1978, p. 918)

The second reason appeals to the ease with which people habituate to the new pleasures their winnings afford:

> Eventually, the thrill of winning the lottery will itself wear off. If all things are judged by the extent to which they depart from a baseline of past experience, gradually even the most positive events will cease to have impact as they themselves are absorbed into the new baseline against which further events are judged. Thus, as lottery winners become accustomed to the additional pleasures made possible by their new wealth, these pleasures should be experienced as less intense and should no longer contribute very much to their general level of happiness. (Brickman et al., 1978, p. 918)

Together, these tendencies neutralize the impact the new wealth has on a subject's levels of happiness:

> In sum, the effects of an extreme stroke of good fortune should be weakened in the short run by a contrast effect that lessens the pleasure found in mundane events and in the long run by a process of habituation that erodes the impact of the good fortune itself. (Brickman et al., 1978, p. 918)

While some worry about the limited longitudinal reach of this particular study,[4] there is little debate that adaptation occurs and that it occurs particularly with respect to wealth and income.

Adaptation has a far-reaching effect on happiness. The effects of adaptation threaten to mitigate not only the influence of wealth on happiness but also the influence of external conditions more generally. This has significant impact for the pursuit of happiness, which we will consider in Chapter 11.

The Limits of External Sources of Happiness

Our capacity for adaptation suggests that whether or not we experience happiness depends not exclusively on external conditions of life but to a perhaps surprising extent on the degree to which those conditions have changed. There is not a direct input/output relationship between the external conditions of our life and our subjective well-being. We've seen so far that there is a complex relationship between money and happiness. A *lack* of money interferes with our capacity to experience subjective well-being, and *changes* to our level of income might translate to temporary changes in happiness, but, contrary to popular opinion, more money is not always better. Our mind seems to have much more control over whether or not we are happy than most of us probably realize.

Psychologist Tim Kasser (2003) explores this theme in his analysis of materialism and the limits of materialism. What he finds is that once we are past subsistence levels, it isn't the possession of material goods that necessarily affects our happiness but rather how we *view* and *value* the possession of material goods. His research finds that embracing materialistic goals and structuring our life around them negatively affects our happiness.

Kasser's particular research on materialism operates within a larger field of psychology that explores the impact the content of goals has on their pursuit and obtainment. According to this line of research, desiring or wanting something isn't enough to make one happy when one successfully obtains it. Wanting to be wealthy will not make one happy upon becoming wealthy; rather, whether or not satisfying a desire will make one happy depends heavily on whether that desire is reflective of something that is conducive to one's psychological needs.

This framework, sometimes called a "human nature approach," maintains that there are basic psychological needs that affect how we experience things and specifically that affect the degree to which objects of desire are experienced as rewarding. Experiences are rewarding when they fulfill these needs and are less rewarding to the extent that they do not fulfill or, worse, hamper the fulfillment of needs. When we desire something that fulfills our needs, we experience the satisfaction of that desire as rewarding. When we desire something that does not fulfill our needs, or prevents us from fulfilling our needs, we experience the satisfaction of that desire as less rewarding.

The specific framework Kasser works within is the self-determination perspective (Deci & Ryan, 2000), according to which we have three central innate psychological needs:

- First, we have a need for relatedness: We need social engagement and to feel that we belong. Sometimes called a need for "belongingness," satisfaction of this need is widely recognized to be essential to our psychological development as well as to our experience of cognitive functioning, physical health, and a host of other aspects essential to our general well-being. Deprivation of this need can be devastating for the subject, as seen through the well-documented effects of social isolation. We'll talk much more about this need in Chapter 9.
- Second, we have a need for autonomy: We need to experience our activities as stemming from ourselves. The self-determination framework maintains that we satisfy our need for autonomy to the extent that we can identify with and even internalize the goals/aims of our actions. We satisfy our need

for autonomy when we pursue courses of action that we embrace and so feel
as if we are in control of them.

- Third, we have a need for competence: We need to experience ourselves as
having the ability and skills to accomplish our goals and to make contributions to our environment. We satisfy this need through engaging in activities that challenge us, stimulating us to use and develop our skills.

There are different ways of carving up our psychological needs, and the self-determination perspective Kasser works within presents just one way of framing and understanding them. But there is widespread convergence on the themes self-determination theory identifies in their specification of needs: We need social interaction; we need to experience ourselves as the source of our actions; we need to feel that we are competent at the experiences we engage in. When these needs are fulfilled, we experience psychological well-being and generate positive cycles of need fulfillment. The more we fulfill our needs, the greater psychological well-being we experience, and the greater psychological well-being we experience, the better situated we are to keep fulfilling those needs.[5]

With this background in place, we ought to expect that pursuing goals that fulfill needs benefits us more than pursuing goals that don't. Kasser's research identifies significant differences between the pursuit of "intrinsic" and "extrinsic" aspirations. Intrinsic aspirations tend to involve goals that are internal to oneself. These are goals that we give to ourselves or that we at least identify with—we pursue the goal because we like it, because it satisfies our interests and not because it will lead others to approve of us, or because we think we should be pursuing it. Intrinsic aspirations tend to be ones that satisfy our psychological needs and generate states of intrinsic motivation, in which we experience ourselves as the source of action and are driven to act out of interest.

Extrinsic aspirations, in contrast, tend to involve pursuits of things whose value is external to us; their value lies not in the fact that they satisfy innate psychological needs but rather is determined by features external to us, such as the admiration of others. This structure affects what it feels like when we pursue extrinsic aspirations. Pursuit of extrinsic aspirations tends to involve striving for the admiration or praise of others or other external rewards and tends to lead us to determine our self-worth via our success in obtaining these external rewards. Cumulatively, these features lead subjects who pursue extrinsic aspirations to experience their activities as "controlled" rather than as autonomous. This is one reason why pursuit of extrinsic aspirations fails to satisfy psychological needs.

Wealth seems clearly to be an extrinsic goal whose pursuit is an extrinsic aspiration. Kasser finds that those who value materialistic goals experience less psychological well-being than do those who value nonmaterialistic goals. To determine the extent to which individuals value materialistic goals, Kasser and his colleagues ask subjects to rank how important financial aspirations, such as having a job that pays well, having expensive possessions, and having a job with high social status, are to them. Those who ranked these financial aspirations highly also tended to highly value other extrinsic goals, such as social recognition/fame and appearances. These subjects reported lower well-being, seen through both psychological and physical measures, than subjects who prioritized values centered around self-acceptance and social affiliation or community—representations of intrinsic aspirations. Kasser concludes:

> Adults who focused on money, image, and fame reported less self-actualization and vitality, and more depression than those less concerned with these values. What is more, they also reported significantly more experiences of physical symptoms. That is, people who believed it is important to strive for possessions, popularity, and good looks, also reported more headaches, backaches, sore muscles, and sore throats than individuals less focused on such goals. (Kasser, 2003, p. 11)

How do we explain the negative impact valuing material possessions has on our happiness and well-being?

Following Kasser's line of argument, let's consider what happens when we value material possessions and the fame and image goals with which financial goals are associated. When we value material goods, we create a psychological orientation that looks outside ourselves for affirmation and value. We gauge our self-worth by factors external to us, and this begets a cycle that leads us to pursue experiences for the sake of external rewards rather than pursuing the kinds of experiences we need to satisfy our innate psychological needs. The cycle just described—one in which one's values and aspirations set up a cycle that ultimately disassociates one from fulfilling one's true needs—is a familiar one. Image goals are notoriously like this: When we aspire to maintain a certain image, be it a youthful one or a fashionable one, we focus on things that turn out to deliver very little satisfaction and lead us to neglect the kinds of experiences that do satisfy us. Likewise, taking financial goals to be the marker of happiness encourages us to value wealth too much. If Kasser is right, this leads us to neglect things whose attainment does deeply satisfy and affect one's happiness.

Conclusion

While money is important to our happiness, we've seen research converging on two themes: *more* money is not always better, and *valuing* material goods diminishes your well-being and happiness. The message seems clear: If we want to be happy, we shouldn't value material goods. And as long as we are earning enough to subsist, increases in our income won't make a difference to our happiness, so we might think cautiously before making life decisions for the sake of increased income. Of course, this is easier said than done, particularly for those of us living in societies that value and prioritize materialistic values. The societal transmission of values is easy to catch and hard to resist. As Kasser describes, "society encourages materialistic values, so we adopt them and pursue more and more materialistic aims; such pursuits do not improve our happiness, so we look to society for suggestions on how to be happier; society tells us to become even more materialistic, and on it goes" (Kasser, 2003, p. 100). We'll consider the role public policy can play in directing a society to prioritize happiness over material gain in Chapter 14.

Making decisions about what to prioritize in our society, or in our own lives, involves coming to terms with how important happiness is and what we are prepared to sacrifice for the sake of it. The research we've explored suggests that prioritizing wealth and embracing materialism stands in tension with experiencing happiness so that it is a mistake to pursue and value these things for the sake of being happy. There may be other reasons why these pursuits are important and worthwhile, but their connection to happiness does not seem to be one of them.

Chapter Summary

- The Easterlin paradox observes that increases in a society's GDP do not track corresponding increases in subjective well-being, calling into question the correlation between wealth and happiness.
- Most researchers recognize that there is a "satiation point" of income after which increases in income do not track increases in subjective well-being.
- Our neurological capacity for adaptation can mitigate the effect changes to our income (be they increases or decreases) have on our happiness. More generally, this adaptation effect threatens the impact any change in our circumstances may have on our subjective well-being.
- Valuing wealth and other material goods tends to generate a negative cycle in which one pursues external validation through accumulation of resources, often thereby neglecting to satisfy one's innate psychological needs.

End Notes

1 Frey and Stutzer refer here to the neoclassical field of economics; behavioral economics takes a more complicated view on the relationship between utility and happiness. We'll return to this topic in Chapter 13.
2 Kahneman and Deaton (2010).
3 Jebb et al. (2018) and Kahneman and Deaton (2010).
4 See Diener, Lucas, and Scollon (2006), Lucas (2007), and Chapter 11 for discussion.

5 Notice that the focus on innate psychological need satisfaction is often framed, as it is here, in terms of psychological well-being. Psychological well-being is gauged by looking at behaviors and other indicators of mental health, such as vitality, lack of depression or anxiety, and cognitive functioning. Psychological well-being is highly correlated with subjective well-being and intuitively so: We might see psychological well-being as a precondition for experiencing happiness (Besser-Jones, 2013).

References

Angeles, L. (2011). A closer look at the "Easterlin paradox". *The Journal of Socio-Economics*, *40*(1), 67–73.

Besser-Jones, L. (2013). The pursuit and nature of happiness. *Philosophical Topics*, *41*(1), 103–121.

Brickman, P., Coates, D., & Janoff-Bulman, R. (1978). Lottery winners and accident victims: Is happiness relative? *Journal of Personality and Social Psychology*, *36*(8), 917–927.

Deci, E. L., & Ryan, R. M. (2000). The "what" and "why" of goal pursuits: Human needs and the self-determination of behavior. *Psychological Inquiry*, *11*(4), 227–268.

Diener, E., Lucas, R. E., & Scollon, C. (2006). Beyond the hedonic treadmill: Revising the adaptation theory of well-being. *American Psychologist*, *61*(4), 305–314.

Frey, B. S., & Stutzer, A. (2010). *Happiness and economics: How the economy and institutions affect human well-being*. Princeton, NJ: Princeton University Press.

Jebb, A. T., Tay, L., Diener, E., & Oishi, S. (2018). Happiness, income satiation and turning points around the world. *Nature Human Behaviour*, *2*(1), 33. https://doi.org/10.1038/s41562-017-0277-0

Kahneman, D., & Deaton, A. (2010). High income improves evaluation of life but not emotional well-being. *Proceedings of the National Academy of Sciences United States of America*, *107*(38), 16489–16493.

Kasser, T. (2003). *The high price of materialism*. Cambridge, MA: MIT Press.

Lucas, R. E. (2007). Adaptation and the set-point model of subjective well-being: Does happiness change after major life events? *Current Directions in Psychological Science*, *16*(2), 75–79.

Suggested for Further Reading

On the Easterlin paradox:

Angeles, L. (2011). A closer look at the Easterlin paradox. *The Journal of Socio-Economics*, *40*(1), 67–73.

Easterlin, R. A. (1974). Does economic growth improve the human lot? Some empirical evidence. *Nations and Households in Economic Growth*, 89–95.

Easterlin, R. A. (1995). Will raising the incomes of all increase the happiness of all? *Journal of Economic Behavior & Organization*, *27*(1), 35–47.

Easterlin, R. A., McVey, L. A., Switek, M., Sawangfa, O., & Zweig, J. S. (2010). The happiness–income paradox revisited. *Proceedings of the National Academy of Sciences United States of America*, *107*(52), 22463–22468.

Stevenson, B., & Wolfers, J. (2008). *Economic growth and subjective well-being: Reassessing the Easterlin paradox* (Working Paper No. 14282). National Bureau of Economic Research.

On adaptation:

Brickman, P., Coates, D., & Janoff-Bulman, R. (1978). Lottery winners and accident victims: Is happiness relative? *Journal of Personality and Social Psychology, 36*(8), 917–927.

Diener, E., Lucas, R. E., & Scollon, C. (2006). Beyond the hedonic treadmill: Revising the adaptation theory of well-being. *American Psychologist, 61*(4), 305–314.

Haidt, J. (2006). *The happiness hypothesis: Finding modern truth in ancient wisdom*. New York: Basic Books.

Lucas, R. E. (2007). Long-term disability is associated with lasting changes in subjective well-being: Evidence from two nationally representative longitudinal studies. *Journal of Personality and Social Psychology, 92*(4), 717–730.

Lucas, R. E., Clark, A. E., Georgellis, Y., & Diener, E. (2003). Reexamining adaptation and the set point model of happiness: Reactions to changes in marital status. *Journal of Personality and Social Psychology, 84*(3), 527–539.

On human nature and human needs:

Deci, E. L., & Ryan, R. M. (2000). The "what" and "why" of goal pursuits: Human needs and the self-determination of behavior. *Psychological Inquiry, 11*(4), 227–268.

Ryan, R. M., & Deci, E. L. (2002). Overview of self-determination theory: An organismic dialectical perspective. In E. L. Deci & R. M. Ryan (Eds.), *Handbook of self-determination research* (pp. 3–33). Rochester, NY: University of Rochester Press.

Ryan, R. M., Sheldon, K. M., Kasser, T., & Deci, E. L. (1996). All goals are not created equal. In P. Gollwitzer and J. Bargh (Eds.), *The psychology of action: Linking cognition and motivation to behavior* (pp. 7–26). New York: Guilford Press.

Ryff, C. D., & Singer, B. H. (1998). The contours of positive human health. *Psychological Inquiry, 9*(1), 1–28.

Sheldon, K. M. (2002). The self-concordance model of healthy goal striving: When personal goals correctly represent the person. In E. L. Deci & R. M. Ryan (Eds.), *Handbook of self-determination research* (pp. 65–86). Rochester, NY: University of Rochester Press.

On materialism:

Belk, R. W. (1985). Materialism: Trait aspects of living in the material world. *Journal of Consumer Research, 12*(3), 265–280.

Kasser, T., & Ryan, R. M. (1993). A dark side of the American dream: Correlates of financial success as a central life aspiration. *Journal of Personality and Social Psychology, 65*(2), 410–422.

Kasser, T., & Ryan, R. M. (1996). Further examining the American dream: Differential correlates of intrinsic and extrinsic goals. *Personality and Social Psychology Bulletin, 22*, 280–287.

Kilbourne, W. E., & LaForge, M. C. (2010). Materialism and its relationship to individual values. *Psychology & Marketing, 27*(8), 780–798.

Ryan, L., & Dziurawiec, S. (2001). Materialism and its relationship to life satisfaction. *Social Indicators Research, 55*(2), 185–197.

7
HAPPINESS AND VIRTUE

"Some philosophers say that true happiness comes from a life of virtue." So says Hobbes to Calvin as Calvin is about to throw a snowball at Susie. Calvin stops and proceeds to test this hypothesis. He cleans his room, shovels the driveway, makes his mom a card, and generally is a good boy. But he finds himself frustrated. The next chance he gets, he pegs Susie with a snowball, declaring, "Someday I'll write my own philosophy book." Hobbes agrees, noting, "Virtue needs some cheaper thrills."

The position that with virtue comes happiness is one deeply engrained within the history of philosophy. Aristotle's conception of "eudaimonia" holds that exercising virtue comprises an important part of human flourishing, such that true happiness is unattainable without virtue. While many contemporary philosophers distinguish "eudaimonia" from happiness (and certainly from subjective well-being),[1] the notion that virtue is important to happiness is one to which many are deeply committed.

Ordinary conceptions of happiness and of virtue, however, often see the two as opposed, encouraging something more akin to the view described above, according to which being virtuous stands in the way of being happy. There is an important tension between ordinary conceptions of happiness and deeply engrained philosophical views about happiness regarding the role of virtue within happiness. In what follows, we will work through this tension, beginning by exploring Aristotle's position that virtue is necessary to happiness and then turning to consider how much of this view survives within the framework that takes happiness to consist in subjective well-being.

Eudaimonia

Aristotle's conception of "eudaimonia" focuses on human flourishing and is distinctive insofar as it maintains a connection between human flourishing and virtue. As we saw in Chapter 2, contemporary philosophers disagree about whether "eudaimonia" describes a theory of happiness, with some holding that eudaimonia is best understood as a form of well-being and some holding that eudaimonia is best understood as a robust form of human happiness—something that tracks what we might describe as *true happiness*. If you've ever been compelled by the thought that, even though your life is full of good feelings, you might not be *truly happy*, then a distinction between subjective well-being (feeling happiness) and eudaimonia (experiencing a deeper, more settled form of happiness) might be one way to characterize that thought.

Eudaimonia is at its basis a theory of human flourishing. Aristotle's project in formulating eudaimonia is to explore how it is that human beings can flourish and obtain their most supreme good. Aristotle argues that given the rational capacities distinctive to human beings, in order for human beings to flourish, they must use this rational capacity in its highest, most excellent form. And this, Aristotle argues, is through the exercise of virtue.

Aristotle recognizes that not everyone thinks about happiness in these terms. People often think that happiness consists in a life of money, or a life of pleasure, or, as was particularly true in ancient times, a life of honor. Yet Aristotle delivers powerful arguments calling into question whether any of these approaches can at all approximate what our highest end consists in. To be our highest end, representative of our supreme good, it needs to be a life that we want for its own sake and that for the sake of which we wish other things. And to be the highest *human* end, it must be tied to our humanity.

In his *Nicomachean Ethics*, Aristotle argues that there are three conditions to which a conception of human happiness must conform: First, it must be reflective of distinctively human capacities. Second, it must be good itself. This means it must be a complete good and not lacking in any other desirable aspects. Third, it must be a self-sufficient good and so not depend on anything else. Aristotle argues that these conditions exclude the other conceptions of happiness he took to be commonplace. Our highest end cannot be a life of money or wealth, for wealth is something that is valuable only insofar as it is useful toward something else. It cannot also be a life of pleasure, for pleasure is an end shared by nonhuman animals. And it cannot be a life of honor, for this depends on others bestowing it.

Aristotle argues that only a life of virtue meets these conditions and is our highest end. A life of virtue is distinctively human insofar as it depends on the exercise of reason. A life of virtue is self-sufficient insofar as it doesn't depend on the approval or affirmation of other people or any other goods. A life of virtue is a complete good: One who has a life of virtue finds that it lacks nothing at all and that it is "always worth choosing in itself and never for the sake of something else" (Aristotle, 340 B.C.E., sec. 1097a35).

By "virtue," Aristotle means a mental state that causes its possessors to do good things and to perform their functions well. Virtues are dispositions, which activate in response to virtue-eliciting conditions and allow us to feel the emotions appropriate to the circumstances. "By states," Aristotle writes, "I mean those things in respect of which we are well or badly disposed in relation to feelings. If, for example, in relation to anger, we feel it too much or too little, we are badly disposed; but if we are between the two, then well disposed. And the same goes for the other cases" (Aristotle, 340 B.C.E., secs. 1105b26-29). Virtues are not themselves particular feelings but are dispositions to feel the proper emotions at the appropriate time.

To illustrate, consider the virtue of "courage." Aristotle defines courage in terms of the mean between cowardice and foolhardiness: The coward feels too much fear and becomes frozen in response to danger; the foolhardy fails to feel enough fear and jumps into dangerous situations recklessly. The courageous person, however, feels the amount of fear appropriate to her situation. Her degree of emotion accurately reflects the level of danger presented by the situation and allows her to engage in the situation with a degree of caution. She is neither too scared nor too brash.

Those who possess virtue will feel emotions appropriate to the situation that allow them to act well: The courageous person will be able to jump into a shallow pond and save a drowning girl. Importantly, Aristotle stresses that part of possessing virtue is to feel the appropriate emotion fully and without conflict. A courageous person won't be torn about whether or not to embrace her disposition to help even in the face of danger. She will do so wholeheartedly, and this leads her to feel pleasure in the exercise of virtue. Pleasure, Aristotle maintains, isn't the point of virtuous activity but is that which "completes" the activity: "So long, then, as the objects of intellect or perception, and the faculties of judgment or contemplation, are as they should be, there will be pleasure in the activity" (Aristotle, 340 B.C.E., secs. 1174b32-1175a).

While it isn't a central aspect of his theory, Aristotle does believe the virtuous person will experience pleasure through the exercise of virtue. If this is true, then this ought to count as evidence that exercising virtue is at least one way to experience happiness, be it construed as eudaimonia or subjective well-being. To wrap our heads around what Aristotle means when he says that pleasure completes virtuous activity, it will help to consider how he distinguishes between virtuous and vicious people. He makes this distinction largely in terms of how a person's emotions line up with virtue. A vicious person follows his base appetites—such as a desire to throw a snowball at someone—and takes pleasure in so doing. His emotions are not controlled by reason and may be contradictory to reason. In contrast, a virtuous person lacks such base appetites altogether. She feels no urge to throw snowballs at people, and, in fact, feels "no pleasure contrary to reason" (Aristotle, secs. 1152a2–3).

The virtuous person finds pleasure in the exercise of virtue because she has been successful in bringing her emotional states in line with what reason requires. Developing virtue thus allows her to experience eudaimonia, which she attains through the ongoing exercise of virtue. Unlike Hobbes depicted in the opening cartoon, she has no desires for cheap thrills to be had at the cost of virtue: Her thrills, as it were, come through the exercise of virtue.

While it may seem far-fetched to talk about feeling pleasure in exercising virtue, part of what Aristotle is getting at here are the ways in which developing virtue transforms one's desires such that one's desires aim at virtue. Aristotle's claim is not that the kid who derives pleasure from throwing snowballs at people will also find pleasure in acting virtuously; his point is that if this kid develops virtue, he wouldn't find pleasure in throwing snowballs at people and would find pleasure in exercising virtue. Julia Annas describes this aspect of Aristotle's view as the "transformative role of virtue," which, according to Aristotle, makes possible a form of happiness (eudaimonia) that isn't possible without virtue. Annas explains this transformative role as follows:

> Virtue is not just one disposition among many... Virtue is of more importance than other things in your life because it controls the value that they have for you. Virtue, in a word, can transform a human life. It can do so because it can transform your view of what happiness is. The virtuous person is not tempted to identify happiness with something like having a lot of money, for virtue enables you to correct ordinary valuations and arrive at a true estimate of value... Only the virtuous person properly knows how to put money to use and do the right things with it; and thus only in the virtuous person's life does money make a contribution to happiness. (Annas, 1998, p. 49)

The suggestion is that developing virtue opens up a form of true happiness attainable only by the virtuous. The rest of us may *think* we are pursuing happiness through cheap thrills, but we are mistaken insofar as we neglect to appreciate the distinctively human form of happiness Aristotle frames as eudaimonia. If Aristotle is correct, developing virtue opens up an individual to a deep and robust form of happiness.

Does Being Virtuous Feel Good?

Let's now turn to consider reasons for thinking that virtue is connected to happiness that are independent of Aristotle's particular framework of eudaimonia. The strongest support for thinking there is a connection between virtue and happiness would be if being virtuous feels good. If being virtuous feels good, then it seems we can build a plausible case for the connection between virtue and happiness. We've seen the Aristotelian claim that someone who has fully developed virtue will feel pleasure in the exercise of virtue—a claim that depends on the transformative power Aristotle attributes to the development of virtue and to the successful regulation of our emotional states by reason. There still remains to be seen whether or not, when most of us try to act virtuously, doing so feels good.

There's a common sense in which it does. It feels good to do the right thing. Doing the right thing provides us with a sense of achievement and deep satisfaction. It provides us with a sense of worth and, often, a sense of our connection to others. In his arguments against egoism, Bishop Butler (1726) famously observes that most people do tend to have benevolent desires. We have desires to help the specific people in our lives and desires to help in general. If happiness involves satisfying our fundamental desires—either because desire satisfaction is important or because satisfying desires feels good—then there is no reason to suspect that being benevolent would *not* be an important part of happiness.

Contemporary research affirms this line of thought, and there is empirical support for the claim that acting benevolently satisfies the subject and increases her happiness. Much of this research revolves around the impact performing acts of kindness has upon the actor. Research by Sonya Lyubomirsky and colleagues demonstrates a correlation between engaging in kind acts—construed broadly to include acts that benefit others or that make others happy—and experiencing immediate increases to mood and long-lasting effects on well-being (Lyubomirsky, King, & Diener, 2005). Doing good to others does seem to feel good. Moreover, longer-term data indicate that performing acts of kindness seems to pay off in the long run, creating not just temporary feelings of happiness but reinforcing cycles of positive moods in general.

Lyubomirsky et al. (2005) speculate this effect arises from a combination of factors. First, the positive emotions associated with performing kind acts themselves seem to trigger a mutually reinforcing cycle of experiencing positivity. Second, engaging in kind behaviors seems to satisfy our psychological needs and in particular our need for relatedness. When we engage in acts of kindness, we view ourselves a part of a community that warrants kindness. This leads us to recognize our interdependence and the importance of cooperation. Engaging in kind acts delivers a sense of confidence and optimism. This further connects us to others and inspires others to reciprocate kindness and, more generally, to like us. Both of these factors turn out to have significant influences on subjective well-being.

The experience of positive emotions ("feeling good") is a significant predictor of other good things, such as well-functioning relationships, increased creativity and physical health, and greater career success (Lyubomirsky et al., 2005). Research by Barbara Fredrickson and colleagues (2001) examines the apparent consequences of experiencing positive emotions. They find that experiencing positive emotions generates a self-reinforcing cycle that stimulates the subject to engage in particular experiences, relationships, and activities that generate further positive emotions and reinforce the cycle. Since engaging in acts of kindness generates positive emotions, engaging in acts of kindness sets off a trajectory toward the continued experience of positive emotions.

Fredrickson describes this understanding of positive emotions in terms of a "broaden and build model." The idea is that experiencing positive emotions shapes an individual's thought patterns in ways that allow her to experience more positive emotions. For example, feelings of joy tend to create an urge to play and so make an individual more apt to recognize opportunities for play. Embracing those opportunities generates more feelings of joy and moreover aids in the development of physical, emotional, and intellectual skills (Fredrickson & Joiner, 2002). Initial experiences of joy thus influence the individual's mindset, and further engagement in joyful activities prompt skill development that enhances future engagement and experiences of positive emotions. The general correlations we see associated with positive emotions are significant to subjective well-being and include greater career success, better relationship functioning, increased creativity, enhanced physical health, and longer life expectancy (Fredrickson, 2001).

Sometimes when we do good things, we feel good—and given the upward spiral feeling good promises to stimulate, it seems we ought to allow ourselves to feel good when we do good things. This explains the high correlations we see between a commitment to moral values and life satisfaction: Volunteer work, in particular, stands out as something that is correlated with higher rates of life satisfaction (Argyle, 2003; Meier & Stutzer, 2008). While sometimes people worry that attaching benefit to moral behavior diminishes the moral value of those actions, the reality is that this is just a feature of our psychology; feeling good when we do good things doesn't have to taint the moral goodness of our actions.

That performing acts of kindness generates positive emotions suggests virtue is important to happiness. But does virtue *always* feel good? I think it is important to acknowledge that doing good things sometimes does not feel good at all. It is often the case that acting virtuously involves sacrifices and so often feels like a sacrifice, an interference with our happiness that, however worthwhile and important, is still something that diminishes our happiness—at least in the short term. We've promised a friend a ride to the airport, yet when the time comes and we realize all that we have to give up to fulfill the promise, doing so may feel like a chore. We know that we should help the stranger who has dropped her papers on the sidewalk during a windy, rainy storm, but helping also involves getting wet ourselves. The logistics involved in doing the right thing are not always the kinds of things that generate good feelings.

Consider, for example, the experience of "whistleblowing." The moral demand to report unethical or illegal behavior is a strong one but notoriously one that requires significant personal cost to the whistleblower, who must jeopardize her career, her relationship with her employer, and so on, in order to do the right thing. Whistleblowing may be the right thing to do, but, let's face it, it doesn't feel good. In these cases, there seems to be a tension between virtue and happiness. "Feeling good," however, is only one aspect of happiness and on some accounts is not even the most important part of happiness. It is possible that, even if virtue doesn't always feel good, it is still important to happiness. We'll consider one such account in the next section, wherein we consider from a psychological perspective the overall impact committing to virtue has on an individual.

Virtue: An Intrinsic Aspiration

In Chapter 6, we discussed the distinction between intrinsic and extrinsic aspirations and the impact pursuit of these aspirations has on our happiness. Extrinsic aspirations, such as materialistic, fame, and image goals, are goals that focus on gaining reward and praise, while intrinsic aspirations, such as community growth and affiliation, are ones whose benefit is obtained internally. Intrinsic aspirations involve goals that satisfy our fundamental psychological needs, whereas extrinsic aspirations involve goals for things outside of oneself. Given their structure, the more we pursue extrinsic aspirations, the more we focus on external signs of self-worth. Where we seek out materialistic goals, for example, we often tend to do so as a means toward seeking the approval of others—something that is contingent and ultimately out of our control.

While we all have extrinsic aspirations, the more we value them, the more we set up a dynamic where we end up placing our focus and energies on things that are ultimately external to us. And, as we saw in the case of wealth, this has a negative, albeit indirect, effect on our happiness. Those who value materialistic goals tend to experience higher rates of depression and anxiety, are more prone toward anger and unpleasant emotions and less prone to experiencing pleasure, and overall experience less vitality in life (Kasser, 2003).

There are two plausible reasons for this effect: First, the pursuit of extrinsic aspirations is reward based. This means that when one is pursuing extrinsic aspirations, one is focused on the rewards to come at the end of the day and not on whether or not the activities one engages in are themselves rewarding. This mindset leads individuals to make sacrifices to their day-to-day experiences premised on the promise of a big reward at the end. Second, because the reward is placed outside of oneself, whether or not one gets the desired payoff, or finds the desired payoff to be rewarding, is questionable. We often find that the promotion we have sacrificed and worked for doesn't end up being as rewarding as we once thought; we quickly adjust to bigger paychecks, and whether or not we increase our image in the eyes of others is a contingent matter.

Whereas extrinsic goals have negative effects on those who pursue and value them, intrinsic goals tend to have positive effects on those who pursue and value them. In contrast to extrinsic aspirations whose reward is separate from the activity, intrinsic aspirations are such that the "reward" is found within the activity insofar as the activity itself taps into features of the individual. Kasser and Ryan explain the content of intrinsic goals as being "expressive of desires congruent with actualizing and growth tendencies natural to humans" (1993, p. 280). As such, intrinsic goals tend to be ones that satisfy basic psychological needs.

There is a plausible case to be made that virtue-related goals, such as aspiring to treat others well, to go out of one's way to help and support others, and to be honest, just, and fair, are intrinsic aspirations. The intrinsic aspirations identified by Kasser's line of research include affiliation, community feeling, and self-acceptance. By taking a deeper look at these, we see that virtue-related goals are either included in the above groupings or, at a minimum, share the same structure.

An aspiration for "affiliation" refers generally to desires to have satisfying relations with family and friends. The specific goals tested under the umbrella of affiliation include being able to share your life with someone you love, having people around that care about you and are supportive, and having people around to have fun with. Finally, affiliation aspirations include having good friends that you can open up to and with whom you can share personal information. While we don't often think of virtue in the context of friendships, it is easy to see how virtue-related goals, such as treating others with care and respect, inform and shape our affiliations.[2]

An aspiration for "community feeling" tracks more directly common conceptions of virtue and seems to be invoked in Lyubomirsky et al.'s analysis of the impact of acts of kindness. The specific goals measured in this context include goals to donate money or time to charity, to work for the betterment of society, and to make the world a better place. They also include goals directed at the betterment of individuals—helping others to improve their lives and to more generally help people in need. These goals are clear-cut examples of virtue-related goals. And, most importantly, their pursuit is associated with increased psychological well-being—something that may not be happiness itself but is pretty important to happiness.

In focusing on virtue, and especially on treating others well and on helping to improve one's society, we direct our energies toward pursuits that fulfill our psychological needs and so are experienced as inherently rewarding, independently of the contingent reactions of those around us.

So far, we've seen that virtue contributes to happiness in several ways. Some acts of virtue, such as volunteering or doing kind things for others, stimulate positive emotions directly, emotions that themselves comprise a state of happiness and generate an upward spiral of positive emotions. Other acts of virtue, such as whistleblowing or keeping promises, may not deliver immediate positive emotions but nonetheless satisfy innate psychological needs and so make important yet indirect contributions to happiness.

Virtue and Relationships[3]

The above discussion suggests framing virtue-relating goals as intrinsic aspirations and shows how doing so supports the thesis that virtue is important to happiness. This support does not establish that virtue is *necessary* to happiness, which is what many take Aristotle to advocate. But, as we've seen, it is difficult to maintain that virtue is necessary to happiness without departing from ordinary conceptions of happiness and embracing something more robust, such as eudaimonia. Working within an understanding of happiness as subjective well-being, the question becomes more modest: For most of us, will the development and exercise of virtue be important to happiness? Framing virtue-related goals as intrinsic aspirations provides us with some insight into how and why virtue is important to happiness: Because pursuing virtue enables us to satisfy basic psychological needs, regardless of whether or not it generates the approval of others or other external rewards. When we commit to virtue, and desire to pursue virtue-related goals, we bring that which we desire into alignment with what, psychologically speaking, we need.

The above line of argument rests largely on virtue's role in connecting us to others. Affiliation aspirations to form various sorts of meaningful relationships represent this clearly, as do aspirations toward community feeling. Striving to make the world a better place and to help those in need are ways in which we can locate ourselves within a larger social context and see ourselves as making vital contributions to others around us. This pays off in significant and often underappreciated ways.

The suggestion is that virtue allows us to meaningfully locate ourselves within a social context and to connect with others and that this is important to our happiness. This is something we know intuitively, but the psychological explanation of it provides a helpful analysis of its plausibility. This explanation revolves around the psychological basis driving our need for "relatedness." The earliest discussions of our social needs come in the context of attachment theory. Famously, psychologist Harry Harlow (Harlow & Zimmerman, 1958) somewhat accidentally discovered the importance of attachment during his lab work on monkeys. Discouraged at the rate at which monkeys in his lab kept getting sick, he decided to raise monkeys in isolation to ensure their health. He discovered that the monkeys raised in isolation failed to develop social and cognitive prob-lem-solving skills. Thus began a line of research stimulating "attachment the-ory," which emphasizes the developmental importance of forming attachments at a young age. Developing attachment to a caregiver allows infants and children to feel safe and secure. When a child feels that she has a secure base, she feels more comfortable exploring on her own. This exploration is necessary for skill development.

Subsequent research reveals a robust connection between relationships and cognitive, physical, and psychological development, and something akin to a need for relatedness appears on all lists of fundamental psychological needs.[4] Most of us are not surprised to learn of the benefits of feeling like we belong. And we are not surprised to learn the harms involved in feeling excluded. Durkheim's groundbreaking research on suicide finds that the strongest predic-tor of suicide is the number of social attachments one has formed. And it isn't just having lots of social attachments that counts; numerous studies attest to the importance of developing close personal relationships and of feeling loved. Studies of mental illness, for example, consistently reveal significantly higher rates of mental illness among divorced people than married people.[5] While the causal direction of this correlation is worth paying attention to, the numbers still attest to the importance of feeling the close, personal connections distinctive to long-term romantic relationships.

It may not be that surprising to observe that we experience greater psy-chological health and well-being when we feel included and loved, yet lest we think the importance of relationships is solely derived on the "receiving" end of things, we need to consider the importance of being on the "giving" end of things. There is significant research attesting to the benefits of *including* others and of *giving* love and respect to others. Here is where the moral implications of the need for relatedness may be most significant. If treating others poorly harms our psychological health and by extension our subjective well-being, then this indicates the importance of treating others well to our subjective well-being and further strengthens the claim that acting virtuously comprises an important aspect of our subjective well-being.

The first line of research draws on the effects of being in a one-sided rela-tionship, understood as a relationship in which one person gives love and the other takes love without reciprocating. Researchers find that one-sided relationships fail to satisfy the need for relatedness for *either* party involved (Baumeister & Leary, 1995; Baumeister, Wotman, & Stillwell, 1993). Regardless of whether one is the recipient of love and care or the giver, both parties tend to experience the relationship overall as an aversive one. There seems to be something about opening up oneself to others, and directing one's positive affection to others, that is deeply important to our psychologi-cal health and that we find deeply rewarding. Research on the connection between experiencing compassion and experiencing subjective well-being directly supports this thesis: The simple extension of love and warmth to others allows one to develop feelings of connectedness to others—a point we will discuss further in Chapter 10.

The second line of research explores the effects of actively excluding others. We often see this kind of behavior reinforced through a group mentality: A member of a dominant group seems to find it easy to exclude others. His own membership in the group allows him to feel safe, and, ironically, the act of excluding others seems to strengthen his bond with the group. But the psychological effects of ostracizing others suggests that these feelings do not satisfy one's need for relatedness and so do not buttress the ostracizer from the negative effects that arise from a failure to satisfy one's need for relatedness. Williams and Sommer (1997), for example, found that subjects tasked with ostracizing find it very hard to do, an effect that arises even when they have been primed to dislike those they are supposed to ostracize (Ciarocco, Sommer, & Baumeister, 2001). Ciarocco et al. also find a correlation between ostracizing and diminished cognitive performance (which is symptomatic of need frustration).

Including others and caring about them is an important component of our need for relatedness and may be just as important as feeling included and cared for. Virtue allows us to do so; indeed, it is often through the exercise of virtue that we find ourselves developing connections to others—especially others with whom we do not have a previous relationship or with whom we may have had aversive relationships. Even absent close personal bonds, it is important to extend our love and concern to others. Insofar as exercising virtue, and being a good person more generally, allows us to do so, it seems intimately connected to our psychological health and our subjective well-being.

Conclusion

We've seen that the connection between virtue and happiness is an important one but one that takes a little work to unpack. Aristotle argued that virtue is necessary for eudaimonia, but there are important differences between eudaimonia and happiness understood in terms of subjective well-being, and his arguments have limited applicability to subjective well-being. In thinking about how virtue is related to subjective well-being, research suggests that many virtuous acts generate the kind of positive emotions that are typically associated with happiness and that pursuing virtue-related goals, and being a good person more generally, is conducive to happiness. Developing virtue ensures that we treat others with care and respect and thereby fulfill our deeply rooted needs for relatedness, a point we'll discuss more in Chapter 8.

So does virtue really need some cheaper thrills? Subjective well-being may very well require cheap thrills, but the reality is there is no reason to suspect that cheap thrills come at the cost of virtue. Committing ourselves to virtue doesn't have to entail a boring, dull life. We've seen that many virtuous acts do feel good, and the experiences of positive feelings they stimulate are important to sustaining happiness. There is no reason to think that being virtuous interferes with being happy and lots of reasons to think that being virtuous will enhance our happiness.

Chapter Summary

- Eudaimonia represents a form of flourishing that is connected to the exercise of our rational capacities. Because Aristotle believes that the exercise of virtue is the most excellent way in which we can exercise our rational capacities, developing virtue is necessary to eudaimonia.
- Eudaimonia departs from ordinary understandings of happiness that hold happiness to be something akin to subjective well-being but deliver something closer to "human happiness," or even simply well-being.
- Psychological research shows a correlation between performing acts of kindness and experiencing positive emotions. It also shows that positive emotions themselves can spiral, allowing the subject to see and experience things in ways that generate further positive emotions.
- Virtue-related goals are examples of intrinsic aspirations, the pursuit of which is correlated with enhanced psychological well-being, likely because they satisfy innate psychological needs.
- Virtue seems most important to the development and sustaining of relationships and other social interactions that fulfill our need for relatedness.

End Notes

1 See Chapter 2.
2 See Besser (2020) for further development of this line of argument.
3 This section follows closely Besser-Jones (2014).
4 We'll expand on this in Chapter 8.
5 Baumeister and Leary (1995) and Bloom et al. (1978).

References

Annas, J. (1998).Virtue and eudaimonism. *Social Philosophy and Policy*, *15*(01), 37–55.
Argyle, M. (2003). 18 causes and correlates of happiness. *Well-Being: The Foundations of Hedonic Psychology*, 353.
Aristotle. (340 C.E.). *Nicomachean ethics* (R. Crisp, Ed.). Cambridge: Cambridge University Press.

Aristotle. (2014). *Nicomachean ethics* (R. Crisp, Ed.; revised). Cambridge: Cambridge University Press.

Baumeister, R. F., & Leary, M. R. (1995). The need to belong: Desire for interpersonal attachments as a fundamental human motivation. *Psychological Bulletin, 117*(3), 497–529.

Baumeister, R. F., Wotman, S. R., & Stillwell, A. M. (1993). Unrequited love: On heartbreak, anger, guilt, scriptlessness, and humiliation. *Journal of Personality and Social Psychology, 64*(3), 377–394.

Besser, L. L. (2020). Learning virtue. *Journal of Moral Education.* DOI: 10.1080/03057240.2020.1714564

Besser-Jones, L. (2014). *Eudaimonic ethics: The philosophy and psychology of living well.* New York: Routledge Press.

Bloom, B. L., Asher, S. J., & White, S. W. (1978). Marital disruption as a stressor: A review and analysis. *Psychological Bulletin, 85*(4), 867–894.

Butler, J. (1726). *Five sermons* (S. Darwall, Ed.). Indianapolis, IN: Hackett Press.

Ciarocco, N. J., Sommer, K. L., & Baumeister, R. F. (2001). Ostracism and ego depletion: The strains of silence. *Personality and Social Psychology Bulletin, 27*(9), 1156–1163.

Fredrickson, B. L. (2001). The role of positive emotions in positive psychology: The broaden-and-build theory of positive emotions. *American Psychologist, 56*(3), 218.

Fredrickson, B. L., & Joiner, T. (2002). Positive emotions trigger upward spirals toward emotional well-being. *Psychological Science, 13*(2), 172–175.

Harlow, H. F., & Zimmermann, R. R. (1958). The development of affectional responses in infant monkeys. *Proceedings of the American Philosophical Society, 102*(5), 501–509.

Kasser, T. (2003). *The high price of materialism.* Cambridge, MA: MIT Press.

Kasser, T., & Ryan, R. M. (1993). A dark side of the American dream: Correlates of financial success as a central life aspiration. *Journal of Personality and Social Psychology, 65*(2), 410–422.

Lyubomirsky, S., Sheldon, K. M., & Schkade, D. (2005). Pursuing happiness: The architecture of sustainable change. *Review of General Psychology, 9*(2), 111–131.

Meier, S., & Stutzer, A. (2008). Is volunteering rewarding in itself? *Economica, 75*(297), 39–59.

Williams, K. D., & Sommer, K. L. (1997). Social ostracism by coworkers: Does rejection lead to loafing or compensation? *Personality and Social Psychology Bulletin, 23*(7), 693–706.

Suggested for Further Reading

On Aristotle's conception of virtue and eudaimonia:

Annas, J. (1993). *The morality of happiness.* New York: Oxford University Press.

Annas, J. (1998). Virtue and eudaimonism. *Social Philosophy and Policy, 15*(01), 37–55.

Chappell, T. (2013). Eudaimonia, happiness, and the redemption of unhappiness. *Philosophical Topics, 41*(1), 27–52.

Keyes, C. L. M., & Annas, J. (2009). Feeling good and functioning well: Distinctive concepts in ancient philosophy and contemporary science. *The Journal of Positive Psychology, 4*(3), 197–201.

Russell, D. C. (2012). *Happiness for humans.* New York: Oxford University Press.

Waterman, A. S. (1990). The relevance of Aristotle's conception of eudaimonia for the psychological study of happiness. *Theoretical and Philosophical Psychology, 10*(1), 39–44.

On understanding the exercise of virtue as a flow experience:

Annas, J. (2008). The phenomenology of virtue. *Phenomenology and the Cognitive Sciences*, 7(1), 21–34.

Besser-Jones, L. (2012). The motivational state of the virtuous agent. *Philosophical Psychology*, 25(1), 93–108.

Csikszentmihalyi, M. (1990). *Flow: The psychology of optimal experience*. New York: Harper & Row.

On the correlation between virtuous acts and positive emotions:

Fredrickson, B. L. (1998). What good are positive emotions? *Review of General Psychology*, 2(3), 300–319.

Fredrickson, B. L., & Joiner, T. (2002). Positive emotions trigger upward spirals toward emotional well-being. *Psychological Science*, 13(2), 172–175.

Lyubomirsky, S., King, L., & Diener, E. (2005). The benefits of frequent positive affect: Does happiness lead to success? *Psychological Bulletin*, 131(6), 803.

Meier, S., & Stutzer, A. (2008). Is volunteering rewarding in itself? *Economica*, 75(297), 39–59.

Sheldon, K. M., & Lyubomirsky, S. (2007). Is it possible to become happier? (And if so, how?). *Social and Personality Psychology Compass*, 1(1), 129–145.

On virtue considered as an intrinsic aspiration:

Kasser, T., & Ryan, R. M. (1996). Further examining the American dream: Differential correlates of intrinsic and extrinsic goals. *Personality and Social Psychology Bulletin*, 22, 280–287.

Ryan, R. M., & Deci, E. L. (2000). Self-determination theory and the facilitation of intrinsic motivation, social development, and well-being. *American Psychologist*, 55(1), 68–78.

Ryan, R. M., Sheldon, K. M., Kasser, T., & Deci, E. L. (1996). All goals are not created equal. In P. Gollwitzer and J. Bargh (Eds.), *The psychology of action: Linking cognition and motivation to behavior* (pp. 7–26). New York: Guilford Press.

On the need for relatedness and virtue's connection to it:

Baumeister, R. F., Twenge, J. M., & Nuss, C. K. (2002). Effects of social exclusion on cognitive processes: Anticipated aloneness reduces intelligent thought. *Journal of Personality and Social Psychology*, 83(4), 817–827.

Besser-Jones, L. (2014). *Eudaimonic ethics: The philosophy and psychology of living well*. New York: Routledge Press.

Ciarocco, N. J., Sommer, K. L., & Baumeister, R. F. (2001). Ostracism and ego depletion: The strains of silence. *Personality and Social Psychology Bulletin*, 27(9), 1156–1163.

Vohs, K. D., & Ciarocco, N. J. (2004). Interpersonal functioning requires self-regulation. In R. F. Baumeister & K. D. Vohs (Eds.), *Handbook of self-regulation: Research, theory, and applications* (pp. 392–407). New York: Guilford Press.

8

RELATIONSHIPS AND HAPPINESS

A quick Internet search reveals an overwhelming number of bold claims about the importance of relationships to happiness. "Want to Be Happy? Make Your Relationships Exceptional," reads one headline,[1] followed by "Why Other People Are the Key to Our Happiness."[2] The idea is quite straightforward, as one article presents it: "How can you be healthier, happier, more successful, and live longer? The answer is positive relationships. Positive relationships form a foundation for happiness and success."[3]

Research does affirm that relationships may be the most important predictor of happiness. In a landmark study of the characteristics of happy people, Diener and Seligman (2002) found that the greatest discrepancy between very happy people and very unhappy people was the degree and quality of social relationships. Very happy people spend the least amount of time alone and the most time socializing relative to averagely happy people. Conversely, very unhappy people have significantly worse social relationships relative to averagely happy people. This leads Diener and Seligman to stipulate "that good social relationships are, like food and thermoregulation, universally important to human mood" (Diener & Seligman, 2002, p. 83).

If we want to be happy, we probably should make our relationships exceptional. But what kinds of relationships are most conducive to happiness? And why exactly are relationships so conducive to happiness? This chapter will explore these questions.

Why Relationships Matter[4]

We initially discussed the importance of relationships to happiness in the context of virtue, and we explored in Chapter 7 why treating others well seems to be so important to our happiness and well-being. Here, we discuss research tracing the importance of relationships to early developmental needs to attach oneself to a caregiver. This is the main premise of attachment theory, which stresses the importance of developing feelings of safety and security in early childhood. When infants and the young attach to their caregivers, these attachments serve as a safe, secure base from which the child feels comfortable exploring the world. These explorations are essential to their overall development. Attachment theory anchors reflection on the importance of relationships throughout one's life with research showing that while the nature of one's social needs may evolve throughout one's life, one's basic need to relate to others remains constant. There is significant convergence on the stipulation that we have a deeply rooted need to engage, belong, and relate to others (e.g., Baumeister & Leary, 1995; Reis, Sheldon, Gable, Roscoe, & Ryan, 2000).

This "need for relatedness" drives us to engage with others and maintain social relations. We know from experience the pleasures of social engagement and the pains of loneliness and the contributions these feelings make to our happiness. Extensive research on the need for relatedness shows the contribution of social interactions extends far beyond subjective feelings and that how we interact with one another significantly affects our basic functioning.

On a psychological level, we find significant correlations between healthy psychological functioning and social interactions, and, conversely, between social exclusion and mental illness. When we have a close relationship with another, or when we feel included within a community, we are more likely to experience higher levels of positive affect and life satisfaction (Baumeister, 1991) and significantly lower rates of mental illness than those who lack these kinds of relationships (Bloom, Asher, & White, 1978). The figures are often astonishing; as Baumeister and Leary report, they show that "mental illness is at least 3 and possibly up to 22 times higher among divorced people than among married people" (1995, p. 509). But when we don't have close relationships, and suffer more generally from social exclusion, we face higher rates of mental illness and suicide. Some suggest that social exclusion itself is a primary cause of negative feelings such as anxiety, grief, depression, and guilt (e.g., Rothberg & Jones, 1987; Trout, 1980).

On the physical level, we find significant correlations between social integration and overall health, as seen through decreased mortality rates[5] and higher survival rates among cancer patients (Goodwin, Hunt, Key, & Samet, 1987). Those with social connections tend to have better-functioning immune systems (Kiecolt-Glaser et al., 1984), lower mortality rates (Lynch, 1979), and are better able to bear the effects of stress (DeLongis, Folkman, & Lazarus, 1988).[6] While one explanation of these correlations is that positive social relationships are instrumental in providing coping support during times of need, research finds that there is in addition a distinct generalized beneficial effect of social integration that typically occurs whether or not a person is under stress.[7] Being a member of a large social network can enhance happiness and well-being directly, likely in virtue of the ways in which this network serves as a source of positive affect, comfort, and stability and affirms one's worth (Cohen & Wills, 1985, p. 311).

On the cognitive level, we find correlations between social inclusion and cognitive functioning. Much of this research explores the effects social exclusion has on a subject's executive functioning, which includes her ability to organize tasks, manage frustration, focus, make memories, and self-regulate. In one series of studies, researchers found individuals facing social exclusion performed poorly on cognitive tasks and found themselves unable to regulate their behaviors effectively (Baumeister & DeWall, 2005; Baumeister, DeWall, Ciarocco, & Twenge, 2005; Baumeister, Twenge, & Nuss, 2002).

This overview of the ways in which social interaction influences our psychological, physical, and cognitive functioning shows a clear correlation between engaging in social interaction and being able to function in ways that are important to the experience of happiness. It is harder to be happy when we are sick, when we find it difficult to complete basic tasks, when we feel rejected by others, and when we don't have a source of support. Making and establishing relationships aids us in our essential functioning, which is important in its own right and without which happiness seems off the table.

All this suggests that we ought to prioritize our relationships; let us now consider how to do this with particular respect to happiness. What kinds of relationships are important to happiness?

Community

We are all part of a number of communities, ranging from our neighborhoods, to our workplaces, to the gym, to the gang at the coffee shop on Monday mornings, to mom groups, to the friends of friends, and so on. While we tend to identify more with some communities of which we are a part than others, for most of us, operating within a community is the norm. Some communities we actively seek out and cherish the relationships we develop within them. Other communities we may simply find ourselves in by circumstance. Being part of communities may be unavoidable, but how we interact with those in our communities is up to us, and research suggests that whether or not these interactions are a source of happiness may also be up to us.

Membership within a community involves primarily "weak ties" between individuals rather than the "strong ties" that are distinctive to one-on-one relationships. Your community includes your neighbors, your barista, your coworkers and classmates, even that guy you see walking down the street at noon every day. That community often involves weak ties rather than strong ties makes it tempting to overlook their importance and attach a lower priority to the interactions that sustain them. Research suggests this is a mistake. Social interactions, in general, are a significant predictor of subjective well-being, even when those interactions are with weak ties.

For example, Sandstrom and Dunn (2014) tracked college students' feelings of positive affect and sense of belonging during class periods. They found that the more interactions students had with their classmates, the happier they were, and that whether those interactions were with strong or weak ties did not seem to have an impact on their subjective well-being:

> Students who typically interact with more classmates are happier and experience greater feelings of belonging. Furthermore, students are happier and experience greater feelings of belonging during classes when they interact with more classmates than usual. These results emerged even though participants described most of their classmates (64%) as weak ties, and our findings held up even for people who had no strong ties at all in class. (Sandstrom & Dunn, 2014, p. 913)

This research suggests that social interactions in general are importantly correlated with happiness. Moreover, there is reason to think this correlation is explainable not solely by whom one is interacting with but rather by the tone of those interactions and explicitly whether one's interactions are characterized by warmth.

One study of elementary school children conducted by Ryan and Grolnick (1986) showed that where teachers were perceived to be warm and accepting, children's feelings of self-worth, competence, and control were higher than in classroom climates marked by an absence of warm feelings. A related study showed that when children were asked to perform tasks in the presence of an experimenter who avoided eye contact with them, their levels of intrinsic motivation dropped. The failure of the person in the room to acknowledge the children limited their capacity to find an otherwise fun exercise of free drawing interesting and enjoyable (Anderson, Manoogian, & Reznick, 1976). Anderson and colleagues describe this situation as painful and uncomfortable for both parties, observing that "while the experimenter was (rather painfully) striving to avoid eye contact, conversation, or attending to the child's drawing, the child was striving equally hard to elicit some recognition or validation from the experimenter for what he was doing" (Anderson et al., 1976, p. 917). When, in different groups, the experimenter watched the children draw, his presence had no effect on their levels of interest and motivation.

Being around cold-hearted people negatively affects us. It generates negative feelings and inhibits us from engaging in ways that generate subjective well-being. There's also reason to think that cold interactions have a cyclical effect on people, making it the case that even an isolated instance of social rejection can lead one to feel more vulnerable to future rejections.[8] A simple smile may be enough to turn an everyday interaction into a positive one, which helps both parties feel that they belong in the community. Those who feel like they belong to a community are able to engage in warm social interactions and stimulate positive cycles that strengthen this sense of belonging and the happiness that is associated with it. They build strong emotional connections that allow them to see their needs as capable of being met from within the community; they find that they can exert control over the community while also being themselves influenced by the community; they build social capital that serves to help them cope and overcome challenges. Establishing these bonds, even among weak ties, is significantly correlated with feelings of happiness (Davidson & Cotter, 1991).

Friendships

The ancient philosopher Epicurus (325 B.C.E.) famously thought friendships were pivotal to the happy life. He argued that developing friendships and engaging with friends is one of the most important things we can do to become happy; friends rescue us from a life of unpleasant solitude. Through forming friendships, learning to trust one another, and treating others as well as we treat ourselves, Epicurus believed we can live the quintessential pleasant life. Epicurus thought the best way to do this was by living within communities that make these friendships possible.[9] Friendships allow for ease of communication, sharing and supporting of values, and company.

Contemporary philosophical discussions of friendship focus on what it means to be a friend and why friendships are important. Most define friendships as relationships marked by mutual caring. In any given relationship, the level of mutuality naturally varies over time, and there is often a delicate balancing act involved in sustaining this mutual caring. Sometimes being a good friend requires giving more, particularly in times when one's friend is undergoing struggle. But an absence of reciprocation over time sets up an imbalance in the relationship, which hampers its qualitative feel. Lack of reciprocation gives rise to feelings of resentment and anxiety, which in some cases may prove strong enough to make that relationship an unhealthy one.

Friendships involve a degree of intimacy. In platonic friendships—our focus in this section—this intimacy is understood largely in terms of sharing intimate thoughts and feelings. Friends vent to one another about their jobs, their room-mates, their partners. Friends share secrets with one another, share their hopes and dreams, and, in their best instantiations, share their true feelings. This letting down of one's guard and opening up of oneself may be one of the features of friendships that is most conducive to happiness.

Finally, fundamental to friendships are shared experiences. We develop friendship bonds over the course of shared experiences. These shared experiences come in all forms and often stand out as our happiest moments. When spending time with friends, we often pursue leisure activities and set aside obligations and other stressors. We see concerts, go on hikes, eat together, and so forth. These kinds of shared experiences can deliver pure enjoyment. But not all the shared experiences between friends are enjoyable ones. Part of being a friend is being there in times of loss and conflict, supporting a friend while she grieves, and helping her pick up the pieces after a devastating setback. While these shared experiences may not be enjoyable, they help to define and strengthen the friendship. They allow us to feel connected to our friends in deep, nonsuperficial ways.

These features of friendship aren't at all surprising to those of us lucky enough to have strong friendships. And, as Valerie Tiberius has argued, it is clear that forming friendships is something to which we are naturally suited: "Most of us human beings are naturally social and sympathetic; we like to share experiences with each other, we need support, we suffer loneliness. When we care about others for their own sakes, then, we are engaging in an activity that suits us psychologically" (Tiberius, 2018, p. 143).

In this quote we see perhaps the most striking feature of friendship and the most paradoxical to consider with respect to its connection to happiness: This is that friendship involves caring about others for their own sake. Because caring about others does seem to be something to which we are naturally suited, it feels good. Being a friend is thus prudentially valuable for us, although this can't be our motive within the friendship. We can't develop a friendship if we are in it just to make ourselves happy.[10] That friendship is correlated with happiness is important to recognize and to appreciate, but this correlation shouldn't—and perhaps cannot—serve as the foundation for the friendship. In order for a relationship to constitute a friendship, it must involve caring for others for their own sakes.

Cocking and Kennett (1998) emphasize the ways in which friendship involves not only this kind of selfless caring about others but also a willingness to be shaped by one's friends and to be responsive to the interests and opinions of one's friends. They argue that "as a close friend of another, one is characteristically and distinctively receptive to be directed and interpreted and so in these ways drawn by the other" (Cocking & Kennett, 1998, p. 503). Being a friend affects one's choices insofar as one sees the other's interests as reason-giving. Being a friend also affects how it is that one conceives of oneself. We build our self-conception through social interactions in general, but Crocking and Kennett argue that there is a specific role friendships have in shaping one's self-concept:

> Consider how we often recognize and highlight aspects of our close friend's character. So, for example, Judy teasingly points out to John how he always likes to be right. John has never noticed this about himself, however, now that Judy has pointed it out to him he recognizes and accepts that this is indeed a feature of his character. Seeing himself through Judy's eyes changes his view of himself. But beyond making salient an existing trait of character, the close friend's interpretation of the character trait or foible can have an impact on how that trait continues to be realized. Within the friendship John's liking to be right may become a running joke which structures how the friends relate to each other. John continues to insist that he is right; however, his insistences are now for the most part treated lightheartedly and take on a self-consciously ironic tone. And John may be led by Judy's recognition and interpretation of his foibles to more generally take himself less seriously. Thus, John's character and his self-conception are also, in part, drawn, or shaped, by his friend's interpretation of him. (Cocking & Kennett, 1998, p. 505)

This example shows the positive and unique influence friends can have on how one thinks of one's self. Friendships can help one accept one's flaws and put them into perspective, thereby bolstering one's self-esteem and mitigating the impact a lack of self-esteem can have on one's subjective well-being.

This reflection on the ways in which friendships improve our lives shows the depth of our sociality and bolsters the thesis that we do have a fundamental need to relate to others. Various features of our psychology are structured so that they develop through social engagement, and this helps to explain why forming friendships is positively correlated with subjective well-being.

There is a further explanation of this correlation between friendships and subjective well-being that appeals to the cyclical effect of positive emotions we first explored in Chapter 7 and will expand on in Chapter 9. The emotions involved in forming friendships and in being a friend are ones that themselves tend to generate positive feelings. Being friendly makes one happier; and happy people are more likely to see others in a positive light and to express desires to be friends. The cycle replicates and extends, building on the power of positive affect.

All the signs indicate that friendships are essential to happiness. This point is well confirmed within empirical research and, as we have seen, philosophical discussion of friendship identifies much of the nuances of friendship that help to explain and support this correlation.

Romantic Relationships

Romantic relationships take priority in many people's lives, and by their nature romantic relationships are importantly different from friendships and community ties. Within most romantic relationships, one person is expected to fill many roles, which makes romantic relationships among the most precarious. A fulfilling romantic relationship can serve as a life-sustaining, highly rewarding source of happiness, yet an unhealthy romantic relationship can be among the most harmful to one's happiness and well-being.

In committing to a romantic relationship, partners take on a shared commitment to happiness. Michael Martin argues that, in the context of marriage, this shared commitment transforms both the content of one's happiness and one's pursuit of it:

> Marriage partners pursue happiness together. This means three things. First, they pursue a happy marriage, a marriage that both partners are happy with and happy in. Second, they pursue the overall happiness of both partners, not only their domain happiness within their marriage. Third, and even more inclusively, they undertake a shared pursuit of happiness, that is, happiness in a shared life pursued together in love—with shared activities and agency, shared intimacy and identity, shared virtue and luck, and shared enjoyment and meaning. (Martin, 2012, p. 119)

While Martin references the specific institution of marriage, there is no reason to think this important point is limited to any one kind of marriage; rather, it generalizes to any two people committed to a long-term romantic relationship.

Some reflection on the philosophy of love will help us to understand why it is that forming a committed relationship based on romantic love is so transformative and has such an impact on one's happiness. In one influential understanding of love, partners form a shared union: In coming together, they form a "we." Forming a shared union requires pooling together one's interests in happiness as well as one's autonomy in making pivotal decisions about one's happiness. Robert Nozick defends this view, writing,

> People who form a *we* pool not only their well-being but also their autonomy. They limit or curtail their own decision-making power and rights; some decisions can no longer be made alone. Which decisions these are will be parceled differently by different couples: where to live, how to live, who friends are and how to see them, whether to have children and how many, where to travel, whether to go to the movies that night and what to see. Each transfers some previous rights to make certain decisions unilaterally into a joint pool; somehow, decisions will be made together about

how to be together. If your well-being so closely affects and is affected by another's, it is not surprising that decisions that importantly affect well-being, even in the first instance primarily your own, will no longer be made alone. (Nozick, 1990, pp. 70–71)

In virtue of coming together as a "we," partners open themselves up to the rewards of a long-term relationship, but, as the above quote suggests, these rewards come with distinctive challenges.

Forming a shared union requires being vulnerable; successful shared unions require trust. These features are essential to friendships as well, but in the scope of a romantic relationship, where one sees one's happiness as intimately connected with one's partner and where one makes decisions from the "we" perspective, these features are magnified and besot with emotions. This delivers romantic relationships a rocky connection to happiness. At their best, long-term romantic relationships provide a person with the opportunity to grow as an individual and as a partner and experience deep, stable levels of happiness and well-being. At their worst, long-term romantic relationships can rob a person of his individuality and autonomy and sow abusive conditions.

Long-standing feminist critiques of the institution of marriage express concern that it perpetuates patriarchal power differentials and gender norms that limit women's range of opportunities and threaten oppression. There is a history of viewing marriages as private zones, which are excluded from the norms of justice that we take to regulate our societal interactions. And despite the growing awareness of the problems of spousal abuse and the ways in which marriages can perpetuate inequalities, the problem—the large extent to which women are more vulnerable within marriages than men—remains (Okin, 1989). While more women are now in the workforce, they still tend to take on the greater share of childcare and household responsibilities. This unpaid labor contributes to a "dual burden" that arises when women work both outside and inside the house, a burden to which men overwhelmingly are not subject.

These disparities may explain why it is that women's levels of subjective well-being have declined since the 1970s, both absolutely and relative to men, despite the generally agreed-upon fact that their objective standards of welfare have increased dramatically during that time (Stevenson & Wolfers, 2009). Women enjoy higher wages and levels of education attainment and participate more in the labor force than ever before, but they are less happy. Their dual burden may explain some of the decline; Stevenson and Wolfers also find relevant the ways in which women's expectations and reference groups have transformed. Increased opportunities to work outside of the house engender new expectations about so doing and what the rewards of so doing look like. When women view themselves as on an equal playing field with men, their reference group shifts. Women start to judge their positions relative to men rather than relative to other women; this may lead them to view themselves as unhappy or as less happy than they think they ought to be.

One cross-sectional study of gender roles and inequality across 26 European countries corroborates the impact of expectations and reference groups on reported subjective well-being (Mencarini & Sironi, 2012). The study found that while performing the larger share of housework negatively affects working women, this effect is mediated by societal norms:

> We found that being engaged in housework that exceeds the median amount recorded in a specific country affects respondents' happiness in a negative way: a woman, living in a country where partners usually share household chores equally, feels more unhappy if she has to perform the bulk of total housework; conversely, where women are, on average, in charge of almost all housekeeping (e.g., Greece), sharing part of it with the partner decreases the negative effect of housework on respondents' happiness. (Mencarini & Sironi, 2012, p. 216)

Despite the potentially negative impacts of the institution of marriage, particularly on women, research affirms that most people are happier within marriages (and other long-term relationships) than living alone. With respect to happiness, the rewards of companionship, in most instances, seem to be worth it. Yet, given the established challenges that women experience in marriages, it behooves us to learn more about them and to address them both as individuals and as a society.

Conclusion

There is, indeed, a reason why we hear so much public discourse about the importance of relationships to happiness. Good relationships provide support systems, are sources of positive affect, and allow parties to feel vulnerable, affirmed, and connected to others; bad relationships fail at all these things and serve as a continual source of stress. These connections hold for both close ties and weak ties; whomever we are interacting with, those interactions can be conducive to happiness when they are marked by care and respect.

As social distancing policies become increasingly important to the health of our society, it becomes increasingly important to nurture and cherish the relationships we have. We know the effects of social isolation can be devastating, and there's no question that the social isolation required during the Covid-19 pandemic will be detrimental to people's mental health and well-being. In times where social distancing is necessary, it behooves us to prioritize our relationships and engage in creative ways to connect with one another. Connecting is harder in the absence of physical proximity, or where smiles are hidden by masks, but we have a lot to lose by not making the effort and much to gain by trying.

Chapter Summary

- The quality and quantity of one's relationships is an important predictor of happiness.
- Forming relationships and developing a sense of belonging fulfills one's need for relatedness, a need whose frustration negatively affects not just one's happiness but also one's physical, cognitive, and psychological functioning.
- Social engagement is itself a source of positive feelings, and the emotions involved in successful social interactions (friendliness, etc.) are themselves ones that tend to generate a cyclical network of positive emotions.
- Interactions with weak ties are important to our subjective well-being; negative interactions with anyone threaten our sense of belonging and are a source of negative emotions. The most important aspect seems to be that our interactions are marked by warm feelings and lead the subject to feel recognized by the other.
- Establishing friendships and forming long-term romantic relationships are important to subjective well-being.
- Both sorts of relationships require parties to be vulnerable, be it in terms of sharing deep thoughts and emotions or in terms of forming a shared union and pooling together one's stake in the important things in life. This vulnerability opens up potential harmful space that ought to be managed with care and with a commitment to equality.

End Notes

1 https://greatergood.berkeley.edu/article/item/want_to_be_happy_make_your_relationships_exceptional
2 https://www.psychologytoday.com/us/blog/ulterior-motives/201407/why-other-people-are-the-key-our-happiness
3 https://www.connectinghappinessandsuccess.com/overview/happiness-concepts/3-positive-relationships/
4 This section draws on Besser-Jones (2014).
5 Berkman and Syme (1979), House, Robbins, and Metzner (1982), and Vogt, Mullooly, Ernst, Pope, and Hollis (1992).
6 See Baumeister and Leary (1995, pp. 508–509) for discussion of these effects and more.
7 See Cohen and Wills (1985) and Schwarzer and Leppin (1989, 1991).
8 Baumeister and DeWall (2005, p. 56) and Zadro, Williams, and Richardson (2004, p. 567).
9 Interestingly, Epicurus favored friendships over intimate relationships. He worried that being too attached to any one person is a recipe for anxiety.
10 This is true of many things, a point we will discuss in Chapter 11.

References

Anderson, R., Manoogian, S. T., & Reznick, J. S. (1976). The undermining and enhancing of intrinsic motivation in preschool children. *Journal of Personality and Social Psychology, 34*(5), 915–922.

Baumeister, R. F. (1991). *Meanings of life.* New York: The Guilford Press.

Baumeister, R. F., & DeWall, C. N. (2005). The inner dimension of social exclusion: Intelligent thought and self-regulation among rejected persons. In K. Williams, J. Forgas, & W. von Hippel (Eds.), *The social outcast* (pp. 43–76). New York: Psychology Press.

Baumeister, R. F., & Leary, M. R. (1995). The need to belong: Desire for interpersonal attachments as a fundamental human motivation. *Psychological Bulletin, 117*(3), 497–529.

Baumeister, R. F., DeWall, C. N., Ciarocco, N. J., & Twenge, J. M. (2005). Social exclusion impairs self-regulation. *Journal of Personality and Social Psychology, 88*, 589–604.

Baumeister, R. F., Twenge, J. M., & Nuss, C. K. (2002). Effects of social exclusion on cognitive processes: Anticipated aloneness reduces intelligent thought. *Journal of Personality and Social Psychology, 83*(4), 817–827.

Berkman, L. F., & Syme, S. L. (1979). Social networks, host resistance, and mortality: A nine-year follow-up study of Alameda County residents. *American Journal of Epidemiology, 109*(2), 186–204.

Besser-Jones, L. (2014). *Eudaimonic ethics: The philosophy and psychology of living well.* New York: Routledge Press.

Bloom, B. L., Asher, S. J., & White, S. W. (1978). Marital disruption as a stressor: A review and analysis. *Psychological Bulletin, 85*(4), 867–894.

Cocking, D., & Kennett, J. (1998). Friendship and the self. *Ethics, 108*(3), 502–527. https://doi.org/10.1086/233824

Cohen, S., & Wills, T. A. (1985). Stress, social support, and the buffering hypothesis. *Psychological Bulletin, 98*(2), 310–357.

Davidson, W. B., & Cotter, P. R. (1991). The relationship between sense of community and subjective well-being: A first look. *Journal of Community Psychology, 19*, 246–253.

DeLongis, A., Folkman, S., & Lazarus, R. S. (1988). The impact of daily stress on health and mood: Psychological and social resources as mediators. *Journal of Personality and Social Psychology, 54*(3), 486–495.

Diener, E., & Seligman, M. E. (2002). Very happy people. *Psychological Science, 13*(1), 81–84.

Epicurus. (325 C.E.). In L. P. Gerson & B. Inwood (Eds.), *The Epicurus reader selected writings and testimonials.* Indianapolis, IN: Hackett Press.

Goodwin, J. S., Hunt, C., Key, C., & Samet, J. (1987). Relationship of marital status to stage at diagnosis, choice of treatment and survival in individuals with cancer. *Journal of the American Medical Association, 258*, 3125–3130.

House, J. S., Robbins, C., & Metzner, H. L. (1982). The association of social relationships and activities with mortality: Prospective evidence from the Tecumseh Community Health Study. *American Journal of Epidemiology, 116*(1), 123–140.

Kiecolt-Glaser, J. K., Garner, W., Speicher, C., Penn, G. M., Holliday, J., & Glaser, R. (1984). Psychosocial modifiers of immunocompetence in medical students. *Psychosomatic Medicine, 46*(1), 7.

Lynch, J. J. (1979). *The broken heart: The medical consequences of loneliness.* New York: Basic Books.

Martin, M. W. (2012). *Happiness and the good life.* New York: Oxford University Press.

Mencarini, L., & Sironi, M. (2012). Happiness, housework and gender inequality in Europe. *European Sociological Review, 28*(2), 203–219. https://doi.org/10.1093/esr/jcq059

Nozick, R. (1990). *Examined life: Philosophical meditations.* New York: Simon and Schuster.

Okin, S. M. (1989). *Justice, gender, and the family.* New York: Basic Books.

Reis, H. T., Sheldon, K. M., Gable, S. L., Roscoe, J., & Ryan, R. M. (2000). Daily well-being: The role of autonomy, competence, and relatedness. *Personality and Social Psychology Bulletin, 26*(4), 419–435.

Rothberg, J. M., & Jones, F. D. (1987). Suicide in the US Army: Epidemiological and periodic aspects. *Suicide and Life-Threatening Behavior, 17*(2), 119–132.

Ryan, R. M., & Grolnick, W. S. (1986). Origins and pawns in the classroom: Self-report and projective assessments of individual differences in children's perceptions. *Journal of Personality and Social Psychology, 50*(3), 550–558.

Sandstrom, G. M., & Dunn, E. W. (2014). Social interactions and well-being: The surprising power of weak ties. *Personality and Social Psychology Bulletin, 40*(7), 910–922.

Schwarzer, R., & Leppin, A. (1989). Social support and health: A meta-analysis. *Psychology & Health, 3*(1), 1–15.

Schwarzer, R., & Leppin, A. (1991). Social support and health: A theoretical and empirical overview. *Journal of Social and Personal Relationships, 8*(1), 99–127.

Stevenson, B., & Wolfers, J. (2009). The paradox of declining female happiness. *American Economic Journal: Economic Policy, 1*(2), 190–225.

Tiberius, V. (2018). *Well-being as value fulfillment: How we can help each other to live well.* New York: Oxford University Press.

Trout, D. L. (1980). The role of social isolation in suicide. *Suicide and Life-Threatening Behavior, 10*(1), 10–23.

Vogt, T. M., Mullooly, J. P., Ernst, D., Pope, C. R., & Hollis, J. F. (1992). Social networks as predictors of ischemic heart disease, cancer, stroke and hypertension: Incidence, survival and mortality. *Journal of Clinical Epidemiology, 45*(6), 659–666.

Zadro, L., Williams, K. D., & Richardson, R. (2004). How low can you go? Ostracism by a computer is sufficient to lower self-reported levels of belonging, control, self-esteem, and meaningful existence. *Journal of Experimental Social Psychology, 40*(4), 560–567.

Suggested for Further Reading

On relationships and subjective well-being in general:

Diener, E., & Seligman, M. E. (2002). Very happy people. *Psychological Science, 13*(1), 81–84.

Gable, S. L., Reis, H. T., Impett, E. A., & Asher, E. R. (2004). What do you do when things go right? The intrapersonal and interpersonal benefits of sharing positive events. *Journal of Personality and Social Psychology, 87*(2), 228–245.

Leung, A., Kier, C., & Sproule, R. A. (2014). Happiness and social capital. In A. C. Michalos (Ed.), *Encyclopedia of quality of life and well-being research* (pp. 2650–2654), Dordrecht: Springer Netherlands.

Schwarzer, R., & Leppin, A. (1991). Social support and health: A theoretical and empirical overview. *Journal of Social and Personal Relationships, 8*(1), 99–127.

On the need for relatedness:

Baumeister, R. F., & Leary, M. R. (1995). The need to belong: Desire for interpersonal attachments as a fundamental human motivation. *Psychological Bulletin, 117*(3), 497–529.

Davidson, W. B., & Cotter, P. R. (1991). The relationship between sense of community and subjective well-being: A first look. *Journal of Community Psychology, 19*, 246–253.

Demir, M., & Özdemir, M. (2010). Friendship, need satisfaction and happiness. *Journal of Happiness Studies, 11*(2), 243–259. https://doi.org/10.1007/s10902-009-9138-5

Hornsey, M. J., & Jetten, J. (2004). The individual within the group: Balancing the need to belong with the need to be different. *Personality and Social Psychology Review, 8*(3), 248.

Reis, H. T., Sheldon, K. M., Gable, S. L., Roscoe, J., & Ryan, R. M. (2000). Daily well-being: The role of autonomy, competence, and relatedness. *Personality and Social Psychology Bulletin, 26*(4), 419–435.

On weak ties and the importance of community:

Kingdon, G. G., & Knight, J. (2007). Community, comparisons and subjective well-being in a divided society. *Journal of Economic Behavior & Organization, 64*(1), 69–90.

Sandstrom, G. M., & Dunn, E. W. (2014). Social interactions and well-being: The surprising power of weak ties. *Personality and Social Psychology Bulletin, 40*(7), 910–922.

On friendships:

Badhwar, N. K. (1993). *Friendship: A philosophical reader.* Ithaca, NY: Cornell University Press.

Cocking, D., & Kennett, J. (1998). Friendship and the self. *Ethics, 108*(3), 502–527.

Demir, M., & Weitekamp, L. A. (2007). I am so happy 'cause today I found my friend: Friendship and personality as predictors of happiness. *Journal of Happiness Studies, 8*(2), 181–211.

Demir, M., Jaafar, J., Bilyk, N., & Mohd Ariff, M. R. (2012). Social skills, friendship and happiness: A cross-cultural investigation. *The Journal of Social Psychology, 152*(3), 379–385.

Thomas, L. (1987). Friendship. *Synthese, 72*, 217–36.

Tiberius, V. (2018). *Well-being as value fulfillment: How we can help each other to live well.* New York: Oxford University Press.

On love and romantic relationships:

Friedman, M. (1998). Romantic love and personal autonomy. *Midwest Studies in Philosophy, 22*, 162–81.

Haidt, J. (2006). *The happiness hypothesis: Finding modern truth in ancient wisdom.* New York: Basic Books, chapter 6.

Kim, J., & Hatfield, E. (2004). Love types and subjective well-being: A cross-cultural study. *Social Behavior and Personality: An International Journal, 32*(2), 173–182.

Kolodny, N. (2003). Love as valuing a relationship. *The Philosophical Review, 112*, 135–89.

Setiya, K. (2014). Love and the value of a life. *Philosophical Review, 123*, 251–80.

On marriage and gender:

Kleingeld, P. (1998). Just love? Marriage and the question of justice. *Social Theory and Practice*, *24*(2), 261–281.

Mencarini, L., & Sironi, M. (2012). Happiness, housework and gender inequality in Europe. *European Sociological Review*, *28*(2), 203–219.

Okin, S. (1989). *Justice, gender, and the family*. New York: Basic Books.

Stevenson, B., & Wolfers, J. (2008). Happiness inequality in the United States. *The Journal of Legal Studies*, *37*(S2), S33–S79.

Sunstein, C., & Thaler, R. (2008). Privatizing marriage. *The Monist*, *91*(3–4), 377–387.

Young, I. M. (1995). Mothers, citizenship, and independence: A critique of pure family values. *Ethics*, 105, 535–556.

9

THE MINDSET OF HAPPINESS

Think for a moment about the happiest people you know. They are enjoyable to be around and bring a sense of positivity to the table. Happy people are often described as having a particular glow, as shining out from the bunch. They probably seem to have a secure sense of their position and are not often driven by envy or jealousy. They are satisfied with what they have, and if things don't go their way, they likely are able to shrug off the disappointment and not let it get them down.

What is their secret? It is tempting to see happiness as a response to the objective conditions of our lives. We see happy people and often assume that they are happy because they have it easy, because they don't have to worry about money, because their children must be well-behaved and on the honor role, and so on. While these things count, their effect goes only so far: No one's life is truly perfect, and yet people are still happy.

As we've seen in our discussions of wealth and virtue, research suggests that happiness has less to do with the external circumstances of our lives than it does with how we go about living and how we feel about our lives. The happiest people have mindsets, by which I mean a collection of attitudes that sustain their happiness. They tend to be more grateful and compassionate toward others. They tend to be more optimistic and better able to avoid negative emotions. This chapter explores the mindset of happy people. We'll examine the attitudes correlated with happiness and what these correlations tell us about happiness and about ourselves.

Religiosity and Spirituality

We begin with consideration of the connections between religiosity, spirituality, and happiness. Being part of an organized religion and engaging in religious practices is an important aspect of many people's lives, as is having faith in higher powers and other spiritual beliefs. These commitments are often a source of happiness, although, as we will discuss, the relationship between them seems to be mediated by other aspects of religiosity and spirituality.

"Religiosity" describes one's adherence to a particular religious faith and institution, while "spirituality" describes a belief or acknowledgment of a nonmaterial force that permeates one's world and one's interactions (King & Crowther, 2004). These two dimensions are separable: One can be religious yet not spiritual, and one can be spiritual yet not religious. But often the two come together. In a 2017 survey of spirituality and religiosity among Americans, researchers found that 29% were both spiritual and religious, 18% were spiritual yet not religious, 22% were religious yet not spiritual, while the remaining 31% were neither spiritual nor religious (Rany, Cox, & Jones, 2017).

Religiosity is correlated with happiness, although the nature of this correlation is not clear-cut. A review article by Koenig (2008) found a significant correlation between religiosity and well-being (measured both subjectively and objectively) but found that the correlation itself isn't as strong as we might have expected. A cross-cultural study by Diener, Tay, and Myers (2011) finds that the correlation is mediated by the degree to which religiosity is itself valued by a culture. In cultures that value religion, the correlation is stronger.

It may be the case that the correlation between religiosity and happiness is best explained by a subject's involvement with a religious institution and its practices rather than the subject's psychological commitment to that institution. These lines of research suggest that we don't see a correlation between religiosity and happiness because believing in and committing to a particular religion brings happiness but because religious institutions provide the community, involvement, and social support we have already seen to be essential to happiness.

This observation explains why the correlation between religiosity and happiness is highest in cultures that value religion. In places where religiosity is valued, religion (and its affiliated practices and institutions) is promoted and encouraged as a source of social support. In contrast, places that don't value religion tend to have other practices and institutions in place that deliver social support. For example, in the Netherlands, where religiosity is less valued, there is a weak correlation between religiosity and happiness, and there are more state-sponsored sources of social support (Snoep, 2008).

A second mediating factor influencing the relationship between religiosity and happiness is positive emotions. This factor varies significantly between particular religious institutions, but religious practices often emphasize awe, ecstasy, and gratitude and induce these emotions through prayer and song. The experience of these positive emotions (within or without a religious practice) is widely known to be a predictor of subjective well-being—a point we will return to shortly.

The experience of positive emotions also seems to mediate the correlation between spirituality and happiness. In contrast to religiosity, spirituality is defined in terms of a subject's beliefs and faith in a higher power, commitments that generate a particular framework for understanding the world and one's place in it. In the spiritual person, these commitments inform her identity and provide her with a sense of a rich engagement with the world as well as a sense of purpose and meaning.

Because spirituality is deeply connected to other positive states, including optimism, forgiveness, and gratitude, it is difficult to isolate the distinct role spirituality itself plays with respect to subjective well-being (Koenig, 2008). Often, measures that test for spirituality take these emotions as indicators of spirituality. This makes it difficult to determine whether or not spirituality directly and distinctively influences subjective well-being or does so indirectly through its association with positive emotions.

One distinctive aspect of spirituality is the degree to which it involves a sense of deeper connection with the world. Our very brief overview of Hinduism, Buddhism, and Confucianism in Chapter 1 showed the importance of understanding one's place and connection within the world to these religions' consequent understandings of happiness. Delle Fave et al. find that spirituality is often defined by subjects in terms of this connection:

> Spirituality was variously described as a subjective experience of sacredness and transcendence, the search for existential meaning, a contact with the divine within the self, and as a broader conceptual system which also includes the feelings of connectedness and integration—with a transcendent power, with oneself, with nature, with one's community—and the process of meaning-making. (Delle Fave, Massimini, & Bassi, 2011, p. 253)

These feelings of connectedness—with oneself, with others, with a larger sense of meaning and person, with a higher power—lie at the heart of spirituality.[1] Spirituality allows one to locate oneself within a system that makes sense and to appreciate the limits of one's egocentric concerns for self.

The importance of getting outside oneself by feeling connected to others, or to the world at large, is becoming a common theme in contemporary literature on the mindset of happiness, as we will see clearly in our discussions of compassion and gratitude later in this chapter. We have seen already the impact feeling included within one's community, and feeling connected to those one interacts with, has on our subjective well-being. The kind of connectedness invoked in spirituality is both more abstract and more far-reaching, but it may be just as important to our happiness.

Mindfulness

While mindfulness originates within meditative traditions specific to Buddhist philosophy, contemporary research increasingly highlights the power of mindfulness to happiness and well-being. This research highlights the promise of mindfulness to help us to live in the moment and to control our thoughts and reactions to things going on both inside and outside of our selves.

What exactly is mindfulness? Mindfulness describes a state of consciousness as well as how apt a given individual is to experience mindful states of consciousness (the latter is sometimes called "trait mindfulness"). Mindful states are characterized by a nonjudgmental and nonevaluative awareness of one's cognitive states and of the transitions between one's thoughts and attention. We can helpfully understand mindfulness as a state of "meta-cognitive awareness" in which subjects are aware of and witness to their mental states without engaging in them. Mindfulness involves not necessarily controlling one's thoughts but controlling one's reactions to those thoughts. Through developing mindfulness, subjects learn to see their thoughts as processes rather than as facts that trigger emotional responses. When something is seen as a fact, it tends to trigger an emotional response; but when something is seen as a process, it can more easily be accepted as such without triggering an emotional reaction.

Mindfulness is indeed correlated with subjective well-being and may be one of the most firmly established correlates we see with respect to subjective well-being (Schutte & Malouff, 2011). This correlation is primarily a mediated one; mindfulness leads to a number of skills and traits of mind that themselves seem directly correlated with happiness.

Prevention of negative thoughts. One of the most prominent features of mindfulness is its effectiveness in preventing a subject from engaging in negative thought patterns that spiral. A tendency toward rumination predicts the onset of depression and low levels of subjective well-being (Deyo, Wilson, Ong, & Koopman, 2009). Training in mindfulness helps individuals focus on the present, accept thoughts as they come, and let them go. These processes lessen the impact of negative thoughts and forestall rumination. Instead of dwelling on a negative thought and letting that thought multiply, mindfulness trains a person to recognize that she is having a negative thought and to let it go.

One interesting line of research explores specifically how it is that mindfulness helps to overcome or mitigate a tendency toward neuroticism. Neuroticism is an attitude characterized by negative affective states such as fear, anxiety, and worry. These affective states are clear reactions to thoughts and especially to chains of negative thoughts. Consider Ted, who at the end of the day thinks he hasn't performed very well at his job. If Ted is neurotic, the thought that he hasn't done his job well triggers a set of thoughts and emotional reactions. His neuroticism may trigger fear that he will get fired from his job or worry that his poor performance will mean that his colleagues may have to take on extra work and may hold it against them and so on. People high in neuroticism tend to be low in subjective well-being, and Wenzel, von Versen, Hirschmüller, and Kubiak (2015) find that a lack of mindfulness mediates this correlation. This finding is consistent with the general acknowledgment of mindfulness's powerful role in preventing negative thoughts in general and so in paving the way for the experience of the positive thoughts and feelings that are indicative of subjective well-being. Consider: Were Ted to be mindful rather than neurotic, he may very well still think that he didn't do his job well that day. This thought, however, wouldn't generate many other thoughts or negative emotions. Ted might be aware of the thought, decide he should try harder tomorrow, and go on with the rest of his night. This one negative thought would be contained and not affect his happiness.

Resilience. A related aspect of mindfulness is its capacity to promote resilience. Resilient people withstand adversity and bounce back from traumatic experiences. Resilience is instrumental to subjective well-being and is highly correlated with both positive affect and life satisfaction. Some even define resilience in terms of its connection to subjective well-being (e.g., Ryff & Singer, 2003); on this account, resilience is that which allows us to sustain well-being and to flourish despite the challenges life throws at us.

Mindfulness seems to promote resilience insofar as it helps individuals control their reactions to difficult situations rather than respond automatically in ways that encourage wallowing in them. Bajaj, Gupta, and Pande (2016) find that mindfulness helps to explain why resilience is positively correlated with life satisfaction and positive affect:

> Pausing and observing the mind may resist getting drawn into wallowing in a setback. Mindfulness produces emotional balance and may help in faster recovery from setbacks. High levels of mindfulness may help people maintain a decentered attitude toward difficult situations and foster resilience, and that may lead to wellbeing. Mindful people are better able to respond to difficult situations without reacting in automatic and non-adaptive ways. They are open to new perceptual categories, tend to be more creative, and can better cope with difficult thoughts and emotions without becoming overwhelmed or shutting down. (Bajaj & Pande, 2016, p. 66)

One explanation of why mindfulness has such an important impact in strengthening and promoting resilience (as well as in preventing negative thoughts) has to do with the ways in which practicing mindfulness retrains the brain. Research by Davidson and Begley (2013) finds that mindfulness meditation weakens the neural connections that encourage obsessive thoughts while strengthening the connections that promote equanimity. This means that it will be easier and more natural to develop equanimity while harder and less likely to develop obsessive thoughts.

Emotional intelligence. Finally, mindfulness also appears to be instrumental in helping individuals to enhance their capacities for emotional intelligence. Emotional intelligence is typically understood as the ability to identify and understand one's own emotional states and others', which requires recognizing emotional cues as well as the ability to regulate and harness one's emotions so that they are utilized functionally toward other ends. Emotional intelligence is significantly correlated with positive affect and life satisfaction for understandable reasons: Having emotional intelligence allows us to make the best of what is going on with us and those around us. Emotional intelligence enables us to become aware of negative emotions brewing within us and to know ways in which these emotions can negatively affect us. Emotional intelligence also enables us to know how to harness one's emotions such that we can build on the positive and direct ourselves away from the negative.

In a study tracking the correlations between (1) emotional intelligence and subjective well-being (measured through positive affect and life satisfaction); (2) mindfulness and emotional intelligence; and (3) mindfulness and subjective well-being, Schutte and Malouff (2011) find that emotional intelligence mediates the correlation between mindfulness and subjective well-being. This research suggests that mindfulness enhances emotional intelligence, and that this explains its correlation with subjective well-being.

The meta-cognitive awareness that is essential to mindfulness allows individuals to develop awareness of their emotional states. Mindfulness's emphasis on living in the moment and being aware of the present allows a person not just to develop emotional cues but also to develop awareness of the transitions their mind makes as it engages with and responds to various stimuli. It makes sense that mindfulness aids in the development of emotional intelligence, which in turn aids in the development of subjective well-being.

Compassion

Being compassionate involves adopting an attitude of care and support toward those around you who are struggling. A compassionate person understands that suffering is a part of life to which no one, including herself, is immune. She allows herself to empathize with others, but rather than drowning in the other's sorrow, she responds with warm wishes for others to be released from their burdens and to be happy.

We experience compassion when we desire the happiness of others in response to their suffering. While historically compassion has often been equated with other affective reactions to suffering, such as pity, recent discussions highlight the uniqueness of compassion as an emotion that is highly correlated with happiness. Experiencing compassion increases positive affect directly and motivates helping behavior, which is also a positive source of happiness.

Contemporary scientific interest in compassion arose largely due to the work of Mathieu Ricard, a former genetic scientist who became a Buddhist monk. Ricard worked in conjunction with the neurologist Richard Davidson to explore the neurological effects of experiencing compassion as it is induced through the Buddhist practice of loving kindness meditation. Brain scans of Ricard reveal significantly more brain activation in areas associated with subjective well-being than in nonmeditators, to the extent that headlines declared Ricard to be "the happiest man in the world." These initial studies set off a series of studies investigating the benefits of experiencing compassion.

Central to the Buddhist understanding of compassion is an appreciation of the ways in which living beings are bound together and a commitment to affirming these connections through the practice of compassion. The "loving kindness meditation" (LKM) is a meditative practice through which an individual stimulates the experience of compassion by extending other-regarding concern to a circle of others, both real (their child, coworkers) and imagined (a stranger). Within the Buddhist tradition, this other-regarding concern ultimately extends to all living things and takes the shape of an objectless form of caring. LKM walks an individual through this process. A standard LKM begins with understanding oneself as the object of loving kindness, as the receiver of kind feelings of warmth, goodwill, and kindness from others, such as his child, parents, or partner. Through the meditation, the meditator then begins to take those feelings of loving kindness and direct them to others. Most instances of LKM begin the extension by having the meditator direct loving kindness toward a specific loved one and then increase this circle of attention to include those he might feel antagonistic toward, to those unknown to him personally, and potentially to all living beings, culminating in a kind of objectless desire for the happiness of all.

Hutcherson, Seppala, and Gross (2008) find the act of mentally extending affection toward others has a positive impact on one's mood. Upon examining the effects of LKM in comparison with a meditative process that preserves the imagery of LKM (imagining other beings) but not the affective component (of directing warm feelings to those beings), they found significant correlations between LKM and increased positive feelings as well as a reduction in negative feelings. Those engaging in imagery only showed no changes with respect to positive or negative feelings. This suggests a distinct and direct correlation between compassion and positive affect that we don't find as strongly within other forms of meditation, such as mindfulness.

Experiencing compassion itself seems to make people happy. It is also true that experiencing compassion tends to motivate altruistic helping behavior and so contributes to subjective well-being in this sense as well. Intuitively, the more we desire to enhance another's welfare, the more apt we are to take steps to do so. C. D. Batson's long-standing research on altruism demonstrates enhanced altruistic helping behavior within individuals who exhibit empathic concern for others, which he describes "as an other-oriented emotional response elicited by and congruent with the perceived welfare of someone in need involving feelings *for* the other such as sympathy, compassion, tenderness, and the like" (Batson, Duncan, Ackerman, Buckley, & Birch, 1981).

More recent investigations target compassion specifically and look at the longer-term effects experiencing compassion has on prosocial behavior. Leiberg, Klimecki, and Singer find that subjects who underwent short-term compassion training engaged in more prosocial behaviors than those in the control group who underwent memory training and that these effects exceeded the immediate target of compassion and led to helping other people more generally. They conclude that "even a short-term compassion training may not only have benefits for the practitioner's health and subjective well-being but also for other people and society in general as it increases the propensity to act pro-socially even toward people one has never met" (Leiberg, Klimecki, & Singer, 2011).

How does this relate back to happiness? Let us not forget that helping behavior itself is a source of subjective well-being. We've seen repeatedly that engaging in helping behavior, and more generally being kind to others, is significantly correlated with positive affect and life satisfaction. Schwartz, Meisenhelder, Ma, and Reed (2003) find that those who provide helping behavior experience greater gains in mental health than those receiving the help. Lyubomirsky, Sheldon, and Schkade (2005) find that individuals instructed to perform acts of kindness experienced enhanced levels of subjective well-being, whereas individuals instructed to refrain from performing acts of kindness showed declines in happiness. And, perhaps most promising, Mongrain, Chin, and Shapira (2011) find that participants instructed to practice compassion through interacting with others in a supportive, caring way for a period of one week experienced enhanced levels of subjective well-being for a six-month period following their compassionate practice. While in its nascent states, this research suggests that compassion may be among the emotional states most highly correlated with subjective well-being.

Gratitude

Gratitude is another emotion highly correlated with happiness, and the practice of gratitude has been lauded in both academic and nonacademic contexts as an important source of subjective well-being. We can learn a lot about the nature of gratitude through reflection on the contrast between non-grateful and grateful people. While most everyone experiences episodes of feeling grateful, what sets grateful people apart from others is that they experience feelings of gratitude more frequently than others. They have a lower threshold for gratitude, meaning that it takes less for a grateful person to experience gratitude than it does for a non-grateful person to do so. A non-grateful person is more apt to take for granted certain benefits. They feel that their raise in salary is "owed" to them rather than an act of generosity, that the stranger who holds the door open for them is just doing what is expected rather than being kind, and so on. But grateful people view these things as benefits for which they ought to be thankful.

Watkins, Woodward, Stone, and Kolts (2003) identify three characteristics of grateful people: First, grateful people don't feel that they are deprived and rather feel a sense of abundance. Instead of focusing on what they do not have, grateful people focus on what they have and feel that they have a lot. Second, grateful people have a tendency to appreciate the simple pleasures in life, the ones that are readily available. Grateful people know that abundance doesn't require extravagance. They learn to see moments of quietness, a smile on their child's face, a home-cooked meal, as benefits that make their life full. Third, grateful people acknowledge the contributions others make to their own well-being. They don't give up ownership of their own role in the good things they experience, but they readily acknowledge the help of others.

Many analyses of gratitude emphasize this last factor, arguing that acknowledging a benefactor is a distinctive component of gratitude and that this component is central to gratitude's connection to happiness. Robert Emmons, for example, writes that

> we recognize the sources of this goodness as being outside of ourselves. It didn't stem from anything we necessarily did ourselves in which we might take pride. We can appreciate positive traits in ourselves, but I think true gratitude involves a humble dependence on others: We acknowledge that other people—or even higher powers, if you're of a spiritual mindset—gave us many gifts, big and small, to help us achieve the goodness in our lives. (Emmons, 2010)

Recognizing that you are receiving a benefit *from a benefactor* helps to explain the relationship-strengthening aspect of gratitude. This no doubt plays an important role in gratitude's connection to happiness and factors heavily into Robert Roberts's philosophical analysis of gratitude (2004). Roberts argues that gratitude involves seeing oneself as a beneficiary of some benefit granted by a benefactor whom one sees as benevolent. On this analysis, gratefulness amounts to an expression of indebtedness and attachment to a benefactor; expressing gratitude is one way of returning the benefit.

As we've seen, feeling grateful encourages us to acknowledge and appreciate our connections with others and the ways in which our own well-being is enhanced through these connections. There is also evidence that experiencing gratitude is inversely correlated with a number of negative traits, most notably depression and narcissism (Watkins et al., 2003). While it is challenging to establish the direction of this correlation (are we less depressed because we are more grateful or are we more grateful because we are less depressed?), research suggests that gratitude inductions, such as maintaining gratitude lists or writing letters of gratitude, does promote higher levels of subjective well-being (e.g., Lyubomirsky et al., 2005).

Research on gratitude induction shows that gratitude enhances our experience of positive events. Feeling grateful adds an extra boost to the experience of the good things in life. It enhances our ability to cope with negative events by helping us put those things into perspective. The perspective delivered through the experience of gratitude moreover helps us to recognize events as positive ones and to recall them as such. All these features deliver a sense of positivity that is characteristic of happy people.

Optimism

Our discussion of the mindset associated with happiness points to a unifying thread: Each attitude or emotion buffers the subject against negative thought patterns and fosters the development of positive thoughts. The last state we will consider, one of optimism, generalizes on these themes. Optimism involves adopting an attitude of positivity toward one's experiences and one's life overall. Optimistic people find the good in the bad and see the bad times as temporary. They are resilient and more likely to spring back from bad times. Unsurprisingly, then, optimistic people tend to experience greater levels of subjective well-being than those less optimistic.

One distinct aspect of optimism is a belief in one's power to succeed. Long-standing research on self-regulation finds that these beliefs play a powerful role in helping us to be successful. When we think we can succeed in our goals, we'll be more likely to succeed (Bandura, 1977). This effect has been studied in many different contexts and suggests important correlations between feeling optimistic and experiencing subjective well-being.

For example, in analyzing the role of optimism within patients before and after surgery, researchers found that an optimistic attitude greatly enhances a patient's subjective well-being throughout the process:

> Presurgically, optimists reported lower levels of hostility and depression than did pessimists. In the week following the operation, optimists reported feeling greater relief and happiness. At the same time, they reported greater satisfaction with the level of medical care they had been receiving, and with the amount of emotional support and backing they had been receiving from friends. (Scheier & Carver, 1992, p. 204)

Whatever one is facing—be it surgery, an exam, or even a wedding—taking on an optimistic attitude can transform those experiences. Optimism helps a subject to see her experiences a as conducive to her happiness. This is one reason Martin Seligman (2006) describes optimism as an "explanatory style" that defines how it is that we wrap our heads around life's events. An optimist will explain "bad" events as temporary setbacks caused by fleeting events, whereas a pessimist will explain those events as permanent ones that generate a sense of hopelessness.

Finally, optimism seems to trigger a self-perpetuating cycle that is characteristic of many of the positive feelings and emotions associated with happiness. Feeling optimistic makes us happier; happier people feel more optimistic, which helps them feel more happy, and so on.[2] The experience of positive thoughts infiltrates our perspective and changes our very thought patterns so that they are more conducive toward seeking out moments of positivity and experiencing them. This effect is so significant that it leads Michael Bishop (2015) to argue that we ought to understand well-being itself in terms of the development of these positive causal networks. To have well-being, on his account, is "to be 'stuck' in a self-perpetuating cycle of positive emotions, positive attitudes, positive traits, and successful engagement with the world" (Bishop, 2015, p. 8). Within these positive causal networks, optimism plays a pivotal role.

Conclusion

This discussion reveals the centrality of our mindset to our experience of subjective well-being. While positive affect and life satisfaction may be constitutive markers of happiness, whether we experience these states depends significantly on how it is that we view our experiences and the attitude we take toward them.

We've also seen the importance of developing control over our affective reactions to our thoughts and over our thought patterns themselves. Practicing mindfulness helps with this and particularly can help overcome a tendency toward the ruminative thinking associated with depressive states.

Throughout, we've seen that many of the mental states associated with happiness are ones that strengthen and highlight our connections to others. This underscores a theme we've seen at several points in this book, which is that healthy social relationships are fundamental to subjective well-being. We've learned that we do better when we help others and are helped by others, that developing emotional states that strengthen this connection generates positive affect and makes us feel good.

Chapter Summary

- One's mindset may be one of the most influential components of our subjective well-being. How it is that we respond to life's events may be more important than what those events are.
- Religiosity, defined as a commitment to a particular religious institution, can be an important source of social support and of positive emotions, although these factors vary depending on the particular religion and degree to which religion is valued by one's culture.

- Spirituality, defined as a belief in some kind of higher power or force, gener- ates feelings of connectedness to the world, to others, and to a higher power.
- Mindfulness involves nonjudgmental and nonevaluative awareness of one's cognitive states; training in mindfulness helps individuals to see thoughts as processes rather than as representative of facts and helps them to control their affective reactions to those thoughts.
- While highly correlated with happiness, the correlation between mindful- ness and subjective well-being is largely a mediated one. Mindfulness aids in the development of certain skills, such as resilience and emotional intel- ligence, that are directly correlated with subjective well-being.
- Compassion is the emotion we experience when desiring to enhance the welfare of others. When compassion is induced, it generates enhanced levels of positive affect. Experiencing compassion also motivates us to help others and so strengthens social bonds.
- Gratitude involves adopting a perspective through which we see life as full of good things and through which we appreciate the role that others play in helping us attain these good things. The experience of gratitude delivers a source of positive emotions as well as a sense of positivity directed toward ourselves and others.
- Optimism, or a will: belief that things go well, changes how it is that we view and understand our experiences in ways that generate positive out- comes. Optimism often triggers positive causal networks that reinforce its connection to subjective well-being.

End Notes

1 Bellingham, Cohen, Jones, and Spaniol (1989) advocate developing feelings of connect- edness as a means toward spiritual well-being.
2 Watkins (2004) discusses this cycle with respect to gratitude. See also Kesebir and Diener (2013), who explore the cycle generated between virtue and happiness.

References

Bajaj, B., & Pande, N. (2016). Mediating role of resilience in the impact of mindfulness on life satisfaction and affect as indices of subjective well-being. *Personality and Individual Differences, 93*, 63–67.

Bajaj, B., Gupta, R., & Pande, N. (2016). Self-esteem mediates the relationship between mindfulness and well-being. *Personality and Individual Differences, 94*, 96–100.

Bandura, A. (1977). Self-efficacy: Toward a unifying theory of behavioral change. *Psychological Review, 84*(2), 191–215.

Batson, C. D., Duncan, B. D., Ackerman, P., Buckley, T., & Birch, K. (1981). Is empathic emo- tion a source of altruistic motivation? *Journal of Personality and Social Psychology, 40*(2), 290–302. https://doi.org/10.1037/0022-3514.40.2.290

Bellingham, R., Cohen, B., Jones, T., & Spaniol, L. (1989). Connectedness: Some skills for spiritual health. *American Journal of Health Promotion, 4*(1), 18–31. https://doi.org/10.4278/0890-1171-4.1.18

Bishop, M. A. (2015). *The good life: Unifying the philosophy and psychology of well-being.* New York: Oxford University Press.

Davidson, R. J., & Begley, S. (2013). *The emotional life of your brain: How its unique patterns affect the way you think, feel, and live—and how you can change them.* New York: Plume.

Delle Fave, A., Massimini, F., & Bassi, M. (2011). Optimal experience and religious practice. In A. Delle Fave, F. Massimini, & M. Bassi (Eds.), *Psychological selection and optimal experience across cultures: Social empowerment through personal growth* (pp. 253–272). Dordrecht: Springer Netherlands. https://doi.org/10.1007/978-90-481-9876-4_12

Deyo, M., Wilson, K. A., Ong, J., & Koopman, C. (2009). Mindfulness and rumination: Does mindfulness training lead to reductions in the ruminative thinking associated with depression? *Explore, 5*(5), 265–271.

Diener, E., Tay, L., & Myers, D. G. (2011). The religion paradox: If religion makes people happy, why are so many dropping out? *Journal of Personality and Social Psychology, 101*(6), 1278.

Emmons, R. A. (2010). *Why gratitude is good.* Greater Good. https://greatergood.berkeley.edu/article/item/why_gratitude_is_good

Hutcherson, C. A., Seppala, E. M., & Gross, J. J. (2008). Loving-kindness meditation increases social connectedness. *Emotion, 8*(5), 720.

Kesebir, P., & Diener, E. (2013). *A virtuous cycle: The relationship between happiness and virtue. SSRN Electronic Journal.* Available at SSRN 2309566.

King, J. E., & Crowther, M. R. (2004). The measurement of religiosity and spirituality: Examples and issues from psychology. *Journal of Organizational Change Management, 17*(1), 83–101.

Koenig, H. G. (2008). Concerns about measuring "spirituality" in research. *The Journal of Nervous and Mental Disease, 196*(5), 349–355.

Leiberg, S., Klimecki, O., & Singer, T. (2011). Short-term compassion training increases prosocial behavior in a newly developed prosocial game. *PLOS ONE, 6*(3), e17798. https://doi.org/10.1371/journal.pone.0017798

Lyubomirsky, S., Sheldon, K. M., & Schkade, D. (2005). Pursuing happiness: The architecture of sustainable change. *Review of General Psychology, 9*(2), 111–131.

Mongrain, M., Chin, J. M., & Shapira, L. B. (2011). Practicing compassion increases happiness and self-esteem. *Journal of Happiness Studies, 12*(6), 963–981. https://doi.org/10.1007/s10902-010-9239-1

Roberts, R. C. (2004). The blessings of gratitude: A conceptual analysis. In R. A. Emmons and M. E. McCullough (Eds.), *The Psychology of Gratitude,* (pp. 58–78). New York: Oxford University Press.

Ryff, C. D., & Singer, B. (2003). Flourishing under fire: Resilience as a prototype of challenged thriving. In J. Haidt (Ed.), *Flourishing: Positive Psychology and the Life Well-Lived, 1st ed,* (pp. 15–36). Washington, D.C.: American Psychological Association.

Scheier, M. F., & Carver, C. S. (1992). Effects of optimism on psychological and physical well-being: Theoretical overview and empirical update. *Cognitive Therapy and Research, 16*(2), 201–228.

Schutte, N. S., & Malouff, J. M. (2011). Emotional intelligence mediates the relationship between mindfulness and subjective well-being. *Personality and Individual Differences, 50*(7), 1116–1119.

Schwartz, C., Meisenhelder, J. B., Ma, Y., & Reed, G. (2003). Altruistic social interest behaviors are associated with better mental health. *Psychosomatic Medicine, 65*(5), 778–785.

Rany, A, Cox, D., & Jones, R.P. Searching for Spirituality in the U.S.: A New Look at the Spiritual but Not Religious. (2017). *PRRI.* https://www.prri.org/research/religiosity-and-spirituality-in-america/

Seligman, M. E. (2006). *Learned optimism: How to change your mind and your life.* New York: Vintage.

Snoep, L. (2008). Religiousness and happiness in three nations: A research note. *Journal of Happiness Studies, 9*(2), 207–211.

Watkins, P. C. (2004). Gratitude and subjective well-being. In R. A. Emmons & M. E. McCollough (Eds.), *The psychology of gratitude.* New York: Oxford University Press.

Watkins, P. C., Woodward, K., Stone, T., & Kolts, R. L. (2003). Gratitude and happiness: Development of a measure of gratitude, and relationships with subjective well-being. *Social Behavior and Personality: An International Journal, 31*(5), 431–451.

Wenzel, M., von Versen, C., Hirschmüller, S., & Kubiak, T. (2015). Curb your neuroticism— Mindfulness mediates the link between neuroticism and subjective well-being. *Personality and Individual Differences, 80*, 68–75.

Suggested for Further Reading

On spirituality and religiosity:

Delle Fave, A., Brdar, I., Vella-Brodrick, D., & Wissing, M. P. (2013). Religion, spirituality, and well-being across nations: The eudaemonic and hedonic happiness investigation. In H. H. Knoop & A. Delle Fave (Eds.), *Well-being and cultures: Perspectives from positive psychology* (pp. 117–134). Dordrecht: Springer Netherlands. https://doi.org/10.1007/978-94-007-4611-4_8

Delle Fave, A., Massimini, F., & Bassi, M. (2011). Optimal experience and religious practice. In A. Delle Fave, F. Massimini, & M. Bassi (Eds.), *Psychological selection and optimal experience across cultures: Social empowerment through personal growth* (pp. 253–272). Dordrecht: Springer Netherlands. https://doi.org/10.1007/978-90-481-9876-4_12

Stavrova, O., Fetchenhauer, D., & Schlösser, T. (2013). Why are religious people happy? The effect of the social norm of religiosity across countries. *Social Science Research, 42*(1), 90–105.

Tay, L., Li, M., Myers, D., & Diener, E. (2014). Religiosity and subjective well-being: An international perspective. In C. Kim-Prieto (Ed.) *Religion and spirituality across cultures* (pp. 163–175). New York: Springer.

Wirtz, D., Gordon, C. L., & Stalls, J. (2014). Gratitude and spirituality: A review of theory and research. In C. Kim-Prieto (Ed.), *Religion and spirituality across cultures* (pp. 287–301). New York: Springer. https://doi.org/10.1007/978-94-017-8950-9_15

On mindfulness:

Brown, K. W., & Ryan, R. M. (2003). The benefits of being present: Mindfulness and its role in psychological well-being. *Journal of Personality and Social Psychology, 84*(4), 822.

Brown, K. W., Ryan, R. M., & Creswell, J. D. (2007). Addressing fundamental questions about mindfulness. *Psychological Inquiry, 18*(4), 272–281.

Ivtzan, I., & Lomas, T. (2016). *Mindfulness in positive psychology: The science of meditation and wellbeing*. New York: Routledge.

Malinowski, P. (2013). Flourishing through meditation and mindfulness. In I. Boniwell, S. David, & A. Ayers (Eds.), *Oxford library of psychology. The Oxford handbook of happiness* (pp. 384–396). New York: Oxford University Press.

On compassion:

Blum, L. A. (1980). Compassion. In A. O. Rorty (Ed.), *Explaining emotions* (pp. 507–518). Berkeley and Los Angeles: University of California Press.

Goetz, J. L., Keltner, D., & Simon-Thomas, E. (2010). Compassion: An evolutionary analysis and empirical review. *Psychological Bulletin, 136*(3), 351.

Mongrain, M., Chin, J. M., & Shapira, L. B. (2011). Practicing compassion increases happiness and self-esteem. *Journal of Happiness Studies, 12*(6), 963–981. https://doi.org/10.1007/s10902-010-9239-1

Neff, K. D. (2011). Self-compassion, self-esteem, and well-being. *Social and Personality Psychology Compass, 5*(1), 1–12.

Ricard, M. (2015). *Altruism: The power of compassion to change yourself and the world*. London: Atlantic Books.

Snow, N. E. (1991). Compassion. *American Philosophical Quarterly, 28*(3), 195–205.

On gratitude:

Gulliford, L., Morgan, B., & Kristjánsson, K. (2013). Recent work on the concept of gratitude in philosophy and psychology. *The Journal of Value Inquiry, 47*(3), 285–317.

Roberts, R. C. (2004). The blessings of gratitude: A conceptual analysis. In R. A. Emmons & M. E. McCollough (Eds.), *The psychology of gratitude* (pp. 58–78). New York: Oxford University Press.

Roberts, R. C., & Telech, D. Eds. (2019). *The moral psychology of gratitude*. New York: Rowman & Littlefield.

Watkins, P. C. (2004). Gratitude and subjective well-being. In R. A. Emmons & M. E. McCollough (Eds.), *The psychology of gratitude* (pp. 167–193). New York: Oxford University Press.

On optimism and positive causal networks:

Bishop, M. A. (2015). *The good life: Unifying the philosophy and psychology of well-being*. New York: Oxford University Press.

Fredrickson, B. L. (1998). What good are positive emotions? *Review of General Psychology, 2*(3), 300–319.

Peterson, C. (2000). The future of optimism. *American Psychologist, 55*(1), 44.

Scheier, M. F., Carver, C. S., & Bridges, M. W. (2001). Optimism, pessimism, and psychological well-being. In E. Chang (Ed.), *Optimism and pessimism: Implications for theory, research, and practice* (pp. 189–216). American Psychological Association. https://doi.org/10.1037/10385-009

Seligman, M. E. (2006). *Learned optimism: How to change your mind and your life*. New York: Vintage.

10

AUTHENTICITY AND DECEPTION

There is a good chance that at some point you've been wrong about an important aspect of your life. Maybe you thought you were a fast runner, until you ran your first organized race. Maybe you thought your teenager was healthy and on track for success, until you checked her texts. Maybe you thought your friendships were solid and secure, until no one showed up in your time of need.

We see within these experiences a pattern. You form a belief and then, at a later time, find out you were mistaken. Depending on the timing, such beliefs can make a significant impact on how we think about ourselves and the degree of happiness we experience. If there is a significant time lag between forming the beliefs and then finding out they were wrong, it is likely that a person bases her happiness on false beliefs. And if she never finds out those beliefs are false, then those beliefs might sustain her happiness over a long period of time.

It is not that unusual for happiness to be predicated on some kind of deception. We might block out the negative aspects of our upbringing and choose to focus only on the good memories. We might find ourselves so in love that we convince ourselves that the object of our love loves us back just as much. We might choose to believe our family is perfect and take satisfaction in this belief. If we feel happy on the basis of false beliefs, is this really happiness? It often feels like it—as long as the deception holds.

This chapter explores the relevance of deception to happiness, and specifically whether or not deception prevents one from being happy. The contrast we will work with is between happiness based on some form of deception and "authentic happiness" in which there is no deception. Authentic happiness describes a state of subjective well-being that is predicated on full information about the circumstances of our lives. We'll begin by considering some influential philosophical arguments in defense of authenticity. We'll then turn to explore some philosophical and psychological explanations of why authenticity might not be that important to subjective well-being, after all.

The Experience Machine and the Deceived Businessman

Imagine a machine that could deliver whatever experiences you desired. The machine needs to be programmed, of course, and you would be involved in the setup of it, but once you are in the machine, you simply experience without any awareness that those experiences are not real. Because, let's say, you've programmed the machine to deliver exactly the kinds of experiences that make you happy, you experience perfect happiness while in the machine.

Robert Nozick (1990) devises this thought experiment as an argument against hedonism, which maintains that only pleasant experiences are good, and, as a view of happiness, maintains that happiness consists in pleasant experiences. Nozick argues that most of us would not enter into the experience machine, and, as we discussed in Chapter 3, he thinks this speaks against the plausibility of hedonism.

One way to view the experience machine is as delivering inauthentic experiences: Experiences we believe we are having but that we are in fact not having as we experience them to be. The experience machine here serves as an instrument of deception. While Nozick's arguments against embracing the experience machine are intended as challenges to hedonism, the specific considerations he raises speak also to the importance of authenticity. Nozick argues that when we think about what we want to do, and what will make us happy, it is important to us that we *do* those things. We don't just want the experience of falling in love; we want to fall in love. If our experience of falling in love is not reflective of actual love that mutually develops between two parties, then our experience falls short, and, if Nozick is correct, its impact on our lives is limited.

But just how much does the "fake" delivery of this experience limit our happiness?

How much do the kinds of considerations Nozick raises realistically affect our experiences of *subjective well-being*? Subjective well-being describes an experiential state of the individual: It describes the degree to which an individual experiences positive affect and life satisfaction. Put this definition together with the plausibility of the experience requirement, which maintains that something doesn't affect our happiness unless it enters into our experiences,[1] and this may mitigate the kinds of concerns raised by the experience machine. We might care about "actual contact with reality," but if we *believe* we have actual contact with reality (as we would within the machine), this belief may be all that matters to our subjective well-being.

Appeals to the experience machine, and discussion of deception in the context of happiness more generally, are often used to reject a purely subjectivist analysis of happiness, such as hedonism and some forms of life satisfaction. A subjectivist approach takes happiness to consist solely in a mental state; if the mental state itself is constitutive of happiness, the conditions under which it arises shouldn't matter. It shouldn't matter whether or not our partners love us to the degree we think, as long as we believe they do and are able to sustain this belief as a stable one.

This consequence is a hard pill to swallow. Many do think the actual conditions of our life affect subjective well-being and that authentic happiness is important. Shelly Kagan develops this line of argument by reflecting on the deceived businessman who never learns the depth of his deception:

> Imagine a man who dies contented, thinking he has everything he wanted in life: his wife and family love him, he is a respected member of the community, and he has founded a successful business. Or so he thinks. In reality, however, he has been completely deceived: his wife cheated on him, his daughter and son were only nice to him so that they would be able to borrow the car, the other members of the community only pretended to respect him for the sake of the charitable contributions he sometimes made, and his business partner has been embezzling funds from the company, which will soon go bankrupt. (Kagan, 1998, pp. 34–35)

Kagan argues that this example gives us reason to think happiness cannot consist solely in a mental state:

> In thinking about this man's life, it is difficult to believe that it is all a life could be, that this life has gone about as well as a life could go. Yet this seems to be the very conclusion mental state theories must reach! For from the "inside"—looking only at the man's experiences—everything was perfect. We can imagine that the man's mental states were *exactly* the same as the ones he would have had if he had actually been loved and respected. So if mental states are all that matter, then—since this man got the mental states right—there is nothing missing from this man's life at all. It is a picture of a life that has gone well. But this seems quite an unacceptable thing to say about this life; it is surely not the kind of life we would want for ourselves. So mental state theories must be wrong. (Kagan, 1998, p. 35)

We might respond to these examples of deception by questioning whether or not false beliefs can have the impact the examples claim them to have: If your partner really doesn't love you, there's reason to think this affects your subjective well-being even if you (falsely) believe they do. This line of response may temper the concern. But it doesn't eliminate the pressing question: Does authenticity matter to happiness, and if so, to what degree? If your happiness is based on deception, is it still happiness?

These thought examples test the range and depth of our ordinary understandings of happiness. Is subjective well-being the kind of thing we can get from a machine or from a drug? Can we be happy when we are deceived about the most important aspects of our lives, or is this form of happiness lacking the depth distinctive to authentic happiness?

The topic of authenticity is particularly critical for life satisfaction theories of happiness: Whether or not one is satisfied with one's life depends to some extent on what one believes to be true about one's life. As the example of the deceived businessman illustrates, we can have false beliefs about the nature of our lives. Other forms of subjective well-being, such as hedonism, are also vulnerable: Pleasure arises under a number of conditions, and oftentimes a person's beliefs about those conditions prompt this pleasure. Pleasure is not just a physical on/off button; we feel pleased that the object of our affection loves us back; we feel pleasure upon completing a deadline; we feel pleased upon learning that our family members are happy, and so on. Certain conditions give rise to pleasure, and our experience of pleasure is contingent on our perception of those conditions and the beliefs we form about them.

Why Authenticity Might Matter

Our question becomes whether or not, if happiness consists in subjective well-being, authenticity counts. Does it matter whether the beliefs that inform a person's life satisfaction or experience of pleasure are true? Defenders of authenticity claim that the truth of these beliefs matters significantly. Intuitively, it seems that whatever kind of happiness the deceived businessman experiences would be better were it to be authentic. It also seems clear that where happiness lacks authenticity, it is more fragile and likely to be thrown off at any time.

Consider the following experience I recently had, ironically while writing this book and teaching a course on happiness. I come to class prepared and excited to lecture on one of my favorite topics—the connection between compassion and happiness. The class goes well: I'm on it, my students asked questions and raised good objections, all the while delivering nods indicative of shared understanding. I left class feeling successful, impressed with both my students' grasp of the difficult material and my ability to teach it to them. Teaching such a successful class had made me happy. The next day, I walk into class, and one student raises her hand to tell me, apologetically, that the class never had access to the paper that I had so eloquently lectured on the day before.[2] Turns out I had forgotten to circulate the reading, and the students, feeling bad for me, followed along in class as if they had all read it when in fact not a single person had.

I felt deflated. The sense of happiness I'd experienced so robustly the day before felt punctured as I realized I was in my own Truman show and that my happiness rested on false beliefs and a lack of information. I began to question so many of the things I take for granted and began to wonder how many other things I am routinely wrong about. Coming to have knowledge of such deception and inauthenticity is indeed painful and obstructive of happiness. But when I reflect on the feelings I had in the moment, which rested on deception and so were "inauthentic," I'm not sure that my inauthentic happiness really felt different, on the inside, from authentic happiness. It felt really good—until the deception was revealed.

Reflecting on similar cases wherein a subject's happiness is based on false information that was later revealed, L. W. Sumner notes that even though learning full information can deflate one's happiness, it is hard to see how it can change the fact that, in the moment, the subject was happy.

> If you ask her during this period [of deception] whether she is happy, she will say that she is; if you ask her whether her life is going well for her, she will say that it is. If you ask how she sees the same period after the delusion has been exposed, she will probably say that it now seems to her a cruel hoax and waste of that part of her life. Clearly she *now* thinks her life was not going well *then*; she has retrospectively re-evaluated her well-being during that period. But will she now deny that she was *happy* then? To do so would seem a mistake, a rewriting of a piece of her personal history. She may resent the fact that her happiness was bought at the price of an elaborate deception, but happy she was all the same. Wasn't she? (Sumner, 1996, p. 157)

Within these kinds of everyday cases, where one's happiness might be inauthentic insofar as it is based on mistaken information, the biggest concern with respect to one's happiness may be the extent to which this happiness is made more fragile, and liable to be deflated, upon realizing one's beliefs are mistaken.

Sometimes it can be relatively easy to accept the situation, even upon recognizing its inauthenticity, and move on. I don't have to dwell on my students' deception and redefine my happiness in light of it. I can laugh it off and go on. Sumner agrees: "We always have the alternative available of accepting the good times we enjoyed with little or no regret and then moving on with our lives" (Sumner, 1996, p. 158).

But other times we might have false beliefs that penetrate more deeply and come to affect how we think of ourselves. We might think we deserve to be subjugated; we might think we are meant for a hard life of turmoil and poverty.

A subject plagued with these beliefs comes to form a conception of happiness so premised on false beliefs that it becomes harder to accept that she is happy.

Literature on "adaptive preferences" focuses on instances wherein subjugated or otherwise oppressed individuals come to form preferences that are grounded within their oppressive circumstances and the false beliefs that structure those circumstances. This problem also arises with respect to individuals facing disabilities, who may scale back their expectations in light of their diminished capacities and so may take as a "happy life" something that is less so.

In some situations, adapting to one's circumstances and adjusting one's preferences to it can be beneficial. From a psychological perspective, the phenomenon of adaptation reveals the powerful ways in which our minds adjust and recalibrate to changes in our situation. Sometimes to be happy we have to adapt, and, as we've seen, often we adapt whether we want to or not. Yet the class of "adaptive preferences" tracks a problematic species of adaptation in which individuals come to form false, distorting views of their selves and form preferences from this point of distortion. Polly Mitchell describes adaptive preferences as "typically characterized by a number of features, including changes in self-perception; incorrect judgement about the appropriateness of the actions of others, or judgement based on incorrect standards; and pursuit of self-destructive or self-deprecating ends" (Mitchell, 2018, p. 1003). In these cases one's preferences are predicated on deception about one's own value and status.

The phenomenon of adaptive preferences warrants attention from many different perspectives. When we think about adaptive preferences within the context of happiness, the concern is that happiness that results from adaptive preferences is problematic for the subject insofar as it fails to reflect her genuine nature. This case is seen clearly within the example of a subjugated woman, whose preferences have been grounded within beliefs about her own inferior status. These preferences, and whatever feelings and mental states they give rise to, seem misaligned and lead the woman to embrace a distorted view of herself and to allow herself to be treated by others in ways that support this distorted view of herself.

These considerations support the importance of authenticity to happiness and so emphasize the importance of being fully informed to being happy. Sumner defends this line of thought; he argues that we ought to question the authenticity of a subject's happiness when it is grounded in deception or delusion:

> Where someone is deceived or deluded about her circumstances, in sectors of her life which clearly matter to her, the question is whether the affirmation she professes is *genuine* or *authentic*. In order for a subject's endorsement of her life to accurately reflect her own priorities, her own point of view—in order for it to be truly *hers*—it must be authentic, which in turn requires that it be informed. (Sumner, 1996, p. 160)

Requiring that an individual be informed ensures that whatever happiness she derives from those circumstances is authentic, insofar as her attitudes are "genuinely hers" (Sumner, 1996, p. 139). Notably, however, Sumner recognizes that the resulting theory of "authentic happiness" is more a theory of well-being than it is of happiness, precisely because it goes beyond a mental state view.[3]

Recognizing that happiness does not always equate with well-being provides another resource from which to analyze the impact of adaptive preferences. That human beings can have false beliefs—be they imposed on them by others or created by themselves—from which their subjective well-being may spring is a feature of our psychology and of the nature of happiness. When pressed with concerns about deception, accepting the fact that a person could experience happiness (subjective well-being) but not necessarily well-being is a possible route to take. This possibility invites debate over which is more important—happiness or well-being—and encourages us to keep perspective on the importance we attach to happiness.

Why (and When) Authenticity Might Not Matter

As our discussion so far has made clear, discussion of authenticity within philosophical analyses of happiness explores deep questions about the foundations of happiness. These questions arise given the possibility that a person's subjective interpretation of his life could fail to mirror the actual conditions of his life, be it because he has been actively deceived, as in the deceived businessman, or because he has internalized the (often harmful) attitudes of those around them.

While we've been discussing cases of deception that give rise to significant discrepancies between the actual conditions of one's life and one's perception of them, psychological literature reveals more everyday instances in which our minds filter the actual conditions of our lives in ways that are deceptive yet nonetheless often conducive to subjective well-being. This suggests our minds simply may have the power to create happiness, absent the "normal" conditions we expect to generate happiness. We've seen a glimpse of this already in our discussions of adaptation. When faced with changes in our situations, our minds readily adapt, thereby mitigating the impact some circumstances of our lives have on our subjective well-being.

Daniel Gilbert argues that this kind of phenomenon extends beyond adaptation and that our minds have a capacity to create happiness. He distinguishes between "natural happiness," which derives from getting what one wants, and "synthetic happiness," which is solely a function of one's mind. Gilbert argues that we tend to prioritize natural happiness, but the reality is that most of us are very bad at predicting what will make us happy and that synthetic happiness might warrant more appreciation.

Natural happiness develops akin to something like life satisfaction: We think about what will make us happy, pursue those things, and feel happy as a result. For all of this to go through, and for natural happiness to develop, we need to be pretty good at thinking about what will make us happy. This involves "affective forecasting"—predicting the impact something will have on our affective states. Gilbert and colleagues find that most of us are pretty bad at this.

First, affective forecasting is subject to an "impact bias" (Wilson & Gilbert, 2005). When thinking about the impact of future events, individuals tend to overestimate the effect those events will have on their emotional states. We may know that receiving a promotion will generate good feelings, but the impact bias leads us to expect a greater intensity and duration of those good feelings than typically occurs.

A number of lines of research affirm the prevalence of the impact bias.[4] In one study, researchers tracked college students' expected happiness following dorm assignments. Students who perceived their assignments favorably expected to be happy (estimating on average a 6 on a 1–7 scale), and those who perceived their assignments as undesirable expected not to be happy (estimating on average of 3.5/7). A year later, both groups of students, on average, ended up reporting identical scores (5.5/7). Their predictions were skewed, likely because both groups overestimated the impact of their dorm assignments.

Second, this tendency to overestimate the impact of circumstances goes hand in hand with a tendency to underestimate one's own resiliency and capacity to respond to negative situations. Gilbert describes this as the "psychological immune system," whose job it is to help us bounce back and adapt to negative changes in our environment. The psychological immune system, he argues, defends "the mind against unhappiness in much the same way that the physical immune system defends the body against illness" (Gilbert, 2006, p. 162).

Gilbert draws on this research and more to argue that synthetic happiness warrants more attention. We tend to prioritize natural happiness, but given most people's limited capacity to predict what will make them happy, and given the existence of our psychological immune system, there is no reason to do this. Happiness that our minds create with the help of our psychological immune system, be it by viewing the world through rose-colored lenses or by blocking out potential threats to one's happiness, can be just as important, even if it is synthetic and even if it lacks authenticity. But one important takeaway from Gilbert's research is that the more aware we are of the synthetic aspects of our happiness, the less effective those aspect are in making us happy: "When people catch themselves in the act of bending the truth or shading the facts, the act may fail" (Gilbert, Pinel, Wilson, Blumberg, & Wheatley, 1998, p. 635).

This line of thought goes hand in hand with ongoing research regarding the power of optimism, or choosing to believe things will go well. Optimism is widely recognized to predict subjective well-being. We've seen in Chapter 9 its potential to stimulate and perpetuate cycles of positive emotions as well as its potential to help us succeed—the latter of which becomes increasingly important in the context of synthetic happiness. There seems to be power in believing things will go well. Reflecting on this role, Karademus observes that optimism shapes one's reality: "The mediatory role of optimism, even if partial, is remarkable and revealing of the possible relations between cognitive representations and human functioning" (Karademas, 2006, p. 1289). When we are optimistic, we represent our reality in a certain way, which proves to be conducive to our physical, psychological, and subjective well-being.

Optimism can often be a form of deception, yet it is one that we embrace and advocate for, upon recognition of the impact it can have. A similar point can be made with respect to illusions, which the 18th-century philosopher Emilie Du Châtelet describes as one of the "great machines of happiness." She draws on an analogy between situations, such as the theater, where illusion is required for enjoyment and everyday situations in which illusions help us to enjoy life:

> To be happy one must be susceptible to illusion, and this scarcely needs to be proved, but, you will object, you have said that error is always harmful: is illusion not an error? No: although it is true, that illusion does not make us see objects entirely as they must be in order for them to give us agreeable feelings, it only adjusts them to our nature. Such are optical illusions: now optics does not deceive us, although it does not allow us to see objects as they are, because it makes us see them in the manner necessary for them to be useful to us. Why do I laugh more than anyone else at the puppets, if not because I allow myself to be more susceptible than anyone else to illusion ...? Would we have a moment of pleasure at the theater if we did not lend ourselves to the illusion that makes us see famous individuals that we know have been dead for a long time, speaking in Alexandrine verse? Truly, what pleasure would one have at any other spectacle where all is illusion if one was not able to abandon oneself to it? ... I have cited spectacles, because illusion is easier to perceive there. It is, however, involved in all the pleasures of our life, and provides the polish, the gloss of life. Some will perhaps say that illusion does not depend on us, and that is only too true, up to a point. We cannot give ourselves illusions any more than we can give ourselves tastes, or passion; but we can keep the illusions that we have; we can seek not to destroy them. We can choose not to go behind the set, to see the wheels that make flight, and the other machines of theatrical productions. Such is the artifice that we can use, and that artifice is neither useless nor unproductive. (Du Châtelet, 1748/2009, pp. 354–355)

Illusions, like optimism, can be useful and productive of happiness. Does this mean we should forgo examination of our circumstances, view things always from a place of optimism, and let our illusions and psychological immune system take over? Perhaps it does, at least in everyday, ordinary cases. We might be optimistic in the face of adversity, release ourselves from the burdens of over-analyzing our choices and from ongoing self-scrutiny, and just let ourselves be happy. Yet at the same time, we've seen the threats that adopting this attitude may generate, especially when taken to extremes. The happiness of the deceived businessman is fragile and liable to be deflated. The happiness of the subjugated women functions to support the conditions of her oppression and her oppressor and likely comes at the cost of her well-being.

Conclusion

It is common for us to be deceived about aspects of our lives. Sometimes this deception comes from a place of bad will, but more often deception likely arises from harmless habits—from the ways in which we hold on to beliefs in the face of conflicting evidence, or from the ways in which we focus on the good rather than the bad. Just how much do these and other habits of mind taint the happy feelings we derive from them? This remains a difficult question to answer. Insofar as happiness is a mental state, the sources from which it originates may not always affect how it feels for the subject. The most important thing just might be that the subject experiences happiness.

Chapter Summary

- When happiness is taken to consist solely in a mental state of subjective well-being, it is theoretically possible for one to be happy even when one is deceived about the circumstances of one's life.
- Thought experiments, such as Nozick's experience machine and Kagan's deceived businessman, are designed to test the limits of whether or not happiness can consist solely in a mental state or whether we ought to impose further conditions to ensure that a subject's happiness is well-grounded in a picture of reality as it actually obtains.
- Sumner argues that when a subject is deceived about the important things in life, the happiness that results threatens to be inauthentic and not reflective of attitudes genuine to them.
- The problems of deception are particularly problematic for subjects in oppressive conditions, who are vulnerable to adapting to their conditions by internalizing harmful beliefs about themselves.

- Deception may be less problematic when it comes in the form of everyday illusions and attitudes, such as optimism, that allow a subject to experience happiness even when the conditions might not mirror reality exactly.
- Gilbert's conception of the psychological immune system holds that we have an immune system that defends ourselves against threats to our happiness, often through illusions or other forms of deception.

End Notes

1 See Chapter 3 for further discussion.
2 This brave student had clearly been solicited by the group to raise this to my attention. Thank you, Alexis Ryan.
3 See Chapter 5 for further discussion of this aspect of Sumner's view.
4 Mellers and McGraw (2001) and Wilson and Gilbert (2005).

References

Du Châtelet, E. (2009). *Emilie Du Châtelet. Selected philosophical and scientific writings* (J. P. Zinsser, Ed.; I. Bour & J. P. Zinsser, Trans.). Chicago: University of Chicago Press.

Gilbert, D. T. (2006). *Stumbling on happiness.* New York: Random House.

Gilbert, D. T., Pinel, E. C., Wilson, T. D., Blumberg, S. J., & Wheatley, T. P. (1998). Immune neglect: A source of durability bias in affective forecasting. *Journal of Personality and Social Psychology, 75,* 617–638.

Kagan, S. (1998). *Normative ethics.* Boulder, CO: Westview Press.

Karademas, E. C. (2006). Self-efficacy, social support and well-being: The mediating role of optimism. *Personality and Individual Differences, 40*(6), 1281–1290.

Mellers, B. A., & McGraw, A. P. (2001). Anticipated emotions as guides to choice. *Current Directions in Psychological Science, 10*(6), 210–214.

Mitchell, P. (2018). Adaptive preferences, adapted preferences. *Mind, 127*(508), 1003–1025.

Nozick, R. (1990). *Examined life: Philosophical meditations.* New York: Simon and Schuster.

Sumner, L. W. (1996). *Welfare, happiness, and ethics.* New York: Clarendon Press.

Wilson, T. D., & Gilbert, D. T. (2005). Affective forecasting: Knowing what to want. *Current Directions in Psychological Science, 14*(3), 131–134.

Suggested for Further Reading

On the problem of deception:

Martin, M. W. (2009). Happily self-deceived. *Social Theory and Practice, 35*(1), 29–44.

Nozick, R. (1990). *Examined life: Philosophical meditations.* New York: Simon and Schuster, chapter 10.

Van Leeuwen, D. S. N. (2009). Self-deception won't make you happy. *Social Theory and Practice, 35*(1), 107–132.

On the need for full information:

Feldman, F. (2008). Whole life satisfaction concepts of happiness. *Theoria, 74*(3), 219–238.

Heathwood, C. (2005). The problem of defective desires. *Australasian Journal of Philosophy, 83*(4), 487–504.

Sumner, L. W. (1996). *Welfare, happiness, and ethics.* New York: Clarendon Press, chapters 5 and 6.

On adaptive preferences:

Bovens, L. (1992). Sour grapes and character planning. *The Journal of Philosophy, 89*(2), 57–78.

Bruckner, D. W. (2009). In defense of adaptive preferences. *Philosophical Studies, 142*(3), 307–324.

Colburn, B. (2011). Autonomy and adaptive preferences. *Utilitas, 23*(1), 52–71.

Khader, S. J. (2011). *Adaptive preferences and women's empowerment.* Oxford, UK: Oxford University Press.

Nussbaum, M. C. (2000). *Women and human development: The capabilities approach* (Vol. 3). New York: Cambridge University Press.

On the role of optimism and illusion:

Block, J., & Colvin, C. R. (1994). Positive illusions and well-being revisited: Separating fiction from fact. *Psychological Bulletin, 116*, 21–27.

Carver, C. S., & Scheier, M. F. (2002). The hopeful optimist. *Psychological Inquiry, 13*(4), 288–290.

Du Châtelet, E. (2009). Discourse on happiness. *Emilie Du Châtelet. Selected philosophical and scientific writings* (J. P. Zinsser, Ed.; I. Bour & J. P. Zinsser, Trans.). Chicago: University of Chicago Press.

Gilbert, D. T. (2006). *Stumbling on happiness.* New York: Random House.

Taylor, S. E. (1989). *Positive illusions: Creative self-deception and the healthy mind.* New York: Basic Books.

11

THE PURSUIT OF HAPPINESS

The pursuit of happiness is widely regarded as an important and fundamental aim. We want happiness for ourselves and for our loved ones; yet pursuing happiness is a complicated enterprise. It is complicated partly because there are widespread misconceptions about what will make us happy. Those of us living in a materialistic society, for example, live in societies premised upon the assumption that accumulating wealth will, in the end, make us happy—an assumption we now know is not borne out by empirical research. These and other societal ideals tend to push us in directions that we think will make us happy. But, as we've seen already, our ordinary assumptions and thoughts about what will make us happy are at best fallible and often downright wrong.

There's a deeper problem here. Even when we've cleared up our false assumptions and made an effort to learn about the kinds of things that are correlated with happiness, such as virtue and relationships, taking up the pursuit of happiness (by which I mean *actively trying to become happy*) is a complex enterprise, unlike different kinds of pursuits. Think, for a minute, about how the pursuit of happiness varies from other kinds of pursuits. Consider the pursuit of academic success. To pursue academic success, a student first needs to form some understanding of what "academic success" consists in. Jay, a premed student, may define academic success in terms of high grades, completion of an honors thesis, and acceptance into top-tier medical schools. Generally speaking, academic success can be understood in terms of a package of grades and success in the challenges specific to one's discipline, which may involve writing a thesis, pursuing an independent research project, creating a work of art, or being admitted to a graduate program. It ought to be relatively easy to identify the components of academic success for any individual student. And once those components are identified, straightforward lines of pursuit emerge: Devote significant time to academics; work with one's peers and professors to gain insight and direction into one's independent pursuits; take the classes relevant to graduate admissions, work hard in them, and study for applicable entrance exams. While these components may be straightforward, *successful* engagement in them requires knowledge of one's own strengths and limitations and an ability to work in ways that preserve one's strengths while striving to overcome one's limitations. As each individual has different strengths and limitations, her pursuit of academic success will include strategies for building on her strengths while overcoming her limitations.

Now consider something like the pursuit of pleasure. As with academic success, pursuit of pleasure begins with reflection on the target: Pleasure. While feasibly a singular and identifiable target, pleasure comes from a wide variety of sources, and not all deliver equal or even comparable experiences of pleasure.[1] Massages give me pleasure, as does rubbing my puppy's belly, as does sitting around the dinner table talking with my family. If I'm serious about pursuing pleasure, it seems I'll need some insight into the *best* sources of pleasure. This insight seems hard to come by, however, as (a) there seem to be significant individual differences in what kinds of experiences we find most pleasurable, and (b) no one route to pleasure seems infallible. Sometimes I rub my puppy's belly and don't find it pleasurable.[2] Sometimes I sit down to talk with my family over dinner and don't find it at all pleasurable. Sometimes, even, a massage may not deliver pleasure. Successful pursuit of pleasure involves a high level of first personal awareness that may not always be possible.[3] The murkiness of the target, and the fact that experiencing pleasure depends heavily on individuated features of the subject, make the pursuit of pleasure more complicated than it might first appear.

These features magnify when it comes to thinking about the pursuit of happiness. The initial reflection on the target, which seemed so straightforward when thinking through academic success, is complicated to the point that it may be pointless. For most of us, happiness is something (we think) we know when we have, but it is also something very difficult to wrap our heads around in a precise fashion. When we think about happiness, we are probably more likely to think in terms of what we already believe will make us happy. So perhaps we think of financial stability, of having a rewarding career, or having a family, and we think about pursuing these things. But absent deep reflection on their connection to happiness, there's a good chance we get caught up in the pursuit of these things themselves and so lose sight of our target altogether.

Alternatively, say we are able to think about happiness as a general target. After reading Part I, perhaps we identify happiness as a target that involves a combination of life satisfaction and lots of pleasurable experiences—this is akin to how most psychologists understand happiness, which they describe as "subjective well-being." If we've done this work, the next step will be to consider how to obtain this combination. But here we run into an exacerbated problem of what we saw likely to happen when we try to pursue pleasure. What delivers life satisfaction, as well as pleasurable experiences, seems to be a combination of factors specific to the individual, and isolating these factors may be insurmountable. How am I to know what will really deliver, to me, life satisfaction? How am I to know what will really deliver, to me, pleasure? Can I figure out the answers to these questions alone?

The pursuit of happiness is unique. The same strategies we use to pursue other goals may not be the best ones to employ in our pursuit of happiness. In this chapter, we'll explore some of the obstacles that interfere with the pursuit of happiness and what we might be able to do to overcome them. Pursuing happiness, we'll see, is challenging but not unsurmountable when approached in the right way, with the right expectations.

The Paradox of Happiness

Philosophical discussions of the pursuit of happiness often start by struggling with a simple observation, made famous in the 18th century by Bishop Butler. Butler observes that most people who actively pursue happiness end up failing to become happy. There is something familiar to this: Imagine Basia, who, after emerging from a conflicted marriage and a long period of unhappiness, just wants to be happy. She puts all her efforts into "being happy," and "being happy" serves as her primary motive, influencing both day-to-day activities and the important decisions in her life. Yet despite the priority she places on becoming happy, she just can't seem to become happy.

Let us take the "paradox of happiness" to refer to this basic observation.[4] The paradox of happiness holds that direct, intentional efforts to maximize one's happiness will not maximize one's happiness. The direct pursuit of happiness, such as taking "being happy" as one's motive, seems self-defeating.

Why think the paradox of happiness exists? Butler spells out the paradox in terms of self-love, arguing that the more self-love engrosses us, the less likely we are to advance our private good: "Private interest is so far from being likely to be promoted to the degree in which self-love engrosses us, and prevails over all other principles, that the contracted affection may be so prevalent as to disappoint itself, and even contradict its own end, private good" (Butler, 1983, p. 49). Butler's observation is one to which many philosophers are sympathetic, and the phenomenon it points to is likely familiar. As is often said, what is the best advice we can give to the sad person, like Basia, who is desperate to be happy? Stop worrying about being happy and find something else to focus on. Rather than waking up every day thinking that one needs to be happy, it seems a better strategy to set aside active thoughts about happiness and instead focus on pursuing experiences because one finds them interesting, or meaningful, or so on.

The paradox of happiness is based on an empirical, observational claim about the efficacy of direct pursuits of happiness. But philosophical discussions of the paradox move very quickly from this observational claim to make a point about the nature of happiness itself. Thus, for example, Butler's discussion of the paradox goes hand in hand with his philosophical analysis of happiness. Because happiness is not something that can be pursued directly, Butler reasons that happiness itself must be something that arises from other pursuits, which he describes in terms of particular passions.

Particular passions, according to Butler, are passions directed at a specific object. Annie has a particular passion for Nordic skiing. As a particular passion, the object is solely the experience of skiing: Annie wants to ski. She satisfies her particular passion through skiing. Most of us have a wide range of particular passions. According to Butler, it is through the pursuit of particular passions, rather than the pursuit of self-interest or happiness more generally, that we attain happiness. Given the paradox of happiness and its observation that directly pursuing happiness is self-defeating, Butler argues that we ought to set aside concerns for happiness, develop particular passions, and pursue those. This, Butler argues, is the recipe for happiness. Happiness arises from the gratification of particular passions. "The very idea of interest or happiness," he argues, "consists in this that an appetite or affection enjoys its object." Moreover, "the very idea of interest or happiness…implies particular appetites or passions, these being necessary to constitute that interest or happiness" (Butler, 1983, p. 20).

Butler puts forward a view of happiness according to which happiness depends on the satisfaction of particular passions and interests insofar as it is something that arises from their satisfaction. This, he seems to think, is the natural way to think about happiness in light of the paradox of happiness. If what happens when we sit around and try to pursue "happiness" is that we end up failing to become happy, it makes sense to think that we ought to stop worrying about happiness and start thinking about what kinds of passions and interests we have.[5]

This line of reasoning has become somewhat commonplace within contemporary philosophical discussions of happiness, which routinely emphasize the importance of what we are doing and how we feel about what we are doing. The life satisfaction theory does this straightforwardly. By describing happiness in terms of a positive evaluation of how one's life is going, it presents a view according to which happiness depends on what we are doing and how we feel about what we are doing.

Many hedonistic views also tie happiness to the pursuit of passions and interests and so also present a view of happiness according to which happiness depends on what we are doing and how we feel about what we are doing. In this picture, we feel pleasure, and so experience happiness, by engaging in experiences that we find agreeable. The experience of happiness is thus dependent on the attitudes we take toward those experiences. Feldman's influential theory of attitudinal hedonism makes this connection explicit. He describes attitudinal pleasures as the pleasures one takes in a state of affairs "if he enjoys it, is pleased about it, is glad that it is happening, is delighted by it" (Feldman, 2004, p. 56). In a move that ought to remind us of Butler's analysis of particular passions, Feldman writes that "attitudinal pleasures are always directed onto objects, just as beliefs and hopes and fears are directed onto objects" (2004, p. 56).

Philosophers often tend to take the problems of pursuing happiness to be a springboard for understanding happiness itself, with the hope that developing a proper understanding of happiness can help alleviate the problems that subjects face pursuing happiness. Thus, for example, understanding that happiness consists in pleasure that derives from one's attitudes allows us to properly channel our efforts to become happy. While this strategy no doubt helps, empirical research on happiness suggests we are no more successful in pursuing happiness than Butler first observed. Moreover, this research suggests that the problems go deeper than Butler thought. The problems we face in pursuing happiness likely arise not because we are pursuing happiness the wrong way but rather by virtue of the fact that our ability to make lasting changes to our happiness is constrained significantly by basic features of our psychology.

Adaptation and the Set-Point Theory

One of the most widely discussed obstacles to the pursuit of happiness is the process of adaption, in which our minds adapt to changes in our environments. The basic phenomenon of adaptation is a familiar one: We adapt to changes in our lives, thereby mitigating their impact on our emotional states. We know that while ending a relationship can be excruciatingly painful, over time the pain will subside and we will move on. We will adapt.

We've seen already the impact adaptation seems to have on the ways in which wealth contributes to our subjective well-being;[6] this is one instance of a broader phenomenon that calls into question the meaningfulness of pursuing happiness. Studies on adaptation demonstrate that most of us have a remarkable ability to adapt our affective response to significant life changes, be they the most "challenging" changes (e.g., becoming paraplegic) or the most "beneficial" changes (e.g., winning the lottery). Research suggests that while such changes may have a temporary impact on one's happiness levels, they do not seem to have a lasting effect. Brickman, Coates, and Janoff-Bulmans's influential studies on adaptation (1978) showed that while both groups experienced changes in their happiness levels immediately following their life-changing event, the change was not permanent, and individuals in both groups returned to their original levels of happiness within two years.

Why do our affective states seem so quick to adapt? The adaptive process appears to be an important part of how we are able to endure change. Change presents us with stress, and adaptation allows us to alleviate that stress.

The psychologist Jonathan Haidt provides an interesting neurological analysis of adaptation, writing,

> Adaptation is, in part, just a property of neurons: Nerve cells respond vigorously to new stimuli, but gradually they "habituate," firing less to stimuli that they have become used to. It is *change* that contains vital information, not steady states. Human beings, however, take adaptation to cognitive extremes. We don't just habituate, we recalibrate. We create for ourselves a world of targets, and each time we hit one we replace it with another. After a string of successes we aim higher; after a massive setback, such as a broken neck, we aim lower...we surround ourselves with goals, hopes, and expectations, and then feel pleasure and pain in relation to our progress. (Haidt, 2006, p. 26, emphasis in original)

Life changes bring about a change in expectations, and nowhere is this clearer than with respect to one's income. Even a small boost in one's salary generates higher expectations about what one will be able to do with all of that extra money; one's expectations increase as one's salary increases, and the degree of positive affect one experiences ends up remaining the same.

We might be tempted here to think that, with respect to happiness, we can prevent our affective states from adapting by controlling our expectations. Yet the adaptive process seems to be more firmly engrained than this, with much of the adjustments being made automatically and beyond our conscious control. Frederick and Loewenstein (1999), for example, find that adaptation can result from a number of different inputs and arise from a number of different processes and not just from our expectations. These processes range from the automatic adjustment of sensory processes, such as when we adapt to foul smells so much that we may no longer notice them, to the overt actions we take to divert our attention away from troubling thoughts, to a conscious change of goals and expectations in response to frustrated efforts to attain previous goals. Thus, while adaptation is something that we can consciously stimulate, it is also one that happens automatically.

These lines of research suggest that the process of adaptation is central to our experience of happiness insofar as it regulates our affective responses to the events and circumstances of our lives. Through the process of regulation, adaptation ends up neutralizing the impact these factors have on one's happiness. It neutralizes not only the impact a new car or house can have on our happiness but also the impact a new promotion can have. Adaptation even promises to neutralize the impact of attaining any milestone, no matter how much that milestone may be cherished.

The process of adaptation has been discussed widely in the context of the theory that there exists a genetically determined happiness set-point for each individual. According to defenders of this theory, our experience of happiness is hardwired, and variations in happiness between individuals are explainable by appeal to genes rather than to life circumstances. Lykken and Tellegen (1996), for instance, find genetic variability to be the most significant factor in determining happiness levels, accounting for at least between 44% and 52% (and maybe as much as 80%) of variance in levels of happiness, while other factors (socioeconomic status, education, marital status) accounted for only 3% of variance. Twin studies affirm this genetic basis, leading Lykken and Tellegen to claim that 'the reported well-being of one's identical twin, either now or 10 years earlier, is a far better predictor of one's self-rated happiness than is one's own educational achievement, income, or status" (1996, p. 188). Adaptation is often brought up to support this claim; the idea is that a significant reason why lasting changes are elusive is because we so readily adapt to any change in our lives. The adaptation hypothesis thus holds that regardless of what is going on in our lives, we will likely return to the same general level of happiness we started with—we return to our happiness set-point.

The adaptation hypothesis and theory of the happiness set-point paint a dismal view of our ability to pursue happiness in a meaningful way. The obstacles seem worse than Butler thought; even if we respond to the paradox of happiness by trying to pursue things that we are interested in and for their sake alone, it still seems unlikely that such pursuits will pay off in increased happiness. Should we just give up on happiness and let whatever comes, come?

The Limits of Adaptation

Concerns about adaption have significantly influenced psychological discussion and research on happiness. Yet, many psychologists have raised important concerns with respect to the initial studies used to explore adaptation in the context of happiness. These concerns suggest that its effect on happiness may not be as pervasive as first appears.

While the infamous study on lottery winners (Brickman, Coates, & Janoff-Bulman, 1978) challenges the influence of money on one's levels of happiness, the idea that there is *no* correlation between increases in income and increases in happiness has been called into question.[7] The hypothesis that we can completely adapt to disability (suggested by Brickman et al., 1978) has also been contested. While Brickman et al. found that those with spinal cord injuries eventually return to levels of happiness similar to those they started with, their studies didn't compare levels of happiness between those with and without such disabilities, and so its conclusions regarding the impact of disabilities on happiness are limited. Further research shows that those with disabilities do tend to be less happy than those without (Dijkers, 1997) and suggests that being disabled does seem to lower one's subjective well-being. This seems particularly true with respect to disabilities that result from chronic or progressive diseases and suggests that these diseases may be resistant to adaptation.[8]

A more general challenge to the adaptation theory questions the extent to which individual differences affect adaptation. Diener, Lucas, and Scollon (2006) argue that the rate and degree of adaption varies between individuals and is influenced by life events.[9] They criticize earlier studies on adaptation for drawing conclusions without having measures of pre-event levels of happiness and argue that longitudinal studies on happiness levels pre-, during, and post-event are necessary to establish adaptation (Lucas, 2007). Moreover, Lucas's longitudinal studies (Lucas, 2007) suggest that some life events, such as changes in marital, employment, and health status, do generate lasting changes to happiness levels. Forced unemployment, for instance, correlates with lower life satisfaction scores not only during the periods of unemployment but two years (and often longer) after unemployment ends (Lucas et al., 2004).

If these studies prove what many take them to prove, the adaptation hypothesis is less powerful than some have thought; we may not need to give up all hope of pursuing happiness. There may be some things that do influence our happiness levels in important ways, such as whether or not we have enough money to live comfortably, whether or not we are gainfully employed, how our personal relationships are going, and whether or not we are faced with a life-changing disability.

There is also interesting research regarding some specific life circumstances that seem to be resistant to adaptation. Being subject to chronic noise, for example, has ongoing effects on one's affective states. In a longitudinal study of whether or not residents would adapt to noise generated by a recently built highway in their neighborhood, Weinstein (1982) found no evidence of adaptation in a 16-month period and, in fact, found increasing annoyance with noise levels (and associated negative affect) over the course of this time. These results are well replicated, suggesting that noise is something we ought to avoid, for it threatens to continually detract from our happiness.[10]

Similarly, having a lengthy, heavy-traffic-laden commute is another life circumstance that seems resistant to adaptation (Koslowsky & Kluger, 1995). While there is much disagreement about the exact cause of the stress (Is it the time? Is it the traffic?), there is widespread agreement on the negative effects of commuting and its resistance to adaptation.[11] Time, it seems, will not help us adjust, and having this kind of stressful daily commute is likely to have lasting effects on our mood. These circumstances stand out as features of our environments that *do* affect our happiness, suggesting that there are at least some things that we don't seem to adapt to and would be helpful to avoid in our pursuit of happiness.[12]

Happiness Interventions

So far we've considered the difficulties involved in making lasting changes to our levels of happiness, difficulties that show the pursuit of happiness is fundamentally constrained by psychological mechanisms that regulate our affective responses to life changes. We have not seen that pursuing happiness is impossible. With this hope, many have begun to explore the effectiveness of certain happiness interventions.

Lyubomirsky and colleagues pursue this line of research (Lyubomirsky, Sheldon, & Schkade, 2005; Sheldon & Lyubomirsky, 2004). Their research is premised on the idea that happiness consists in a combination of genetics, life circumstances, and intentional activities. While one's genetics suggests that there is a happiness set-point, recognizing the contribution of other factors suggests that we see the constraints genetics places on individuals as establishing a range in which we can move up or down. According to this line of thought, where we move within this range is determined both by one's life circumstances and one's intentional activities. The influence of intentional activities seems to be far greater, estimated at 40%, than is the influence of life circumstances, estimated at 10%.

Sheldon and Lyubomirsky speculate that focusing on one's intentional activities will be most productive, largely because one can control what one chooses to do and when. Among other benefits, this makes intentional activities more resistant to adaptation:

> Because of their intentional character, activities are more resistant to the effects of adaptation. In other words, a person can deliberately vary his or her activities, such that they continually provide new experiences and results. Indeed, some intentional activities (such as meditation or pausing to count your blessings) can serve to directly counter adaptation. Furthermore, intentional activity can create a self-sustaining cycle of positive change, in which invested effort leads the person to further opportunities for satisfying actions and accomplishments. The person can also perform an activity robotically, without variation, or fail to sensitively apply or enact the strategy. In such cases…the benefits are likely to fade over time, just as the impact of positive circumstantial changes dampens. Still, activities have the *potential* to create sustained positive change because of their more dynamic and varying nature and because of their capacity to produce a steady stream of positive and rich experiences. If anything can do it, activities can. (Sheldon & Lyubomirsky, 2004, p. 133)

Here we see optimism regarding the potential intentional activities have to create lasting changes to our happiness levels; while their impact may be constrained by our genetics and life circumstances, there is hope that their impact can nonetheless be significant.

Among the intentional activities showing to be most correlated with happiness are performing acts of kindness and engaging in gratitude exercises (Lyubomirsky et al., 2005). Acts of kindness boost temporary moods and contribute to long-term happiness. Performing acts of kindness leads the actor to see herself as happier; this is perhaps because such acts transform the actor's perception of others. Regularly performing kind acts leads individuals to see others in a more charitable fashion as well as to see one's community in a more charitable fashion. It encourages a sense of cooperation and helps one to recognize one's own good fortune. And when one performs kind acts, one begins to see oneself as altruistic and to develop feelings of confidence and self-efficacy regarding one's ability to help. Others in one's community begin to view that person in these terms as well. All these factors combine to create an interplay of emotions and thought patterns that create an upward spiral of positive emotions, thus enhancing one's degree of happiness.

Expressing gratitude seems to have a parallel impact on one's levels of happiness (Lyubomirsky et al., 2005). As we discussed in Chapter 10, feeling grateful allows one to see one's circumstances in a positive fashion. This focus may help to counteract or prevent the adaptation to the good things in one's life. A disposition to be grateful may also serve as a coping strategy, allowing individuals to interpret their stressful or negative experiences in positive ways; this positivity moreover seems to strengthen one's social relationships. Finally, it seems that feeling grateful, or feeling good about one's life, is itself incompatible with feeling negative about oneself and with the experience of negative emotions, such as anger and greed, which are likely to arise from feeling negative about oneself.

Acts of kindness and gratitude exercises illustrate two intentional activities that build on themselves such that they lead the individuals engaging in them to think about one's life and circumstances in ways that generate positive emotions and positive feedback from others. Other intentional activities have a more limited, yet nonetheless significant, effect. For example, flow activities are widely taken to deliver a pure form of enjoyment yet don't seem to generate upward positive spirals once they are over. Nonetheless, the experience of flow activities itself is such a powerful source of happiness that it seems likely that the more flow experiences you can fit into your life, the happier you will be.

Finally, one of the most promising interventions in happiness may lie in meditation practices, which some believe may even change one's happiness set-point. Davidson and colleagues (2003) use neuroimaging to examine the effects of meditation and found meditation to be correlated with greater activity in the left prefrontal cortex, which is thought to indicate levels of contentment.[13] It just may be that meditation trains our brain in ways that make it more apt to experience happiness, and, as we've discussed in Chapter 10, the impact seems particularly live in the context of the loving kindness meditation practices that inculcate feelings of compassion.

Conclusion

The chapters within this part have explored a wide range of the things that contribute to our happiness and things that stand in the way of our happiness. We've learned that money is helpful but that valuing and pursuing wealth is detrimental to happiness; we've learned that relationships are pivotal to happiness and that while acting virtuously may not be *necessary* to happiness, it doesn't hurt and most likely helps insofar as it strengthens our relationships. We've learned that some attitudes and emotional states are conducive to happiness and that there is power to positive thinking. This discussion shows that even when armed with all this information, there is no secret formula by which we can become happy and that happiness may be one of the most difficult things to actively strive for. As Butler first observed, we can't become happy simply by pursuing "happiness." And even when we know the things that are correlated with happiness, such as relationships, pursuing them for the sake of happiness is likely self-defeating.

Both philosophical and psychological analyses of the pursuit of happiness show that the pursuit of happiness is constrained more by what we bring to its pursuit than any kind of external input. Even in a world where our opportunities are limitless, whether or not we can increase our happiness depends on what we are engaging in, the attitudes that shape our engagement, and the impact these have on our subjective psychological states. Yet this impact is not entirely within our volitional control. We can't just decide to be happy in the face of a new job; whether or not the new job helps us to be happy depends on a host of other factors, such as whether or not it taps into our psychological needs, the degree to which we adapt (or not) to the new circumstances it brings, and the degree to which we scrutinize whether or not we *should* feel happy or just let our psychological immune system kick in.

All this suggests that, rather than focusing on how we can change the circumstances of our lives in order to become happy, the best bet for most of us is to focus instead on how we live our lives and what we bring to our experiences. Are we regularly kind to others? Are we aware of the good things in our life and grateful for them? Do we face challenges with optimism and confidence? These components of how we live day to day seem to have the most influence on our happiness, and they are things within our control.

As we go about making these small but significant changes, however, we should recognize the limits of such pursuits. Due to the influence of genetics and to the process of adaptation, we may not be able to dramatically change the degree of happiness we experience. While this conclusion may seem pessimistic, the reality is that most of us do seem to be happy. Repeated studies show that most of us experience positive affect as our default, such that our set-point is one of happiness rather than unhappiness. This means that the adaptive process might be more likely to bring us up rather than down, a point that makes sense from a functional perspective. As Diener and colleagues (2006) explain, there is much evidence that feeling positive affect makes people feel comfortable exploring their environment, more eager to set new goals, and even more successful in attaining those goals. They conclude that "the ubiquity of a positive emotional set-point, in concert with the less frequent experience of unpleasant emotions, likely results from the adaptive nature of frequent positive emotions" (Diener et al., 2006, p. 307). There is thus good reason to think that the overall process of adaptation is a beneficial one and that we should be optimistic about living happy lives even if pursuing such lives is challenging.

Chapter Summary

- The paradox of happiness maintains that the direct pursuit of happiness is self-defeating. Butler argues that in light of the paradox, we are better off pursuing those things we are interested in.
- The psychological process of adaptation minimizes the extent to which changes in circumstances create changes in our levels of happiness, especially our levels of positive affect.
- Psychologists speculate that most people have a genetically determined happiness set-point that, together with the process of adaptation, constrains their ability to make significant changes to their levels of happiness.
- Recent research reveals the promise specific interventions may hold for helping individuals become happier, such as performing acts of kindness and engaging in gratitude practices.

End Notes

1 See Chapter 3 for extended discussion on the nature of pleasure.
2 To be honest, I'm not sure this has happened. It is certainly theoretically possible, though.
3 Haybron (2008) presents a convincing case for the existence of "affective ignorance"— ignorance about one's own affective states. See Chapters 5 and 12 for further discussion of this phenomenon.
4 The general paradox referred to here has been described by a number of terms, including "the paradox of hedonism," "the paradox of egoism," "the paradox of egoistic hedonism," and so forth.
5 Mill describes a similar view in his autobiography, where he writes that the only people who are happy are those "who have their minds fixed on some object other than their own happiness; on the happiness of others, on the improvement of mankind, even on some art or pursuit, followed not as a means, but as itself an ideal end. Aiming thus at something else, they find happiness by the way" (1873, p. 117).
6 Chapter 6.
7 We'll talk more about these challenges and their implications for the economics of happiness in Chapter 13.
8 Antonak and Livneh (1995) and Livneh and Antonak (1994).

9 See also Lucas (2007) and Lucas, Clark, Georgellis, & Diener (2003, 2004).
10 See Frederick and Loewenstein (1999) for review.
11 See Koslowsky (1997) for review.
12 Haidt (2006) argues that a lack of control and shame are also circumstances that are resistant to adaptation.
13 See also Davidson (2004) and Urry et al. (2004).

References

Antonak, R. F., & Livneh, H. (1995). Psychosocial adaptation to disability and its investigation among persons with multiple sclerosis. *Social Science & Medicine, 40*(8), 1099–1108.

Brickman, P., Coates, D., & Janoff-Bulman, R. (1978). Lottery winners and accident victims: Is happiness relative? *Journal of Personality and Social Psychology, 36*(8), 917–927.

Butler, J. (1726). *Five sermons* (S. Darwall, Ed.). Indianapolis, IN: Hackett Press.

Davidson, R. J. (2004). What does the prefrontal cortex "do" in affect: Perspectives on frontal EEG asymmetry research. *Biological Psychology, 67*(1), 219–234.

Davidson, R. J., Kabat-Zinn, J., Schumacher, J., Rosenkranz, M., Muller, D., Santorelli, S. F. ... Sheridan, J. F. (2003). Alterations in brain and immune function produced by mindfulness meditation. *Psychosomatic Medicine, 65*(4), 564–570.

Diener, E., Lucas, R. E., & Scollon, C. (2006). Beyond the hedonic treadmill: Revising the adaptation theory of well-being. *American Psychologist, 61*(4), 305–314.

Dijkers, M. (1997). Quality of life after spinal cord injury: A meta analysis of the effects of disablement components. *Spinal Cord, 35*(12), 829–840.

Feldman, F. (2004). *Pleasure and the good life: Concerning the nature, varieties and plausibility of hedonism.* Oxford: Clarendon Press.

Frederick, S., & Loewenstein, G. (1999). Hedonic adaptation. In D. Kahneman, E. Diener, & N. Schwarz (Eds.), *Well-being: The foundations of hedonic psychology* (pp. 302–329). New York: Russell Sage Foundation.

Haidt, J. (2006). *The happiness hypothesis: Finding modern truth in ancient wisdom.* New York: Basic Books.

Haybron, D. M. (2008). *The pursuit of unhappiness.* New York: Oxford University Press.

Koslowsky, M. (1997). Commuting stress: Problems of definition and variable identification. *Applied Psychology, 46*(2), 153–173.

Koslowsky, M., & Kluger, A. N. (1995). *Commuting stress: Causes, effects and methods of coping.* New York: Springer.

Livneh, H., & Antonak, R. F. (1994). Review of research on psychosocial adaptation to neuromuscular disorders: I. Cerebral palsy, muscular dystrophy, and Parkinson's disease. *Journal of Social Behavior & Personality, 9*(5), 201–230.

Lucas, R. E. (2007). Adaptation and the set-point model of subjective well-being: Does happiness change after major life events? *Current Directions in Psychological Science, 16*(2), 75–79.

Lucas, R. E., Clark, A. E., Georgellis, Y., & Diener, E. (2003). Reexamining adaptation and the set point model of happiness: Reactions to changes in marital status. *Journal of Personality and Social Psychology, 84*(3), 527–539.

Lucas, R. E., Clark, A. E., Georgellis, Y., & Diener, E. (2004). Unemployment alters the set point for life satisfaction. *Psychological Science, 15*(1), 8–13.

Lykken, D., & Tellegen, A. (1996). Happiness is a stochastic phenomenon. *Psychological Science*, 7(3), 186–189.

Lyubomirsky, S., Sheldon, K. M., & Schkade, D. (2005). Pursuing happiness: The architecture of sustainable change. *Review of General Psychology*, 9(2), 111–131.

Mill, J. S. (1873). *Autobiography* (J. M. Robson, Ed.). London: Penguin Books.

Sheldon, K. M., & Lyubomirsky, S. (2004). Achieving sustainable new happiness: Prospects, practices, and prescriptions. In A. Linley & S. Joseph (Eds.). *Positive psychology in practice* (pp. 127–145). Hoboken, NJ: John Wiley & Sons.

Urry, H. L., Nitschke, J. B., Dolski, I., Jackson, D. C., Dalton, K. M., Mueller, C. J. ... Davidson, R. J. (2004). Making a life worth living: Neural correlates of well-being. *Psychological Science*, 15(6), 367–372.

Weinstein, N. D. (1982). Community noise problems: Evidence against adaptation. *Journal of Environmental Psychology*, 2(2), 87–97.

Suggested for Further Reading

For the paradox of happiness:

Bloomfield, P. (2014). *The virtues of happiness: A theory of the good life*. New York: Oxford University Press.

Butler, J. (1983). *Five sermons* (S. Darwall, Ed.). Indianapolis, IN: Hackett Press.

Eggleston, B. (2013). Paradox of happiness. In H. Lafollette (Ed.), *International encyclopedia of ethics*. Oxford, UK: Blackwell Publishing, Ltd., 3794–3799.

Martin, M. W. (2008). Paradoxes of happiness. *Journal of Happiness Studies*, 9(2), 171–184.

Mauss, I. B., Tamir, M., Anderson, C. L., & Savino, N. S. (2011). Can seeking happiness make people unhappy? Paradoxical effects of valuing happiness. *Emotion-APA*, 11(4), 807.

For adaption and the genetic set-point:

Besser-Jones, L. (2013). The pursuit and nature of happiness. *Philosophical Topics*, 41(1), 103–121.

Brickman, P., Coates, D., & Janoff-Bulman, R. (1978). Lottery winners and accident victims: Is happiness relative? *Journal of Personality and Social Psychology*, 36(8), 917–927.

Diener, E., Lucas, R. E., & Scollon, C. (2006). Beyond the hedonic treadmill: Revising the adaptation theory of well-being. *American Psychologist*, 61(4), 305–314.

Frederick, S., & Loewenstein, G. (1999). Hedonic adaptation. In D. Kahneman, E. Diener, & N. Schwarz (Eds.), *Well-being: The foundations of hedonic psychology* (pp. 302–329). New York: Russell Sage Foundation.

Lucas, R. E. (2007). Adaptation and the set-point model of subjective well-being: Does happiness change after major life events? *Current Directions in Psychological Science*, 16(2), 75–79.

Lucas, R. E., Freedman, V. A., & Cornman, J. C. (2018). The short-term stability of life satisfaction judgments. *Emotion*, 18(7), 1024.

Sheldon, K. M., & Lucas, R. E. (2014). *Stability of happiness: Theories and evidence on whether happiness can change*. San Diego, CA: Elsevier.

For happiness interventions:

Lyubomirsky, S., Sheldon, K. M., & Schkade, D. (2005). Pursuing happiness: The architecture of sustainable change. *Review of General Psychology, 9*(2), 111–131.

Sheldon, K. M., & Lyubomirsky, S. (2006). How to increase and sustain positive emotion: The effects of expressing gratitude and visualizing best possible selves. *The Journal of Positive Psychology, 1*(2), 73–82.

Sheldon, K. M., & Lyubomirsky, S. (2007). Is it possible to become happier? (And if so, how?). *Social and Personality Psychology Compass, 1*(1), 129–145.

Urry, H. L., Nitschke, J. B., Dolski, I., Jackson, D. C., Dalton, K. M., Mueller, C. J., & Davidson, R. J. (2004). Making a life worth living: Neural correlates of well-being. *Psychological Science, 15*(6), 367–372.

PART III
The Context of Happiness

12

THE SCIENCE OF HAPPINESS

While happiness has long been the subject of philosophy, it is only within recent decades that talk of a *science* of happiness began. The science of happiness explores what makes people happy and seeks to understand which pursuits, behaviors, and thought patterns are most conducive to happiness. We've been discussing the science of happiness throughout this book, and we have seen, especially in Part II, its fundamental discoveries. We've learned that developing and nurturing relationships is essential to happiness, while valuing material goods and wealth may hinder our pursuit of happiness; we've learned that human beings have a system of adaptation that mitigates the impact circumstantial changes have on our happiness; we've learned the power of optimism and the importance of feeling connected to others.

In this chapter, we'll explore the science underlying these important findings. We start with discussion of the positive psychology movement, which tracks the advent of scientific investigation into happiness. We'll then focus on the challenges involved in this kind of scientific investigation and specifically on the dynamics involved in measuring happiness. The science of happiness depends on the ability to measure happiness, which is hard. We'll explore some of the challenging involved in measuring happiness, as well as the promises and limitations of the most prominent modes of measuring happiness.

The Positive Psychology Movement

The science of happiness began in earnest with the development of the field of positive psychology. Most trace the emergence of positive psychology to a 1998 address to the American Psychology Association by Martin Seligman, in which

Seligman argued that, as a field, psychology ought to expand its focus to include the study of positive human strengths and flourishing. At the time, the dominant focus of psychology was on understanding abnormal behavior and mental illness. There were humanistic psychologists interested in explaining human potential, notably Abraham Maslow, whose landmark 1943 paper advocated for understanding and discussion of human needs and of self-actualization. The humanistic school had limited reach, however, largely because their methodology invoked what were seen to be philosophical questions about human beings and depended less on the methods standard to natural sciences. Polkinghorne, for example, describes humanistic psychology as committed to developing "a deeper understanding of human beings," which to be successful requires "inquiry systems that differed from the natural science system. It would require systems tailored to reveal the complex meaningfulness of the human realm" (Polkinghorne, 1992, p. 227).[1] The movement toward positive psychology can be seen as capturing the spirit of the humanistic psychologists' interest in human growth and potential and developing the systems required to study it scientifically.

Positive psychology maintains that the positive qualities of human beings can be understood and studied scientifically using the same methods used to understand the pathologies of human beings. As Seligman and Csikszentmihalyi describe the ambitions of positive psychology:

> Our message is to remind our field that psychology is not just the study of pathology, weakness, and damages; it is also the study of strength and virtue. Treatment is not just fixing what is broken; it is nurturing what is best. Psychology is not just a branch of medicine concerned with illness or health; it is much larger. It is about work, education, insight, love, growth, and play. And in this quest for what is best, positive psychology does not rely on wishful thinking, faith, self-deception, fads, or hand waving; it tries to adapt what is best in the scientific method to the unique problems that human behavior presents to those who wish to understand it in all its complexity. (Seligman & Csikszentmihalyi, 2000, p. 7)

We can understand positive psychology as calling for a theoretical shift in the focus of psychology while also affirming a commitment to pursuing questions about the positive dimensions of human beings using the same scientific methods and rigor the field uses to develop its understanding of mental illness and other pathologies.

This theoretical shift in focus, and subsequent development of the field of positive psychology, is not without controversy. Lazarus points out that the very labeling of "positive psychology" misleadingly sets up a dichotomy between the positive and the negative that fails to recognize the indispensability of understanding both positive and negative states and their interplay: "We need the bad, which is part of life, to fully appreciate the good. Anytime you narrow the focus of attention too much to one side or the other, you are in danger of losing needed perspective" (Lazarus, 2003, p. 94).

Others worry that in its study of positive states, positive psychology crosses a line by entering normative territory typically reserved for philosophical as opposed to scientific analysis. We see this tension in Csikszentmihalyi's descriptions of his own struggles to reconcile the "twin imperatives that a science of human beings should include: To understand what *is* and what *could be*" (Seligman & Csikszentmihalyi, 2000, p. 7, emphasis in original). Standardly, psychology is taken to be a descriptive science—of what *is*—while any prescriptive or normative considerations of what *could be* are reserved for philosophical analysis. Positive psychology challenges this dichotomy by taking as its science the study of both what is and what could be.

A final concern, and one that the rest of this chapter will focus on, regards positive psychology's commitment to using scientific methods to study the inner workings of our minds. While the humanistic school seemed to think that efforts to understand the growth and potential of human beings required departing from the methods of natural science, positive psychologists maintain that the study of human strengths and flourishing can be conducted using the same empirical foundations and methodology as other fields in psychology.

This position expresses a higher degree of optimism and confidence in our ability to study and understand mental states than was dominant within psychological discourse of the 20th century. Much empirical research of this century was predicated on the field of behaviorism, which takes behavior to be a product of external stimuli that can be understood by the study of these external inputs rather than by studying any processes internal to the mind. The upshot was that the inner workings of the mind were seen to be less important, and, perhaps, less capable of being understood, than the concrete and observable external inputs to behavior.

We can see this contrast, and the diminished role attributed by behaviorists to the mental states that occupy a primary role within positive psychology, in George Graham's presentation of behaviorism, as follows:

> Behaviorism, the doctrine, is committed in its fullest and most complete sense to the truth of the following three sets of claims.

1. Psychology is the science of behavior. Psychology is not the science of the inner mind—as something other or different from behavior.
2. Behavior can be described and explained without making ultimate reference to mental events or to internal psychological processes. The sources of behavior are external (in the environment), not internal (in the mind, in the head).

3. In the course of theory development in psychology, if, somehow, mental terms or concepts are deployed in describing or explaining behavior, then either (a) these terms or concepts should be eliminated and replaced by behavioral terms or (b) they can and should be translated or paraphrased into behavioral concepts (Graham, 2019).

The field of positive psychology rejects each of these theses: It maintains that we need to understand how the inner mind works in order to understand behavior, and, more importantly, to understand how human beings can flourish. It recognizes that the internal, mental inputs to behavior are important and seeks to understand their contribution without reduction. Moreover, the field of positive psychology maintains that we can study these inner states scientifically—a project many behaviorists were skeptical could ever be successful.

The successful science of happiness depends on our ability to measure inner states, a topic about which cognitive psychology has made significant advances. Yet, while cognitive psychologists have paved the way for the scientific investigation of mental states, the particular mental states pertinent to the science of happiness make their measurement especially difficult. After all, happiness, as the science understands it, is a state of subjective well-being (SWB). The study and measurement of subjective well-being requires not only some capacity to study inner mental states in general but also an assessment of an individual's *subjective experience* of those mental states.

How do we assess whether or not someone is happy? If we are trying to figure out whether a friend is happy, it seems that we would look at a combination of factors. Our first instinct may be to ask them whether or not they are happy, although notice that we might do so with trepidation, knowing that their first response may not be accurate. We thus would probably also think about how they act: We'd look for smiles or signs of stress. We'd also probably look at what is going on in their lives for some indicator: Did they just start a new relationship, lose a job, or are they struggling with a chronic illness?

Within the science of happiness, we find a variety of different strategies for employing these basic modes of assessment to measure happiness formally. Data collected through the measurement of happiness can provide invaluable information about the kinds of things that affect our happiness and, as we will discuss in the remaining chapters, are often used in understanding economic decisions and in making policy decisions. As we will see, however, the measurement of happiness remains an imperfect science.

The first step in measuring happiness is the deceptively simple task of identifying what we are measuring. At this point in the book, we know that this task is deceptively simple because coming to understand "happiness" is a challenging philosophical enterprise made even more challenging when we seek to understand happiness uniformly in a way that is capable of being measured.

While there are some important exceptions, most of the science of happiness has converged on understanding happiness as a form of subjective well-being that combines both life satisfaction and positive affect.[2] We'll continue to stick with that approach here, noting divergences where relevant.

Self-Report Scales

Self-report scales are the most straightforward way to measure a person's happiness, and some think that self-reports are the only way to capture the subjectivity inherent to happiness. Myers and Diener maintain that because the topic is subjective well-being, "the final judge is whoever lives inside a person's skin" (1995, p. 11) and Diener et al. remark that "it is a hallmark of the subjective well-being area that it centers upon the person's own judgments, not upon some criterion which is judged to be important to the researcher" (Diener, Emmons, Larsen, & Griffin, 1985, p. 71). Using self-report surveys to measure a subject's happiness seems to preserve the subjectivity of happiness because it respects and grants the subject first personal authority of his own mental states.

One of the earliest self-report surveys is Cantril's Self-Anchoring Striving Scale (Cantril, 1965), which asks respondents to imagine a ladder in which the bottom rungs represent their worst possible life and the top their best. Respondents then rank where they see themselves now and often also where they predict their lives will be in the future. Cantril's ladder, as it is often called, is meant to track life satisfaction. Gallup World Polls uses Cantril's ladder to study international patterns of happiness and well-being, the results of which are published annually in its World Happiness Report. One particular way in which Gallup uses data from Cantril's ladder is to identify populations that are striving, struggling, or suffering. It takes populations to be striving when respondents rank themselves as high on their ladders both now and in the future (e.g., 7 on a 10-step ladder); struggling when respondents rank their present status moderately or predict that their futures will be moderate or negative; and suffering when ranking of present and future are negative (e.g., under 4 on a 10-step ladder). By identifying populations through these frameworks, researchers can identify those populations whose happiness and well-being are at risk and study features of striving populations to better understand what kind of policy measures support a striving population.

While Cantril's ladder asks individuals only to reflect on "their best possible life," other self-report measures try to ask more specific questions aimed at getting an overall sense of their current satisfaction. One of the most prominent self-report assessments used within psychology is the Satisfaction with Life Scale (SWLS) developed by Diener et al. (1985), included in Figure 12.1.

The SWLS asks subjects to rate the extent to which they agree with five statements, thereby tracking subjects' cognitive judgments about how satisfied

Below are five statements that you may agree or disagree with. Using the 1–7 scale below, indicate your agreement with each item by placing the appropriate number on the line preceding that item. Please be open and honest in your responding.

- 7 - Strongly agree
- 6 - Agree
- 5 - Slightly agree
- 4 - Neither agree nor disagree
- 3 - Slightly disagree
- 2 - Disagree
- 1 - Strongly disagree

_____ In most ways my life is close to my ideal.
_____ The conditions of my life are excellent.
_____ I am satisfied with my life.
_____ So far I have gotten the important things I want in life.
_____ If I could live my life over, I would change almost nothing.

- 31 - 35 Extremely satisfied
- 26 - 30 Satisfied
- 21 - 25 Slightly satisfied
- 20   Neutral
- 15 - 19 Slightly dissatisfied
- 10 - 14 Dissatisfied
- 5 - 9   Extremely dissatisfied

FIGURE 12.1 Satisfaction with Life Scale

Source: Diener, E. D., Emmons, R. A., Larsen, R. J., & Griffin, S. (1985). The satisfaction with life scale. *Journal of Personality Assessment, 49*(1), 71–75.

they are with their lives. The statements are designed to allow subjects to freely interpret what, for them, constitutes their ideal life, or which conditions make it excellent, and so on, to ensure that their rankings reflect *their* satisfaction with life rather than tracking whether or not their lives live up to some external standard of a good or happy life.

While focusing on cognitive judgments captures only one aspect of life satisfaction, and of subjective well-being more generally, other self-report measures look at levels of positive affect, which are often used in conjunction with life satisfaction measures. Most prominent among self-report scales for positive affect is the Positive and Negative Affect Schedule (PANAS) developed by Watson, Clark, and Tellegen (1988). This scale asks subjects to rank how much and how often they experience certain feelings and emotions ranging from feelings of guilt, nervousness, and fear to feelings of enthusiasm, pride, and determination. Although not designed as an explicit measure of subjective well-being, the scale is widely accepted to reliably measure the degree of positive (and negative) affect experienced by subjects.

When measured by empirically validated scales, such as SWLS and PANAS, self-reports of life satisfaction and of positive affect provide helpful indications of a subject's overall sense of happiness. Because these scales are relatively easy to administer across large populations, they have been widely used to ascertain large-scale patterns of subjective well-being and its correlates.

However, self-reports are inherently limited by the artificialities inherent to the task of measurement. While based on the very intuitive idea that the subject is the authority of their subjective well-being, the design of self-report scales presents challenges. To successfully measure subjective well-being, (1) the scale must be shown to be reliable and valid, and (2) the subject must be capable of accurately reporting her subjective well-being. Both of these tasks are more difficult than they might first seem.

Reliability and Validity

The results of any survey can only be as good as the survey itself. To determine whether any empirical measurement is trustworthy, researchers must establish its reliability and validity. While no empirical measurement can be established as perfectly reliable and valid, the more reliable and valid, the less it is prone to err and the more trustworthy its results.

A measurement is reliable if it produces consistent results across subjects and time. Testing for reliability is important to ensure the results of any particular survey administration is not skewed by extraneous factors. Typically reliability is established by looking at the internal consistency of a scale's measures and by looking at a scale's stability over time through testing and retesting. Establishing the internal consistency of subjective well-being scales involves ensuring that similarly grouped items are ranked similarly. For example, we'd expect that someone who is satisfied with her life wouldn't want to change a lot of things in her life. If a measurement ends up attributing to her a strong sense of satisfaction and a strong desire to change things in her life, that's a signal that something has gone wrong. The measurement lacks internal consistency. Test-retest reliability explores the temporal stability of the measurements. It is a sign of an accurate measurement if retesting at a different time delivers the same results. Establishing test-retest reliability is important yet particularly challenging in the context of measuring subjective well-being, which seems to vary over time. Researchers thus must ensure that the retesting conditions are similar enough so that we'd expect similar reports and that respondents haven't experienced major life events in the interim.

A measurement is valid (or salient) if it triggers the responses that it targets; a measurement of subjective well-being is valid if it measures subjective well-being. This means that particular items of self-report surveys must be such that they are interpreted by the subject in the way that they were intended. Part of the difficult process of scale validation is to ensure that the specific items included track subjective well-being such that when, for example, a subject affirms that her life is "close to ideal," we can be confident that this is indicative of her happiness.

One of the things that makes this work so difficult is that there are many other factors beyond what is being asked that influence how it is that subjects interpret what is being asked. It is always a challenge to get someone to focus on what you want them to, and even more so when our efforts to do so occur within the impersonal administration of a survey, where questions must be standardized. As Paul Dolan et al. note:

> Any question focuses attention on something and we must be clear about where we want respondents' attention to be directed, and where it might in fact be directed. We should like to have attention focused on those things that will matter to the respondent when they are experiencing their lives and when they are not thinking about an answer to our surveys. It must also be recognized that the mere act of asking a SWB question might affect experiences. (Dolan, Layard, & Metcalfe, 2011, p. 10)

In asking for self-reports of happiness, we want subjects to focus on their subjective well-being, but deliberate efforts to instruct subjects to do so must proceed carefully and with careful consideration of the range of factors that might influence a subject's interpretation of the items asked within a survey.

Subjective Reporting

Even when a self-report scale succeeds in prompting subjects to reflect on their subjective well-being, subjects still have to *report* their subjective well-being. They still have to decide how strongly they agree with the items on the scale, or to remember how often they've experienced certain emotions, and so on. How can we be sure that their reports genuinely reflect their subjective well-being?

On the one hand, there is compelling reason to question whether or not most people really do enjoy a position of authority over their own mental states. Haybron (2008) presents a compelling case for the prevalence of "affective ignorance," which leads him to conclude that individuals may not have the ability to know whether or not they are happy. This skepticism is backed up by a wealth of research on the prevalence of factors, ranging from the order of the items on the survey to the weather, that can distort a subject's judgments.

For instance, significant research indicates that a subject's present mood can transform her responses. Schwarz and colleagues have found that when subjects are primed with established mood enhancers (finding a dime, receiving a chocolate bar), their reported overall happiness is greatly increased. This suggests that subjective reports of happiness may be a function of much more than that subject's happiness. In this instance, we see that "judgments of well-being are not only a function of what one thinks about, but also of how one feels at the time of judgment" (Schwarz & Strack, 1988, p. 36).

The problems of subjective reporting become magnified when those reports must be quantified in standardized forms. Given that the goal of measuring subjective well-being is to gather data that can be used to make comparisons across populations, or to learn about the correlates of subjective well-being, or to develop policies to enhance subjective well-being, the measurements themselves must be standardized. This adds another, potentially problematic, dimension to subjective reporting.

A dominant way to standardize measurements is through the use of scales. The SWLS, for example, asks subjects to rank their agreement with items on a 1–7 scale, with "1" tracking "strongly disagree" and "7" tracking "strongly agree." And PANAS uses a 1–5 scale to gauge the frequency with which a subject experiences the itemized emotions, where "1" tracks "very slightly, or not at all" and "5" tracks "extremely."

In theory, scaling provides a way of standardizing responses in a manner that allows us to develop meaningful conclusions about the prevalence of happiness among large populations. Yet all scales must be interpreted by the individual subject who is completing them, and there exists significant variation in the ways in which individuals interpret scales. How do *you* weigh the difference between (6) agree and (7) strongly agree? Are you confident that the weights you assign are in alignment with the researchers' analysis of your rankings? If you report 6 and I report 7, what does that information really tell us?

This problem is likely a familiar one; we've all been asked to rank things and are aware of the difficulties in assigning a number to something as subjective as how much pain we are feeling, or how effective we think our professor's teaching is, and so on. The process of ranking invites judgments, comparisons, and biases that, while essential to the process of ranking, nevertheless have the potential to distort those rankings.

The more we can learn about the process of ranking, the better position we are in to analyze the results. And much of the science of happiness involves analysis of the patterns underlying reported subjective well-being. For example, in her study of happiness within Latin America, Carol Graham has found that reports of subjective well-being are significantly influenced by a subject's expectations: Subjects with low expectations tend to report higher levels of subjective well-being than those with high expectations. This gives rise to what she describes as the paradox between the happy peasant and the frustrated achiever: The former reports higher levels of subjective well-being than the latter, for the peasant has lower expectations.

> In this instance, there are many cases where very poor and uninformed respondents, who either have a high set point (cheery nature) or low expectations, report they are very happy, even though they live in destitute poverty. (C. L. Graham & Behrman, 2010, p. 17)[3]

Learning about the common factors that influence how an individual reports her level of happiness can help us better understand those rankings, and in particular can be helpful to interpret widespread trends found within certain populations. It is well known that the norms found within a country influence the nature of self-reported happiness: Diener, Suh, Smith, and Shao (1995), for example, find that individuals within collectivist countries consistently report lower subjective well-being than those within individualist cultures, and they suggest that this difference is explainable by cultural norms governing the experience and expression of emotions.

Despite the limitations of self-reports and the questions these limitations give rise to for the analysis of subjective well-being data, the science of happiness has developed remarkably through the use of self-report measures. The factors that influence self-reports of happiness have not been shown to invalidate the measures themselves and, when considered on the aggregate level, the individual variations often fail to track significant differences (Dolan et al., 2011). Moreover, further research shows convergence between self-reports and other measures of happiness. Measuring happiness via self-reports may not be a perfect science but nonetheless seems to be tracking something meaningful.

Measuring Affect

Self-report surveys offer a measurement of subjective well-being that is indirect insofar as they depend on the subject's report of his happiness. Given the limitations of subjective reporting, many have sought to develop measures of happiness that bypass self-reports and measure SWB more directly. While it is challenging to measure something like "life satisfaction" directly, much progress has been made to measure affect directly. These measures have been used both as a means to understand the occurrence of subjective well-being and to validate and supplement self-reports of happiness.

The most direct way to measure affect is to look at its physiological occurrence. By investigating the brain patterns associated with the experience of positive affect, neuroscientists have by and large reached consensus on the physiological markers of positive affect. This allows researchers to directly measure positive affect through the use of brain-imaging methods such as EEG or MRI studies. These methods provide researchers with a means to measure the occurrence of positive affect and a basis from which to understand the neurological processes underwriting the development of positive affect. One pivotal finding in this regard is the notion of neuroplasticity, or the brain's ability to strengthen neural networks through the exercise of those networks. The neuroscientist Richard Davidson, whose work on compassion we explored in Chapter 9, has used these methods to identify the neural circuits salient to happiness and to explore how these circuits can be strengthened by developing skills such as meditation and resiliency.

While the neuroscience of happiness has taught and will continue to teach us valuable insights into the nature of subjective well-being, the mechanics involved in the neuroscientific study of subjective well-being limit its applicability. Brain-imaging methods are expensive and must be conducted within an experimental setting. This limits their use and scope. An alternative means to study the occurrence of positive affect is through the use of "experience sampling methods" (ESM). These methods seek to study, as best as possible, the affective experience of subjects in the moments in which they occur. While still requiring the subject to report on their affective experiences, experience sampling methods are seen to be more objective than self-report surveys of positive affect (such as PANAS) insofar as they test how a subject feels in that moment and so are less dependent on memory and less susceptible to the problems involved in reporting one's overall subjective well-being.

Csikszentmihalyi is among the first to highlight the important role experience sampling can play in the science of happiness. He describes this role as follows:

> Conceptually, the ESM "exposes" regularities in the stream of consciousness, such as states of heightened happiness or self-awareness, extreme concentration experienced at work, and symptoms of illness. The research aim is to relate these regularities to the characteristics of the person (e.g., age, aptitude, physiological arousal, medical diagnosis), of the situation (e.g., the challenges of a job, the content of a TV show), or of the interaction between person and situation (e.g., the dynamics of a conversation with a friend, the circumstances that lead to a specific event). The objective is to identify and analyze how patterns in people's subjective experience relate to the wider conditions of their lives. The purpose of using this method is to be as "objective" about subjective phenomena as possible without compromising the essential personal meaning of the experience. (Csikszentmihalyi & Larson, 2014, p. 36)

Particular methods of experience sampling range from having subjects complete daily diaries, to having subjects report on their positive affect at random times throughout the day via smart phones, to having subjects wear sensors that relay information automatically and can be used to prompt specific sampling. Whichever means through which this data is collected, the distinctive aspect of experience sampling is that it seeks to measure the subject's experience in the moment so that researchers can draw conclusions both about her overall experiences of positive affect and the contextual features that influence those experiences.

While data collected through ESM are less dependent on subjective reporting than are self-report measures, they also become somewhat more dependent on the researcher's analysis. As Frey and Stutzer note, "Physiological and moment-based measures rely on strongly normative judgments in the sense that happiness is assessed according to fixed rules, although our attitude toward particular pleasures and pains is not a priori given. Individual well-being is not an isolated feeling" (Frey & Stutzer, 2010, p. 6). The threat is that the more objective the measure, the less it measures the subject's happiness and the more it measures the researcher's interpretation of the subject's happiness.

Objective Indicators of Happiness

The most objective way to measure happiness bypasses completely the subject's construal of their experiences and instead measures their subjective well-being indirectly by looking at established correlates of subjective well-being, such as health, employment, and social connectedness. Taking these objective circumstances to be indicators of subjective well-being researchers measure a population's happiness through analysis of their objective circumstances.

This approach works in conjunction with other methods that have first established the significance of the factor to subjective well-being. Thus, for example, reports of life satisfaction consistently show a high degree of correlation between employment and life satisfaction. This information supports taking employment rates as an indicator of subjective well-being such that we can measure a population'ssubjective well-being by looking at their employment rates.

Objective indicators provide an indirect mode of measurement and so may be limited by nature. It will always be problematic to highlight an external circumstance as indicative of an individual's subjective well-being for, fundamentally, an individual's happiness depends on how they interpret and respond to that circumstance. As we have seen in earlier chapters, however, the science of happiness has discovered many robust correlations, and taking these correlations to be indicators of subjective well-being allows for large-scale measurement and the development of data sets that can be of much use to policy making and analysis as well as to enhance our understanding of people's choices and behavior.

Conclusion

While still in its nascent stages, the science of happiness already has made a tremendous impact. The field of positive psychology exhibits how scientific methods can be used to study the inner workings of the human mind and the conditions that seem to be most conducive to the development of happiness and has amassed an unprecedented body of information regarding subjective well-being.

The most prominent measures of happiness are self-report surveys such as Cantril's Ladder or the Satisfaction with Life Scale. These measures can be used to gather information across populations and inform public policies, but they may be problematic insofar as they depend on the subject's ability to gauge and report her levels of happiness without bias and with accuracy. More objective measures, such as neuroscientific measurement of the brain states associated with positive affect and experience sampling methods, may avoid these problems but are still subject to errors involved in the analysis of data and are limited in their use to smaller sample sizes.

As we have seen, the ability to measure happiness is pivotal to the science of happiness. It is also very difficult. Each approach to measurement faces limitations that make it important to explore carefully the conclusions drawn and the impact the limitations of measurement may have on those conclusions. Given the limitations inherent to each method, it makes sense for those measuring happiness to use a combination of methods where possible and doing so can be particularly helpful to fill in the gaps left out by one method. The SWLS could be used in conjunction with daily diaries to develop a better sense of the temporal stability indicated by the SWLS as well as a richer picture of what subjects are reflecting on or reporting on when they say they are "very" satisfied; experience sampling can be used in conjunction with PANAS to provide a more complete picture of a subject's experience of positive affect and so on. Combining measures that themselves have been shown to have high degrees of reliability and validity should only increase the overall reliability and validity of the data.

Chapter Summary

- The field of positive psychology is defined both by a theoretical focus on human strengths and potential and by a commitment to the scientific study of these psychological states.
- Measuring happiness is essential to the science of happiness. The science of happiness generally takes happiness to consist in a combination of life satisfaction and positive affect, and the task of measuring happiness generally involves looking at both the subject's judgments of life satisfaction and the frequency and degree to which they experience positive affect.
- Self-report surveys, such as the Satisfaction with Life Scale, measure happiness in terms of subjective reports. To provide valid information, particular items within self-report surveys must stimulate the subject to think about and report on their subjective well-being.
- Subjective reports of happiness are liable to be influenced by a wide range of factors (societal norms, design of the survey, memory bias, mood, and so on) that should be controlled for as much as possible.

- Neuroimaging tools such as EEG and MRI can provide physiological data regarding the incidence of positive affect. By learning which circuits of the brain are most associated with positive affect, we can seek to strengthen those circuits.
- Experience sampling provides a mechanism to track a subject's experiences of positive affect and satisfaction in the moment. This reduces memory bias and places less weight on subjective reporting than do self-reports, making experience sampling a more "objective" measure of happiness.
- The most objective measure of happiness measures the occurrence of subjective well-being by analysis of the external circumstances known to be correlated with SWB. Identifying objective indicators of subjective well-being allows for large-scale analysis and measurement.

End Notes

1 Somewhat more dismissively, Seligman and Csikszentmihalyi write that "humanistic psychology did not attract much of a cumulative empirical base, and it spawned myriad therapeutic self-help movements. In some of its incarnations, it emphasized the self and encouraged a self-centeredness that played down concerns for collective well-being: ... collective well-being" (Seligman & Csikszentmihalyi, 2000, p. 7).
2 Economist Paul Dolan is one of the few who explicitly advocate reflecting on philosophical theories of well-being in his influential approach to measurement, arguing, for example, that in selecting a theory of well-being to measure, that theory must be "grounded in an accepted philosophical theory" (Dolan, Layard, & Metcalfe, 2011, p. 4). Following Parfit's classic analysis, Dolan focuses on objective list theory, preference satisfaction, and mental state theories, on the ground that these three approaches represent theories of well-being that are well grounded, relevant to policy, and are capable of being measured.
3 Notice that it isn't quite clear how to best interpret this information (do we say that the peasant isn't really happy?), nor is it clear what policy makers ought to do with this information. As Graham reflects with respect to the happy peasant paradox: "The implications of this information for policy are very unclear. Should policy raise the peasant's awareness of how bad her situation is in order to raise expectations, risking making her miserable? Should policy leave the peasant ignorant?" (Graham & Behrman, 2010, p. 17). We'll explore policy-related issues in Chapter 14.

References

Cantril, H. (1965). *The pattern of human concerns.* New Brunswick, NJ: Rutgers University Press.

Csikszentmihalyi, M., & Larson, R. (2014). Validity and reliability of the experience-sampling method. In M. Csiksentmihalyi (Ed.), *Flow and the foundations of positive psychology* (pp. 35–54). Dordrecht: Springer.

Diener, E., Emmons, R. A., Larsen, R. J., & Griffin, S. (1985). The satisfaction with life scale. *Journal of Personality Assessment, 49*(1), 71–75.

Diener, E., Suh, E. M., Smith, H., & Shao, L. (1995). National differences in reported subjective well-being: Why do they occur? *Social Indicators Research, 34*(1), 7–32.

Dolan, P., Layard, R., & Metcalfe, R. (2011). *Measuring subjective well-being for public policy.* Newport, South Wales: Office for National Statistics.

Frey, B. S., & Stutzer, A. (2010). *Happiness and economics: How the economy and institutions affect human well-being.* Princeton, NJ: Princeton University Press.

Graham, C. L., & Behrman, J. R. (2010). How Latin Americans assess their quality of life. In C. Graham & E. Lora (Eds.), *Paradox and perception: Measuring quality of life in Latin America.* Washington, DC: Brookings Institution Press.

Graham, G. (2019). Behaviorism. In E. N. Zalta (Ed.), *The Stanford encyclopedia of philosophy* (Spring 2019). Retrieved from https://plato.stanford.edu/archives/spr2019/entries/behaviorism/

Haybron, D. M. (2008). *The pursuit of unhappiness.* New York: Oxford University Press.

Lazarus, R. S. (2003). Does the positive psychology movement have legs? *Psychological Inquiry, 14*(2), 93–109.

Myers, D. G., & Diener, E. (1995). Who is happy? *Psychological Science, 6*(1), 10–19.

Polkinghorne, D. E. (1992). Research methodology in humanistic psychology. *The Humanistic Psychologist, 20*(2–3), 218–242. https://doi.org/10.1080/08873267.1992.9986792

Schwarz, N., & Strack, F. (1988). *Evaluating one's life: A judgment model of subjective well-being.* Mannheim: Zentrum für Umfragen, Methoden und Analysen -ZUMA-.

Seligman, M. E., & Csikszentmihalyi, M. (2000). Positive psychology: An introduction. *American Psychologist, 55*(1), 5–14.

Watson, D., Clark, L. A., & Tellegen, A. (1988). Development and validation of brief measures of positive and negative affect: The PANAS scales. *Journal of Personality and Social Psychology, 54*(6), 1063.

Suggested for Further Reading

For positive psychology: Overview and criticisms:

Diener, E., Lucas, R. E., & Oishi, S. (2002). Subjective well-being: The science of happiness and life satisfaction. *Handbook of Positive Psychology, 2,* 63–73.

Gable, S. L., & Haidt, J. (2005). What (and why) is positive psychology? *Review of General Psychology, 9*(2), 103–110.

Held, B. S. (2004). The negative side of positive psychology. *Journal of Humanistic Psychology, 44*(1), 9–46.

Kristjánsson, K. (2010). Positive psychology, happiness, and virtue: The troublesome conceptual issues. *Review of General Psychology, 14*(4), 296–310.

Lazarus, R. S. (2003). Does the positive psychology movement have legs? *Psychological Inquiry, 14*(2), 93–109.

Seligman, M. E., & Csikszentmihalyi, M. (2000). Positive psychology: An introduction. *American Psychologist, 55*(1), 5–14.

For the measurement of happiness:

Alexandrova, A., & Haybron, D. M. (2016). Is construct validation valid? *Philosophy of Science, 83*(5), 1098–1109.

Helliwell, J. F., & Barrington-Leigh, C. P. (2010). Measuring and understanding subjective well-being. *Canadian Journal of Economics/Revue Canadienne d'économique, 43*(3), 729–753.

Kahneman, D., & Krueger, A. B. (2006). Developments in the measurement of subjective well-being. *Journal of Economic Perspectives, 20*(1), 3–24.

Krueger, A. B., & Stone, A. A. (2014). Progress in measuring subjective well-being. *Science*, *346*(6205), 42–43.

Layard, R. (2010). Measuring subjective well-being. *Science*, *327*(5965), 534–535.

Veenhoven R. (2017) Measures of Happiness: Which to Choose?. In: Brulé G., Maggino F. (eds) *Metrics of Subjective Well-Being: Limits and Improvements. Happiness Studies Book Series.* Cham: Springer.

For self-report surveys:

Diener, E. (1994). Assessing subjective well-being: Progress and opportunities. *Social Indicators Research*, *31*(2), 103–157.

Diener, E., Emmons, R. A., Larsen, R. J., & Griffin, S. (1985). The satisfaction with life scale. *Journal of Personality Assessment*, *49*(1), 71–75.

Diener, E., Sandvik, E., Pavot, W., & Gallagher, D. (1991). Response artifacts in the measurement of subjective well-being. *Social Indicators Research*, *24*(1), 35–56.

Schwarz, N. (1999). Self-reports: How the questions shape the answers. *American Psychologist*, *54*(2), 93.

Schwarz, N., & Strack, F. (1999). Reports of subjective well-being: Judgmental processes and their methodological implications. *Well-Being: The Foundations of Hedonic Psychology*, 7, 61–84.

Watson, D., Clark, L. A., & Tellegen, A. (1988). Development and validation of brief measures of positive and negative affect: The PANAS scales. *Journal of Personality and Social Psychology*, *54*(6), 1063.

For experience sampling methods:

Csikszentmihalyi, M., & Hunter, J. (2003). Happiness in everyday life: The uses of experience sampling. *Journal of Happiness Studies*, *4*(2), 185–199.

Csikszentmihalyi, M., & Larson, R. (2014). Validity and reliability of the experience-sampling method. In M. Csikszentmihalyi (Ed.), *Flow and the foundations of positive psychology* (pp. 35–54). Dordrecht: Springer.

Dolan, P., Kudrna, L., & Stone, A. (2017). The measure matters: An investigation of evaluative and experience-based measures of wellbeing in time use data. *Social Indicators Research*, *134*(1), 57–73.

Krueger, A. B., & Schkade, D. A. (2008). The reliability of subjective well-being measures. *Journal of Public Economics*, *92*(8–9), 1833–1845.

For the neuroscience of happiness:

Berridge, K. C., & Kringelbach, M. L. (2011). Building a neuroscience of pleasure and well-being. *Psychology of Well-Being: Theory, Research and Practice*, *1*(1), 1–26.

Davidson, R. J., & Begley, S. (2013). *The emotional life of your brain: How its unique patterns affect the way you think, feel, and live—and how you can change them.* New York: Plume.

Kringelbach, M. L., & Berridge, K. C. (2010). The neuroscience of happiness and pleasure. *Social Research*, *77*(2), 659–678.

Urry, H. L., Nitschke, J. B., Dolski, I., Jackson, D. C., Dalton, K. M., Mueller, C. J., … , Davidson, R. J. (2004). Making a life worth living neural correlates of well-being. *Psychological Science*, *15*(6), 367–372.

Yetton, B. D., Revord, J., Margolis, S., Lyubomirsky, S., & Seitz, A. R. (2019). Cognitive and physiological measures in well-being science: Limitations and lessons. *Frontiers in Psychology*, *10*.

13

ECONOMICS AND HAPPINESS

As a field, economics explores the ways in which individuals and societies produce, consume, and distribute goods and services. Fundamentally, the focus of economics is on the choices people make under conditions of scarcity. No one can have it all, and in a world where we cannot have it all, we need to make choices. But what drives those choices? And why are people's choices taken to be so fundamental?

A standard way of framing economics is to see it as the study of rational choice and of the consequences these choices have for the economy as a whole. Standard economics embraces a preference satisfaction model of human behavior, which maintains that rational actors make choices based on their preferences and that we can learn about their preferences by looking at their choices, for rational actors consistently choose to satisfy their preferences. Importantly, as Angner (2016) highlights, this model puts forth a view of decision making that purports to be both descriptively adequate as a theory of how people *do* make decisions and normatively adequate as a theory of how people *ought* to make decisions. Thus, it maintains that people's choices do in fact reflect their preferences and that their choices should be viewed as indicative of their preferences.

While what people prefer and choose certainly has implications for happiness, traditionally economists have not explored these implications and have kept their focus instead on choices and preference satisfaction. The language of "welfare" invoked within standard economics tracks preference satisfaction alone. Rational economic behavior advances people's welfare insofar as it allows them to best satisfy their preferences. Standard economics remains neutral on the question of whether or not rational economic behavior advances subjective well-being.

At this point, readers of this book may find this position surprising. Why would we care about satisfying preferences if preference satisfaction doesn't make one happy? Shouldn't economists focus on what choices make people happy? Increasingly, people inside and outside the field are calling it out for this neglect. Oftentimes, this criticism takes the form of encouraging economists to be more forthright about what is driving them. The economist Andrew Oswald, for example, calls out the field as being fundamentally about happiness while failing to acknowledge this influence:

> Economic performance is not intrinsically interesting. No-one is concerned in a genuine sense about the level of gross national product last year or about next year's exchange rate. People have no innate interest in the money supply, inflation, growth, inequality, unemployment, and the rest. The stolid greyness of the business pages of our newspapers seems to mirror the fact that economic numbers matter only indirectly … Economic things matter only in so far as they make people happier. (Oswald, 1997, p. 1815)

The plausibility of this line of thought, and in general of the notion that economic considerations are important primarily insofar as they make people happier, suggests that economists ought to take seriously questions regarding the impact people's economic choices have on their happiness. In this vein, Bruni and Porta encourage the "return of happiness to economics," emphasizing that the moral justification for the economist is to be found in "the persuasion that increases in wealth, income, or goods generally create the preconditions for greater well-being and happiness" (2005, p. 1).

There is a tension between those economists working within the standard "neoclassical" approach who maintain that economics ought to focus on preference satisfaction and welfare and those who think that considerations of happiness ought to more directly inform economic analysis. Arguments by the latter have stimulated an interest in the economics of happiness, which focuses more directly on the connections between economic choices and happiness. This chapter begins with analysis of neoclassical economics and the commitments central to it. We'll then explore the limitations research within this field has for the study of happiness and conclude with a reflection on how developments within behavioral economics can contribute to the economics of happiness.

Neoclassical Economics

"Neoclassical economics" refers to the standard approach to economics discussed in the introduction, which highlights the role of rationality and preference satisfaction in its analysis of the choices we make as consumers and the efficacy of the market in satisfying our preferences. It frames human beings as rational actors who choose on the basis of preferences. According to this model, when faced with a choice between two options, a rational actor will choose the one she prefers more strongly.

This is a compelling and intuitive picture of how we make choices. If I prefer apples to oranges, then I'll choose the apples; if I have to pay more for the apples than the oranges and I nonetheless choose the apples, this implies that my preference for the apples was proportionately stronger. That I'm willing to pay more for the apples indicates that my preference was that much stronger. The rational choice model at work here maintains that a rational person has a rational ordering of her preferences, both present and future. It allows that some people can be indifferent between two preferences—I can prefer apples and oranges equally and so be indifferent with respect to which is better. In this case, the model stipulates that I wouldn't pay more for the apple, because I can satisfy my preferences at less cost by buying the orange.

One of the benefits of the rational choice model is its ability to understand human behavior simply by looking at what people choose. Because choices are indicative of preferences, we can learn about people's preferences through reflection on their choices. If I see someone pay more for a mango than more cheaply available fruits, I can conclude that he prefers the mango. His behavior alone, seen through his choice, gives me insight into his preferences.

Often informing the rational choice model is the psychological field of behaviorism we first explored in Chapter 12. Behaviorism focuses on observables, maintaining that something must be observable to be the proper object of scientific research. In the context of economics, we can observe the options people are presented with and the choices they make in the face of these options; we can observe how much they are willing to pay for things and the effort they will expend to procure these things. Neoclassical economics takes these observed behaviors to indicate preferences based on the assumptions that (a) most people are rational actors, and (b) rational actors will choose to satisfy their preferences.

This approach leads neoclassical economists to focus heavily on the context of people's decisions—namely, the external stimuli people are confronted with (How much is the mango? How much are the oranges?) and the actual choices people make in response to them (do they buy the mango?). The "typical economist's view," as Easterlin describes it, maintains that these features are the salient ones to consider as opposed to the murky thoughts that might factor into a subject's decisions:

> Economists, as a rule, are not concerned with the internal thought processes of the decision maker or in the rationalizations that the decision maker offers to explain his or her behavior. Economists believe that what people do is more relevant than what they say. (Easterlin, 2004, p. 21)

While reflection on what people *do* delivers important information, some worry that by their focus, economists fail to appreciate the other factors that influence people's decisions, such as their feelings and emotions.

Perhaps these things do count, and the most important information isn't *all* about what we end up choosing. Richard Layard worries about all that gets left out when we focus too much on a person's behavior. If you give a person two choices, and he chooses one, we can infer that he preferred that one to the other. But we can't determine at all "how intense these preferences are, or how happy he is with what he obtains" (Layard, 2005, pp. 133–134). That is, we can't determine the impact that choice has on the subject, for its impact depends on what is going on in the subject's mind and the feelings, emotions, and attitudes that inform his behavior.

Moved by this line of thought, and bolstered by the progress psychologists have made in developing scientific methods for measuring internal states of mind, economists are paying more attention to the ways in which one's feelings and emotions contribute to one's choices and the impact those choices have on the subject, such as whether satisfying one's preferences makes one happy. A new "economics of happiness" is emerging.

Empirical Trends

What happens when we put considerations of happiness into the mix of economic analysis and take seriously the importance of the "unobservables" like our thoughts and feelings? We learn that how much money we have bears little relation to how happy we are. We learn that rarely do our choices simply reflect preferences. We learn that having a preference for something doesn't mean that obtaining that thing will make us happy. These are among the findings central to the economics of happiness, the discovery of which has shaken up the field of economics itself and led many to reject the neoclassical approach in favor of behavioral economics, which we discuss in the following section.

More Income but Less Happiness?

Richard Easterlin's landmark paper "Does Economic Growth Improve the Human Lot?" (Easterlin, 1974) is among the first to explore empirically the connection between happiness and income. His findings challenge decades of assumptions about the relationship between wealth and income, assumptions that are hard to shake even despite evidence to the contrary. We expect that increased wealth increases levels of happiness, at the very least because increased wealth affords greater preference satisfaction; however, Easterlin finds that this expected correlation between wealth and happiness doesn't seem to pan out. There is a general association between income and happiness that we see within a country: The richer tend to be happier than the poorer. But, on the national level, increases in income do not correlate with increases in happiness. Easterlin's findings are often presented as a paradox: If there is a general, positive association between income and happiness, why don't the two increase proportionately?

Reflection on Easterlin's paradox has stimulated much fruitful discussion. Many of the phenomena we discussed in the context of considering wealth and happiness (Chapter 6) have been identified in an effort to make sense of the Easterlin paradox, such as the idea that there is a satiation point after which increases in wealth do not translate to increases in happiness, or the idea that the human capacity for adaptation mitigates the effect of income on happiness.

Easterlin's research is based on analysis of reported happiness within the United States over a period of 24 years, from 1946 to 1970. During this period, the GDP per capita rose significantly, yet on average individuals' reported happiness did not. And it isn't just already relatively wealthy Americans who find that they don't get happier when they make more money; in subsequent research, Easterlin finds this effect across the globe and finds it is consistent across developed and developing countries and independent of the economic growth rates of those countries.[1]

But is the evidence enough to reject the idea that economic growth might help people become happy? Isn't it a hard pill to swallow that economic development really won't pay off in happier citizens? Can empirical research even really show this?

Stevenson and Wolfers (2008) argue that Easterlin's conclusions are not warranted and that he moves too quickly from not finding evidence of a correlation to stipulating that there is no correlation. They maintain that examining data from a wide range of surveys and methods for measuring subjective well-being provides a more nuanced understanding of the relationship between income and happiness. Specifically, Stevenson and Wolfers find the data support the existence of a positive link between GDP and subjective well-being and call into question the notion of a satiation point. Stevenson and Wolfers thus maintain we shouldn't give up on the promise of economic growth to improve the human lot.

While the relationship between income and happiness may not be as straightforward as we first assumed, there is still an important relationship—the details of which are worth figuring out.

Do Choices Reflect Preferences Alone?

Analysis of the Eastern paradox reveals an importance difference between the impact of absolute versus relative income. Relative income describes a person's income as it stands in relation to the income of other members of that person's society and/or country. Relative income can be contrasted with absolute income, which describes a person's income overall, independently of other factors.

Easterlin finds that within a country, the richer tend to be happier than the poorer but that these differences fall apart when considering the relationship between income and happiness between nations. Analyzing these findings and similar data, Richard Layard (2005) argues that the best explanation of this dynamic is the differential effect of relative income on happiness in comparison with absolute income. The actual amount people make seems to matter less to their subjective well-being than how that amount stands in relation to others. Whether or not someone makes $100,000 matters less to their happiness than whether they are making *more* than their neighbors.

The differential effects of absolute and relative income on subjective well-being suggest that it is important to examine a subject's reference group in order to understand how her income affects her happiness. Doing so, Layard proposes, can help us better understand some otherwise counterintuitive results, such as why a group's happiness decreases even while their incomes rise. For example, following the collapse of the Berlin Wall, standards of living rapidly improved in East Germany. But their levels of happiness fell. Why? Layard suggests that this is because East Germans changed their reference groups (Layard, 2005, p. 45). Prior to reunification, they compared themselves with countries in the former Soviet Bloc, but after reunification, they compared themselves with West Germans. The change in reference groups made significant changes to their relative incomes. Relative to Soviet countries, East Germans enjoyed a high income; relative to West Germans, they had a low income.

The change of reference groups seems to be a better explanation of the reported happiness levels than the subject's standard of living—that is, than the numbers alone. While the numbers alone might be taken to indicate that there is no positive correlation between income and happiness, by taking into account the impact of relative income, we are able to develop a better understanding of how income affects happiness. Layard's findings regarding the importance of relative income suggest that income, on its own, does not directly correlate with subjective well-being. Other factors count, such as the role of social comparisons and the significance of a subject's reference groups.[2] When we can't get as much as our neighbors can, this makes us feel bad—even if what we can get is more than enough to satisfy our preferences.

The impact relative income has on reported happiness reveals that the economics of happiness might benefit by moving beyond the neoclassicist's focus on rational choice and preference satisfaction and thinking about happiness directly. That people's levels of happiness are affected more by social comparisons than by their ability to satisfy preferences suggests a divergence between happiness and preference satisfaction. Moreover, that people are so influenced by social comparisons suggests that the ways in which they make decisions are more complicated than the rational choice model suggests. Whether rational or not, we do often make decisions based on factors such as how we are doing with respect to others.

Just How Strong Is the Connection between Preference Satisfaction and Happiness?

Preference satisfaction, as we've seen, informs the conception of welfare embraced by neoclassical economists. While they don't take welfare or preference satisfaction to be proxies for happiness, their focus on preference satisfaction nonetheless attributes weight to preference satisfaction. And most of us do as well. Satisfying our preferences matters! And to the extent that many people value money, it is most often because of the opportunities it affords us to satisfy our preferences.

As intuitive a picture as this is, research on the nature of preference satisfaction calls into question the weight we attribute to it. According to Daniel Gilbert (e.g., Gilbert, Pinel, Wilson, Blumberg, & Wheatley, 1998), the weight most of us attribute to preference satisfaction is fundamentally misguided. It is misguided because we are really bad at predicting what will make us happy.

Part of forming and satisfying preferences is to think through how something will make one feel. If I form a preference for mangos, it is because I expect that I will like eating future mangos. There's a prediction involved in all preference formation: You predict that you will prefer X. Perhaps this is because you've enjoyed X repeatedly before or perhaps because you've enjoyed something similar to it. Some preferences are more informed than others, but even the most well-established preferences still involve a prediction about how the satisfaction of that preference will make one feel. Much data suggest that when it comes to predicting whether or not something will make us happy, we are most often wrong. If so, then forming and satisfying preferences probably won't make us happy. Even the most long-standing and central preferences may not be ones whose satisfaction will make you happy.

In a series of studies, Wilson and Gilbert identify several phenomena that can hamper a person's ability to predict what will make them happy. People do tend to be good at predicting their overall emotional reactions ("people know that a root beer will be more pleasant than a root canal" (Wilson & Gilbert, 2005, p. 131), but Wilson and Gilbert find that when it comes to making the more difficult choices, in which gauging the intensity and duration of one's affective states becomes important, one's predictions are often flawed.

What seems to happen is that people tend to overestimate the impact certain outcomes will have on their affective states. The "impact bias" has been observed in many different contexts and often tracks the decisions we attach the most importance to, such as whether or not to end a relationship, or to switch roommates, or to buy a new car. One study gaining notoriety in academic circles shows that professors err significantly in their predictions of what will happen to them were they to be denied tenure. They tend to think a tenure denial will sentence them to years of unhappiness, but this doesn't pan out.

One explanation of the impact bias is that we take decisions to have much more influence on all areas of our lives than in fact they do. The reality is that our lives are multidimensional, with a number of different aspects influencing our happiness on any given day. Focusing on any one thing, be it a job or a roommate, leads us to underestimate the impact of the other things going on in our lives.

Additionally influencing people's ability to predict how they will feel is a failure to appreciate the lengths their minds will go to keep them feeling happy, a point we've addressed already at several junctures in this book.[3] We've seen that our minds have a remarkable capacity to adapt to changes in our circumstances, thereby mitigating the influence such changes have on our subjective well-being. We've also seen Gilbert (2006)'s research supporting the existence of a psychological immune system that resists the impact of negative changes and encourages resilience in the face of them.

Wilson and Gilbert note that difficulties with prediction arise partly because we overlook the processes our minds engage in to interpret events. When we make a choice, we think about how we will emotionally react to that event; but the emotional reactions salient to our subjective well-being are the reactions to those events as they are interpreted by our minds. We may have immediate emotional reactions that may align with our predictions, but we often "do not consider how quickly their tendency to explain events will reduce the impact of those events" (Wilson & Gilbert, 2005, p. 132). Thus, for example, "when a student tries to predict how she will feel if she receives an unexpected A, she has little trouble imagining herself feeling overjoyed but a lot of trouble imagining herself explaining the event in a way that makes it seem ordinary and predictable" (Wilson & Gilbert, 2005, p. 132).

It is difficult to predict just how something will affect your subjective well-being. Even if you've chosen based on stable preferences, this doesn't guarantee that the satisfaction of those preferences will make you happy. There is a gap between one's expectations of happiness and the actual happiness that one experiences, for there is a multitude of other factors operating, beyond preference, that determine the impact something has on your subjective well-being.

The three central empirical trends we've covered here—that income and subjective well-being are not directly correlated, that relative income counts, that we are not good at predicting what will make us happy—suggest that an economics of happiness needs to move beyond its standard formulation, which limits its focus to understanding rational choice and preference satisfaction.

New Directions for the Economics of Happiness

The findings discussed above suggest that an economics of happiness ought to recognize the number of inputs that influence our choices and explore their connections to happiness. This calls for a departure both from the rational choice model and the focus on preference satisfaction that defines neoclassical economics. This doesn't necessarily mean that the economics of happiness ought to give up these important considerations but that those economists interested in studying happiness might benefit by viewing them through more nuanced lenses informed by the science of happiness.

Many prominent economists advocate for some kind of departure from neo-classical economics on these grounds. Amartya Sen, for example, suggests that even if we limit ourselves to "rational decisions," it is important to broaden our understanding of rationality by recognizing there are a variety of aims that we could rationally pursue: "The demands of rationality need not be geared entirely to the use of only one of those motivations (such as self-love), and there is plenty of empirical evidence to indicate that the presumption of uncompromising pursuit of narrowly defined self-interest is [...] mistaken" (Sen, 1995, p. 15). Daniel Benjamin and colleagues (Benjamin, Heffetz, Kimball, & Rees-Jones, 2012) argue that economists ought to recognize that subjects have a preference for happiness itself in addition to the standard kinds of preferences and to analyze how it is that this preference informs their choices.

Bruno Frey (2008) identifies three commitments essential to the economics of happiness. The first commitment is to take seriously the task of measuring happiness so economists can focus on actual rather than expected utility. The second commitment is to recognize the variety of nonmaterial values that factor into an individual's happiness, factors we've explored at length in Part II. As Frey notes, happiness research shows that "individuals derive utility not only from income (as it is implied in much of received theory) but also from highly valued social relations and from self-determination, as well as using their own competence. Moreover, individuals derive utility from *processes*, not just from outcomes" (Frey, 2008, p. x, emphasis in original). The third commitment consists in taking seriously insights from happiness research and developing policies that are responsive to them. This involves, for example, thinking about how to address the impact of relative income as opposed to absolute income and how to prioritize the nonmaterial values that contribute to our happiness.

Arguing in a similar vein, Layard writes that we "need a new economics that collaborates with the new psychology" (Layard, 2005, p. 135). Layard's own view is that this new economics ought to include the following lessons from psychology: The impact of inequality; the role of external effects, such as the influence of other people on areas beyond our market exchanges; the ways in which our norms and values evolve through the influence of external, societal factors; that people "hate loss more than we value gain"; and—perhaps most important—that we behave in inconsistent ways (Layard, 2005, p. 135).

These kinds of considerations motivate the turn away from neoclassical economics and toward the relatively new field of behavioral economics. While neoclassical economics takes a particular mode of decision making (the rational choice model) to describe both how people do and ought to make decisions, behavioral economics starts with an empirical analysis of how people do make decisions, focusing often on how and when they make errors, in an effort to think about how they can make *better* decisions. The driving idea behind this approach is that by working with a psychologically informed understanding of human behavior, economists can make better predictions, develop better policies, and develop a better theory.

Here's one example of how this approach promises to influence economic thought. There's been a lot of research showing that people tend to become attached to their possessions in a way that challenges the neoclassical economists' assumptions about how to gauge and predict costs and the role of opportunity cost. This is the endowment effect, first identified by Thaler (1980) and illustrated by Kahneman et al. in the following example:

> A wine-loving economist we know purchased some nice Bordeaux wines years ago at low prices. The wines have greatly appreciated in value, so that a bottle that cost only $10 when purchased would now fetch $200 at auction. This economist now drinks some of this wine occasionally, but would neither be willing to sell the wine at the auction price nor buy an additional bottle at that price. (Kahneman et al., 1991, p. 194)

This effect seems to happen regularly (and subsequent research finds that it does) and is difficult to explain using standard notions of the relationships between preferences and costs. What seems to be happening in the endowment effect is that people have a brute attraction to things in their possession that fundamentally skews how it is that they analyze the opportunity cost of giving it up.

Recognizing the prevalence of the endowment effect affords economists better material with which to understand and predict behavior. It allows them to develop alternative models to the rational choice model; these alternative models are more complex but may be more accurate. One such model is the "prospect theory" advocated by Kahneman and Tversky (2013). This theory emphasizes the various framing effects (including the endowment effect) that alter a subject's perception of what counts as a gain and loss and that ought to be factored into our predictions of people's choices in the market.

While many behavioral economists retain the preference satisfaction account of welfare, others use its approach to develop understandings of how income and purchasing power influences our subjective well-being (e.g., Layard, 2005). These understandings situate economists to make more accurate predictions about how people's behavior and market choices influence their happiness. There is a clear role for behavioral economics within the economics of happiness.

Conclusion

The choices people make lay at the foundation of economic analysis. While neoclassical economics interpret these choices through the lens of the rational choice model, behavioral economics more frequently interprets these choices through a psychological lens. The latter strategy invites critical reflection on the choices people make and opens up more space to examine the connection between the choices people make and their happiness. One thing we've learned through this strategy is that people's choices do not straightforwardly represent their preferences and that people's choices do not always track their subjective well-being. Even when people try to choose on the basis of what they think will make them happy, their choices are liable to be skewed by biases and inhibited by the challenges involved in making the predictions necessary to such choices.

The approach of behavioral economics shows significant promise for the economics of happiness. But the models built within behavioral economics will be necessarily fluid and subject to change in light of new research, something that limits the predictive power of those models. This calls to light a certain tension between the aspirations of psychology and economics, which the following reflection from Kahneman captures nicely:

> Much has happened in the conversation between economics and psychology over the last 25 years. The church of economics has admitted and even rewarded some scholars who would have been considered heretics in earlier periods, and conventional economic analysis is now being done with assumptions that are often much more psychologically plausible than was true in the past. However, the analytical methodology of economics is stable, and it will inevitably constrain the rapprochement between the disciplines. Whether or not psychologists find them odd and overly simple, the standard assumptions about the economic agent are in economic theory for a reason: they allow for tractable analysis. The constraint of tractability can be satisfied with somewhat more complex models, but the number of parameters that can be added is small. One consequence is that the models of behavioral economics cannot stray too far from the original set of assumptions. Another consequence is that theoretical innovations in behavioral economics may be destined to be noncumulative: when a new model is developed to account for an anomaly of the basic theory, the parameters that were modified in earlier models will often be restored to their original settings. Thus, it now appears likely that the gap between the views in the two disciplines has been permanently narrowed, but there are no immediate prospects of economics and psychology sharing a common theory of human behavior. (Kahneman, 2003, p. 166)

Kahneman raises important questions regarding the promise and nature of interdisciplinary research. We have seen throughout this book tensions between the theoretical and often normative aims of philosophy and the descriptive aims of psychology, aims that held back psychologists from thinking about happiness for a long time. If Kahneman is right, we also find a tension between the aims of economics and the aims of psychology. To obtain its greater aims, economics needs a model of human decision making and behavior. Yet the more this model is constrained by psychological realism, and so needs to be informed and revised as warranted by psychological research, the more complex and nuanced it will be. The more complex a model, and the more assumptions at work, the more difficult it becomes to use this model to develop stable predictions that can inform policy.

Chapter Summary

- Neoclassical economics embraces a rational choice model that sees agents as rational actors who choose to satisfy their preferences, thereby enabling us to read people's preferences from the choices that they make.
- The psychological field of behaviorism informs early economic models and maintains that scientific inquiry should focus on what it can observe, which is behavior, as opposed to the unobservable components, such as how one feels about one's choices. This leads to a stimulus/response analysis of human behavior that supports the economist's focus on consumer choices.
- Empirical data on the correlations between income and subjective well-being raise questions about whether or not income directly correlates with happiness.
- Relative income—that is, one's income as it is considered in relation to one's reference groups—may be more important than absolute income when it comes to subjective well-being.
- Research on the difficulties of affective forecasting suggests that people struggle to make accurate predictions about what will make them happy, which complicates the relationship between preference satisfaction and happiness.
- Behavioral economics departs from neoclassical economics in its focus on understanding the ways in which people make decisions, the variety of things that influence those decisions, and the mistakes they often make in their decisions.

End Notes

1 In a 2010 article, Easterlin (Easterlin, McVey, Switek, Sawangfa, & Zweig, 2010) finds the scope of the paradox to include 17 Latin American countries, 17 developed countries, 11 Eastern European countries transitioning from socialism to capitalism, and 9 less developed countries scattered across Asia, Latin America, and Africa, including some with quite low growth rates and some with the highest rates of economic growth ever observed.
2 We've seen discussion of these factors throughout this book but particularly in discussions of adaptive preferences (Chapter 10) and of measuring happiness (Chapter 12).
3 See in particular discussions of adaption in Chapter 6 and of immune neglect in Chapter 11.

References

Angner, E. (2016). *A course in behavioral economics* (2nd ed.). New York: Macmillan International Higher Education.

Benjamin, D. J., Heffetz, O., Kimball, M. S., & Rees-Jones, A. (2012). What do you think would make you happier? What do you think you would choose? *American Economic Review, 102*(5), 2083–2110. https://doi.org/10.1257/aer.102.5.2083

Bruni, L., & Porta, P. L. (2005). *Economics and happiness: Framing the analysis.* Oxford, UK: Oxford University Press.

Easterlin, R. A. (1974). Does economic growth improve the human lot? Some empirical evidence. In P. A. David and M. W. Reder (eds.) *Nations and Households in Economic Growth,* (pp. 89–95). Cambridge, MA: Academic Press.

Easterlin, R. A. (2004). *The reluctant economist: Perspectives on economics, economic history, and demography.* New York: Cambridge University Press.

Easterlin, R. A., McVey, L. A., Switek, M., Sawangfa, O., & Zweig, J. S. (2010). The happiness–income paradox revisited. *Proceedings of the National Academy of Sciences of the United States of America, 107*(52), 22463–22468.

Frey, B. S. (2008). *Happiness: A revolution in economics.* Cambridge, MA: MIT Press.

Gilbert, D. T. (2006). *Stumbling on happiness.* New York: Random House.

Gilbert, D. T., Pinel, E. C., Wilson, T. D., Blumberg, S. J., & Wheatley, T. P. (1998). Immune neglect: A source of durability bias in affective forecasting. *Journal of Personality and Social Psychology, 75,* 617–638.

Kahneman, D. (2003). A psychological perspective on economics. *American Economic Review, 93*(2), 162–168.

Kahneman, D., Knetsch, J. L., & Thaler, R. H. (1991). Anomalies: The endowment effect, loss aversion, and status quo bias. *Journal of Economic Perspectives, 5*(1), 193–206.

Kahneman, D., & Tversky, A. (2013). Choices, values, and frames. In W. T. Ziemba & L. C. Maclean (Eds.), *Handbook of the fundamentals of financial decision making: Part I* (pp. 269–278). Singapore: World Scientific.

Layard, R. (2005). *Happiness: Lessons from a new science.* London: Penguin UK.

Oswald, A. J. (1997). Happiness and economic performance. *The Economic Journal, 107*(445), 1815–1831. https://doi.org/10.1111/j.1468-0297.1997.tb00085.x

Sen, A. (1995). Rationality and social choice. *The American Economic Review, 85*(1), 1–24.

Stevenson, B., & Wolfers, J. (2008). *Economic growth and subjective well-being: Reassessing the Easterlin paradox* (Working Paper No. 14282). National Bureau of Economic Research.

Thaler, R. (1980). Toward a positive theory of consumer choice. *Journal of Economic Behavior & Organization, 1*(1), 39–60.

Wilson, T. D., & Gilbert, D. T. (2005). Affective forecasting: Knowing what to want. *Current Directions in Psychological Science, 14*(3), 131–134.

Suggested for Further Reading

On neoclassical economics:

Hicks, J. R. (1939). *Value and capital.* Oxford, UK: Clarendon.

North, D. C. (1989). Institutions and economic growth: An historical introduction. *World Development, 17*(9), 1319–1332.

Prychitko, D. L. (1998). *Why economists disagree: An introduction to the alternative schools of thought.* New York: SUNY Press.

Samuelson, P. (1947). *Foundations of economic analysis.* Cambridge, MA: Harvard University Press.

On behaviorism:

Edwards, J. (2016). Behaviorism and control in the history of economics and psychology. *History of Political Economy, 48*(suppl_1), 170–197.

Lewin, S. B. (1996). Economics and psychology: Lessons for our own day from the early twentieth century. *Journal of Economic Literature, 34*(3), 1293–1323.

Skinner, B. F. (2011). *About behaviorism.* New York: Vintage.

Watson, J. B. (1925). *Behaviorism.* New York: W. W. Norton.

On income and happiness:

Clark, A. E., Frijters, P., & Shields, M. A. (2008). Relative income, happiness, and utility: An explanation for the Easterlin paradox and other puzzles. *Journal of Economic Literature, 46*(1), 95–144. https://doi.org/10.2307/27646948

Easterlin, R. A. (1974). Does economic growth improve the human lot? Some empirical evidence. *Nations and Households in Economic Growth,* 89–95.

Easterlin, R. A., McVey, L. A., Switek, M., Sawangfa, O., & Zweig, J. S. (2010). The happiness–income paradox revisited. *Proceedings of the National Academy of Sciences of the United States of America, 107*(52), 22463–22468.

Stevenson, B., & Wolfers, J. (2008). *Economic growth and subjective well-being: Reassessing the Easterlin paradox* (Working Paper No. 14282). National Bureau of Economic Research.

On decision making:

Gilbert, D. T., Pinel, E. C., Wilson, T. D., Blumberg, S. J., & Wheatley, T. P. (1998). Immune neglect: A source of durability bias in affective forecasting. *Journal of Personality and Social Psychology, 75,* 617–638.

Kahneman, D., Knetsch, J. L., & Thaler, R. H. (1991). Anomalies: The endowment effect, loss aversion, and status quo bias. *Journal of Economic Perspectives, 5*(1), 193–206.

Kahneman, D., & Tversky, A. (2013). Choices, values, and frames. In *Handbook of the fundamentals of financial decision making: Part I* (pp. 269–278). Singapore: World Scientific.

Sen, A. (1995). Rationality and social choice. *The American Economic Review, 85*(1), 1–24.

Thaler, R. (1980). Toward a positive theory of consumer choice. *Journal of Economic Behavior & Organization, 1*(1), 39–60.

Wilson, T. D., & Gilbert, D. T. (2005). Affective forecasting: Knowing what to want. *Current Directions in Psychological Science, 14*(3), 131–134.

On behavioral economics:

Angner, E. (2012). *A course in behavioral economics.* New York: Macmillan International Higher Education.

Angner, E., & Loewenstein, G. (2007). Behavioral economics. *Handbook of the Philosophy of Science: Philosophy of Economics,* 641–690. (U. Mäki, ed.) Amsterdam: Elsevier Press.

Heukelm, F. (2014). *Behavioral economics: A history.* New York: Cambridge University Press.

Kahneman, D. (2003). A psychological perspective on economics. *American Economic Review, 93*(2), 162–168.

14

HAPPINESS AND PUBLIC POLICY

The aim of public policy is to develop strategies that when implemented improve the condition of society. Public policy takes as its focus the group—the "public"—and considers the collective impact particular regulations will have on that group. In making public policy, policy-makers must analyze the problems a given society faces and the degree to which these problems warrant funding priority and then consider specifically which laws or other regulatory practices will help to solve the problems.

Taking scarce resources as a given entails that economic development is often a focus of public policy, and this is especially the case within developing countries. But the rise of the welfare state illustrates a widespread recognition that the government's role goes beyond economic development and includes the welfare of its citizens. Public policies regulating health care and unemployment insurance are examples of policies aimed at improving the conditions of people's lives. Typically, welfare states have focused on improving the objective conditions of people's lives, but as we learn more about the nature and correlates of happiness, many theorists have begun to advocate for policies aimed specifically at improving the subjective conditions of people's lives.

Where happiness is embraced as an aim of public policy, it becomes pressing to understand and explore the impact new policies have on citizens' subjective well-being. Doing so is hard: Policy-makers will need to agree on a working conception of subjective well-being to use as a basis for evaluating the condition of society; they will need access to a reliable system of measurement to determine current levels of subjective well-being and to track changes in these levels; and they will need to justify prioritization of public funds for the promotion of subjective well-being.

We've covered many of these issues already; in this chapter, we limit our focus to thinking about how best to promote happiness through public policy. We'll begin by exploring a long-standing philosophical debate about whether or not protecting individual freedom is the best means to promote happiness. We'll then think through particular policies that have been highlighted as productive of happiness and conclude with analysis of Bhutan, a small country gaining attention for its promotion of the "Greatest National Happiness."

Before moving forward, a caveat is in order. The question of whether happiness *ought* to be the aim of public policy, and the degree of prioritization it warrants, is one whose answer depends on several considerations, including one's preferred political position and view of the role government should play in an individual's life. While recognizing the fundamental role of these political considerations, my discussion will try to be as neutral as possible with respect to these political views. We'll explore some of the theoretical arguments for thinking about whether individuals or policy-makers are best situated to make decisions about an individual's happiness, but I leave it open to the reader to evaluate the implications of these arguments from within their own political framework.

Classical Utilitarianism

We find early efforts to take happiness as the aim of public policy in the writings of classical utilitarians. As we saw in Chapter 1, in the late 18th century, British philosopher Jeremy Bentham defended the radical proposal of using happiness as the basis for public policy. Social reform was necessary, he argued, and the first step in social reform is to reflect on the degree to which current policies promote happiness.

As is distinctive to classical utilitarianism, Bentham defines happiness hedonically in terms of pleasure. He argues that because pleasure and pain serve as fundamental human motivations, it is clear that the promotion of pleasure and the avoidance of pain ought to serve as our aims. Moreover, because pleasure has intrinsic value, the most important goal is the promotion of pleasure in general and not merely the promotion of one's own pleasure. Bentham presents the principle of utility, which maintains that acts are right insofar as they promote the greatest happiness for the greatest number: It is "that principle which approves or disapproves of every action whatsoever, according to the tendency which it appears to have to augment or diminish the happiness of the party whose interest is in question" (Bentham, 1988, p. 12).

Bentham introduces the principle of utility to provide a clear standard from which we can gauge both our behavior and the laws of society. He believed that measuring happiness was possible, and he introduced a framework for gauging expected pleasure. His framework requires us to focus on the intensity, duration, and certainty of the expected pleasure as well as its fecundity (capacity to produce more pleasure) and its purity (the extent to which it is intermixed with pain).

Bentham maintains that we can use this framework as a tool for social reform. His work focused largely on the penal system; notably, Bentham delivers a utilitarian argument against capital punishment that emphasizes that its deterrent effect is less than life imprisonment and introduces his vision of a model prison, the "panopticon," which he took to offer the most efficient system of monitoring and regulating prison activity.

Writing shortly after Bentham, J. S. Mill (2002) develops further the utilitarian framework and explores critically the role it can play in larger discussions of public policy. His arguments regarding how the government can best promote happiness have had a long-standing influence on Western philosophical thought and serve as a foil for contemporary discussion.

Like Bentham, Mill believed that happiness (construed as pleasure and the reverse of pain) ought to serve as our aim; his greatest happiness principle preserves the central thrust of Bentham's principle of utility in taking promotion of happiness to be the criterion of an act's morality:

> The creed which accepts as the foundations of morals "utility" or the "greatest happiness principle" holds that actions are right in proportion as they tend to promote happiness; wrong as they tend to produce the reverse of happiness. By happiness is intended pleasure and the absence of pain; by unhappiness, pain and the privation of pleasure. (Mill, 2002, p. 7)

Mill situates utilitarianism as primarily a moral theory describing the importance of promoting happiness through our individual efforts and social relationships. But, he does think that happiness is a fundamental value resting at the heart of public policy. The catch is that he thinks the individual is best situated to pursue her own happiness; thus, public policies ought to promote the individual's autonomy to make her own happiness-promoting decisions.

This is the general line of argument found within his book *On Liberty* (Mill, 1989). He begins by noting the diversity that exists between individuals, which means that what makes one person happy very well may be different than what makes another person happy. Given this diversity, we shouldn't expect that we will be able to legislate specific policies that promote happiness. Rather, we should prioritize individual authority and the individual's capacity to choose for herself:

> With respect to his own feelings and circumstances, the most ordinary man or woman has means of knowledge immeasurably surpassing those that can be possessed by any one else. The interference of society to overrule his judgment and purposes in what only regards himself, must be grounded on general presumptions; which may be altogether wrong, and even if right, are as likely as not to be misapplied to individual cases. (Mill, 1989 p. 77)

In practice this means that individuals should be granted the greatest degree of freedom possible, limited only by a restriction against harming others. This idea has become known as the "harm principle": "the only purpose for which power can be rightfully exercised over any member of a civilised community, against his will, is to prevent harm to others" (Mill, 1989 p. 13).

Mill's arguments in defense of individual freedom have gained notoriety in the context of free speech, yet here we want to focus on the influence they have had with respect to the role of happiness in public policy. One consequence of Mill's argument is a widespread skepticism toward paternalism. Policies are paternalistic to the extent that they are developed by a third party (here, the government) and are justified by appeal to the subject's best interest. Paternalistic policies are seen to impose a conception of good on individuals insofar as they stipulate what is in a subject's best interest, and the manner in which they do so is by subverting the individual's capacity to determine what is in their best interest and placing these essential decisions in the hands of a third party.

If Mill is correct that individuals are best situated to make decisions about their happiness, then taking happiness into account as a matter of public policy entails what Mill advocated, which are policies that promote and preserve an individual's liberty and restrict the individual only in accordance with the harm principle. But if Mill is wrong about this, and individuals are not the best authorities over their own happiness, then he may be wrong to prioritize individual autonomy. This opens the door for public policies justified on paternalistic grounds.

It is clear that Mill's prioritization of individual liberty has guided much discourse and policy making within Western societies and in particular within the United States and its focus on "life, liberty, and the pursuit of happiness"; the default presumption in many approaches to public policy is to impose high stakes on what justifies infringing on individual liberty and to avoid paternalism as much as possible. Yet the advancement of research on happiness pokes holes in this position, suggesting that individuals may not be the best authorities on their own happiness. This tension between respecting individual authority and promoting that individual's happiness shapes much of the current debates regarding public policy and happiness.

Libertarian Paternalism

The position of "libertarian paternalism" advocates a form of paternalism modified in an effort to capture the spirit of Mill's defense of liberty while also addressing what seems to be a fundamental flaw in Mill's defense of liberty, which is his assumption that granting individuals freedom to pursue their own choices is the most reliable way to help them become happy. If this assumption is false, then this opens the door to justify paternalistic measures. Paternalism maintains that state interventions on behalf of an individual's welfare are justifiable on the grounds that those interventions best promote the individual's welfare. Typically, these interventions involve restrictions on that individual's freedoms. For example, laws requiring the use of seat belts are paternalistic in the sense that they restrict an individual's freedom (by virtue of requiring them to wear a seat belt) and are justified through appeal to that individual's welfare (long-term research showing lowered mortality rates among seat belt wearers). In contrast, laws requiring social distancing restrict an individual's freedom but are not paternalistic insofar as they are justified through appeal to public health.

In the context of the government, and public policy more broadly, paternalism can take many forms: Mandatory seat belt laws, the regulation of narcotics, laws permitting the forced hospitalization of someone in a mental health crisis, and so on. The greater the freedom restricted, the more controversial paternalistic measures become. It is a relatively minor infraction of one's freedom to have to put on a seat belt or a helmet but a much greater infraction on one's freedom to have that person institutionalized against her will. Most plausible forms of paternalism will reflect a delicate process of weighing the coercive aspects of particular policies against their expected impact on an individual's welfare.

All forms of paternalism presuppose that the governing body has some degree of authority over that individual's welfare, a presupposition some find problematic, especially when it is used to justify government interventions in the name of *happiness*: What grounds is there to think an external governing body is best situated to make decisions that will promote an individual's *subjective well-being*? The desire to respect an individual's authority over her subjective well-being is one we've seen repeatedly put forward by psychologists, for whom it is fundamentally important to be able to describe the state of subjective well-being in ways that accurately reflect that state. Psychologists, in short, don't want to be in the business of telling people whether or not they are happy. Yet, as Mill's argument makes clear, in the context of public policy, the importance of respecting an individual's authority over her subjective well-being is contingent on the degree to which doing so is the best way to promote her subjective well-being.

Thaler and Sunstein (2003, 2009) argue that research regarding an individual's capacity to make choices that advance her welfare grounds paternalistic interventions to help direct her choices and that any resistance to paternalism is fundamentally misguided. The first part of their argument criticizes the assumption that "almost all people, almost all of the time, make choices that are in their best interest or at the very least are better than the choices that would be made by someone else" (Thaler & Sunstein, 2009, p. 9). We've seen already a good amount of the research they have in mind here, which calls into question our decision-making skills and the plausibility of maintaining that our choices often/ always/even sometimes reflect preferences that make us better off.[1] One phenomenon we haven't focused on thus far, which plays a central role in Thaler and

Sunstein's argument, concerns how it is that people's decisions are affected by the way in which their various choices are presented. This is of particular interest to Thaler and Sunstein, for it suggests that interventions in choice architecture may be warranted to help individuals make better choices. There are several dimensions to this research and the phenomenon it uncovers.

First, significant research suggests that the *number* of options presented influences a person's very capacity to choose. Other things equal, people find it much easier to make choices when they have to choose from a narrow range of options; widen that range of options and most people find themselves overwhelmed and their capacity to choose impaired. Iyengar and Lepper describe this as the "choice overload hypothesis," which finds that "although the provision of extensive choices may sometimes still be seen as initially desirable, it may also prove unexpectedly demotivating in the end" (Iyengar & Lepper, 2000, p. 996).

For example, in one study, Iyengar and Lepper (2000) tracked purchases of jam made by shoppers following tasting opportunities. In the "limited choice" condition, shoppers were given the opportunity to taste from a range of 6 different flavors; in the "extensive choice" condition, shoppers were given the opportunity to taste 24 different flavors of jam. While 30% of the shoppers given limited choices proceeded to purchase a jar of jam, only 3% of those given extensive choices purchased jam. This significant difference seems explainable only by the difference in the number of choices offered: Having to choose between 24 flavors as opposed to having to choose between 6 flavors serves as an obstacle to choice.

We've all felt frozen in the face of too many choices. Barry Schwartz appeals to this phenomenon, which he describes in terms of the "paradox of choice," to make a larger point with echoes of libertarian paternalism. He argues that Western societies, in particular, tend to highlight the values of autonomy and freedom of choice, yet more choices have not made these groups happy. Freedom is an important aspect of self-respect and is conducive to happiness, he argues, but "increased choice among goods and services may contribute little or nothing to the kind of freedom that counts. Indeed, it may impair freedom by taking time and energy we'd be better off devoting to other matters" (Schwartz, 2009, p. 4). If anyone else has spent too much time in the cereal aisle staring down the options, this probably speaks to you. More choices often seem to weigh one down, taking up time and energy that might be better spent elsewhere.

Second, in addition to consideration of the impact of the *number* of options presented, *how* those options are presented affects what people choose. To take one of Thaler and Sunstein's favorite examples, consider how it is that food is presented within a cafeteria line. When the brownies are laid out before the fruit, more people will choose the brownie. This is an instance of well-known consumer dynamics: People tend to grab what first meets their eye. This is why the most expensive products are often placed at eye level in the store, for people are more likely to choose something at eye level without even noticing the less expensive options; these options tend to be strategically placed on the very bottom or top of the shelves.

Thaler and Sunstein argue that since the number and presentation of choices influences what a subject chooses, we might as well take control of this influence and arrange choices so that consumers make choices that are *better for them*. Any resistance to this suggestion, they think, rests on misconceptions about the nature of paternalism. People tend to see paternalistic measures as cut and dry such that the alternatives are either that we restrict people's freedoms in ways that harm their autonomy or that we don't, so that the individual can enjoy their freedom uncoerced. According to Thaler and Sunstein, this is a false dichotomy. Within most of society, there is no sense in which a person is left completely free to choose, even in the absence of "paternalistic measures." Our choice of cereal is coerced by its placement within the grocery store, our choice of whether to take public transportation is coerced by its availability, and so on.

Part of public policy involves structuring the opportunities that individuals have, and doing so is often unavoidable: "In many situations, some organization or agent *must* make a choice that will affect the behavior of some people" (Thaler & Sunstein, 2009, p. 10) "emphasis in original". Since the very structuring of these choices influences what people will choose, Thaler and Sunstein advocate that organizations take control of this influence and structure choices with an individual's well-being in mind rather than ignore their impact and allow that impact to become negative through their neglect.

Is this paternalistic? Yes. It involves a third party making decisions they think will benefit their subject(s). But is it an offensive form of paternalism? Thaler and Sunstein think no; it is simply a responsible reaction to the impact structuring choices has on an individual's choices. Where choice architecture is unavoidable, structuring choices with the subject's best interest in mind does not involve coercion and so isn't objectionable on these grounds:

> The choice of which order to present food items does not coerce anyone to do anything, yet one might prefer some orders to others on paternalistic grounds. Would many object to putting the fruit before the desserts at an elementary school cafeteria if the outcome were to increase the consumption ratio of apples to Twinkies? Is this question fundamentally different if the customers are adults? If no coercion is involved, we think that some types of paternalism should be acceptable to even the most ardent libertarian. (Thaler & Sunstein, 2003, p. 175)

Thaler and Sunstein describe this view as one of "libertarian paternalism." While seemingly an oxymoron to combine the libertarian's commitment to individual freedom with the paternalist's emphasis on the need to restrict that freedom,

Thaler and Sunstein argue that their approach preserves the best of both: It is paternalistic in that it justifies taking measures to influence the individual's choices yet libertarian in that it preserves the individual's freedom to choose.

Libertarian paternalism presents an alternative way of thinking about how to promote an individual's happiness; while the focus of Thaler and Sunstein's work is primarily on consumer choices and the potential role public policy has to influence those choices, their argument can be extended more broadly to thinking about how public policy might influence subjective well-being. If people are not the best authorities on their subjective well-being, then perhaps there is a need for public policy to help structure their options so that people are more apt to make choices that promote their happiness. And if there is this need, its existence may provide justifiable grounds for enacting such policies.

Promoting Happiness through Public Policy

Having discussed some of the fundamental philosophical concerns underlying the project of taking happiness to be a goal of public policy, let's now consider how public policy might realistically be used to promote happiness. In the context of public policy perhaps more so than other contexts, words like "well-being," "welfare," and "happiness" are often treated as equivalent. From the perspective of public policy, it makes sense to have a broader framework for understanding what makes a particular group of people's life go better. While rates of poverty may, strictly speaking, track objective conditions of welfare, we know that there are strong correlations between poverty and low subjective well-being. Policies aimed at lowering poverty rates plausibly promote both happiness and well-being. And this seems to be the case for many of the policy proposals discussed in this context. Rarely has a particular policy aimed directly at enhancing subjective well-being; rather it is more often the case that policies do so indirectly through enhancing the objective conditions of life.

For example, the United Nation releases an annual "World Happiness Report" ranking the happiest countries. It determines how happy a country is through analysis of six variables: Income, freedom, trust, healthy life expectancy, social support, and generosity. If you've worked your way through this book, you are in a position to see that these variables may not always be good indicators of subjective well-being and that whether or not a given variable is indicative of happiness depends a lot on what particular form of happiness we have in mind. But, in reality, these are complicated issues for policy-makers to have to decide; and there is still much important work that can be done without having to settle on a precise understanding of happiness and its connection to well-being.

Here, I'll consider several contexts in which policy measures have been advocated and justified by appeal to their impact on subjects' happiness. This is by no means an exhaustive examination but is meant to highlight some prominent dimensions of happiness-promoting policy.

Welfare Systems

The origin of the "welfare state" may be one of the clearest examples of policy-driven efforts to promote well-being. Welfare systems are government-sponsored programs dedicated to improving the "welfare" of its citizens, where "welfare" is broadly taken to include economic and social well-being. The traditional components of welfare systems include various forms of social insurance, public education, and state-sponsored health care systems, which offer individuals the opportunities and resources they need in order to live some kind of minimally good life.

While they are not always justified on these grounds, welfare systems are clearly important to subjective well-being. Recent research provides increasing evidence that welfare programs make direct contributions to subjective well-being. Easterlin (2013), for example, finds that citizens of nations with "ultra-welfare" systems display higher rates of life satisfaction in contrast with nations whose welfare systems are less generous.[2] Ultra-welfare states are grouped here according to their levels of unemployment benefits, sickness benefits, and pension benefits.

The impact of unemployment on subjective well-being is significant. Di Tella, MacCulloch, and Oswald (2001) find that at the macro level, nationwide increases in unemployment rates correlate with decreases in reported satisfaction rates and speculate that this results both from lower satisfaction rates by those unemployed and by increased fears of becoming unemployed by those who are currently employed. Clark (2010) cites data from the European Community Household Panel comparing satisfaction rates between the employed and the unemployed that shows that, on a 1–6 point scale, the average satisfaction rates of those employed are between 4 and 4.5, while the average satisfaction rates of the unemployed hover just below 2.5.

This data likely aligns with our intuitions about the impact of unemployment on happiness. It is clear that being unemployed can be a source of unhappiness, yet research shows that the degree to which it does so is influenced by many of the factors we've identified in previous chapters, such as adaptation and one's relative standing to others. The degree to which unemployment affects a person's happiness is also influenced by the social stigma attached to the unemployed within society. Nonetheless, policy measures intended to buffer the financial impact of unemployment are well justified by considerations of happiness, and to the extent that public policy can be used to decrease rates of unemployment, and to reduce the social stigma of those who face unemployment, they too promise to be well justified by appeal to their impact on citizens' happiness.

Beyond providing financial resources, an important aspect of welfare states is a commitment to promoting the health of their citizens. Specific policies run the gamut from ensuring the underemployed and those in poverty have access to health care to ensuring that all individuals have equal health care access. Here again we see an intuitive connection between health and happiness, which is supported by evidence that the more access to health care we have, the happier we will tend to be. Illness affects our functioning and capacity to obtain subjective well-being, and there is a clear correlation between health and subjective well-being, one that Graham finds to be one of the strongest correlations we see with respect to happiness:

> The studies consistently reveal a strong relationship between health and happiness (for example, reported well-being). Indeed, the relationship is more statistically robust than that between happiness and income. Good health is linked to higher happiness levels, and health shocks—such as serious diseases or permanent disabilities—have negative and often lasting effects on happiness. At the same time, a number of studies find that happier people are healthier. Causality seems to run in both directions, most likely because personality traits or other unobservable variables are linked to better health and higher happiness levels. (Graham, 2008, p. 73)

It is difficult to gauge the impact any particular health care system has on subjective well-being. There are a number of mitigating factors that complicate this assessment, such as the percentage of resources devoted to physical health versus mental health, the efficiency of various systems, accident rates within a nation, and so on (Kirkcaldy, Furnham, & Veenhoven, 2005). Nonetheless, Kirkcaldy et al. find that, at the most general level, "nations with more money to spend on health care overall clearly experienced superior physical and psychological well-being" (2005, p. 9).

Considerations of subjective well-being can be helpful in making specific policy decisions regarding health care resources. We see a model for how this might work in discussions of resource allocation. It has long been recognized that when making decisions about where to allocate health care resources, policy-makers ought to take into account the quality of life promised by particular procedures as opposed to focusing solely on the extent to which particular procedures extend life. One prominent way of doing so is through appeal to "quality adjusted life years" (QALY), where these are calculated by considering the anticipated value of years gained to the patient. A particular procedure may extend a patient's life by 20 years, but if she will able to be active for only 3 of those years and spend the majority of the rest hooked up to machines in bed, then it seems that the true benefit of the procedure is closer to 3 than to 20.

Putting the focus on QALY entails appropriating measures to gauge the quality of the expected gains in life years, and there are many ways to interpret the relevant sense of "quality." While this hasn't always been the case, many now advocate using subjective well-being as the framework to evaluate QALY. We determine the quality of life years by thinking about how happy those years will be for the patient. Dolan (2008), for example, defends a QALY approach wherein the quality is analyzed by individual assessments of her subjective well-being, and Veenhoven (2004) advocates focusing on "happiness life years"—a measure he thinks is applicable not only to health care policy but to public policy in general. The intuitive idea behind these proposals is straightforward: Try to devote resources in ways that will make people's lives not just longer but happier.

Health care resources and unemployment benefits provide two stark examples of the ways in which welfare states traditionally seek to promote an individual's welfare and areas in which direct appeal to subjective well-being can support the development of public policy and inform the nature of those policies.

Beyond Welfare States

While we've focused only on two components of welfare states, we can see how considerations of subjective well-being can be used to justify welfare programs, and we've seen some explanation of why nations with robust welfare systems consistently rank higher on measures of life satisfaction. Can happiness justify further policies, which go beyond that which is typically identified as part of a welfare state? Such policies are more complicated from a political perspective insofar as they lean more heavily toward paternalism than do traditionally conceived welfare systems. "Yet, if happiness is a primary consideration for a nation, instituting policies that promote it on the national level may make sense." We'll consider two recent proposals for policies that extend beyond the welfare state.

We've seen throughout this book that interpersonal relationships are highly correlated with subjective well-being.[3] Drawing on these lines of research, the psychologist Jonathan Haidt argues that given the significant contributions community and culture make to happiness, we ought to develop policies that promote them. People need to be a part of moral community that "shares norms and values in order to flourish" (Haidt, Patrick Seder, & Kesebir, 2008, p. S135), he argues, and within that community, the greatest increases to subjective well-being arise when one loses one's sense of self. Thus, Haidt et al. speculate that "the most effective moral communities (from a well-being perspective) are those that offer occasional experiences in which self-consciousness is greatly reduced and one feels merged with or part of something greater than the self" (Haidt et al., 2008, p. S136).

If Haidt is right, then policies that promote the development of community and culture, and experiences that encourage individuals to lose their sense of self and feel a greater sense of belongingness to their community, are justifiable on grounds that they promote happiness. Among the specific policies Haidt highlights are ones that promote local festivals and street dancing by building outdoor amphitheaters and policies that make it logistically easier to close off city streets so that members of the community can gather regularly.

Policies that influence an individual's preferences may also be justifiable by appeal to subjective well-being. The economist Richard Layard (2006) proposes this sort of policy in terms of "tastes." Given that it is easier to satisfy some preferences than others, we are better situated to become happy when we have simple preferences, which are easily satisfied. This point goes back to the ancient philosopher Epicurus, who, as we saw in Chapter 1, emphasizes importance of recognizing that our basic desires are such that they can be easily satisfied. Epicurus worried that the more we develop and pursue unnecessary desires, the less happy we will be, because their pursuit will be a source of anxiety.

Layard argues that since our preferences are inevitably affected by a number of external influences, policy measures ought to be taken to regulate many of these influences so that they help subjects form preferences that are most conducive to their subjective well-being. For example, Layard considers the impact of advertising on preference formation. He notes that advertisements "almost always make us feel we need more money than we should otherwise have felt we need"; because much advertising comes through television, "we find that watching TV makes a person feel poorer, and thus less happy" (Layard, 2006, p. C30). Layard concludes there is thus a role for policy measures intended to regulate advertising as a way to influence people's tastes and preferences away from the expensive things that detract from happiness and toward those things that are more attainable and more supportive of their happiness.

Layard's proposal rings of paternalism and, as he acknowledges, of moralism. But he maintains that some degree of moralism is unavoidable in the context of public policy. Echoing Thaler and Sunstein, he argues that the decisions policymakers make are already moralistic yet currently function to support individualism and threaten overall happiness and so ought to be reexamined.

Environmental Policies

A final area of public policy worth highlighting in the context of happiness regards climate change policies and the preservation of the environment more generally. Our subjective well-being depends on the ability to breathe clean air, to be able to stay within our communities without the ongoing fear of natural disasters, and to be able to exercise outdoors and pursue outdoor activities. Much research has been conducted to track the impact of environmental conditions on subjective well-being. Typically these studies are conducted at the macro level, in which comparisons are made between the environmental conditions of a nation and reported life satisfaction of that nation's citizens, with significant attention focusing on the impact of air pollution and natural hazards such as flooding. This research shows what we would expect, which is that poor environmental conditions predict lower levels of subjective well-being. Here, I'll touch on two central points that have emerged about the relationship between the environment and happiness.

The first is that climate change negatively affects people's well-being and that those in poor nations are less able to bear these effects. Richer nations are better able to support their citizens in the face of natural disasters, air pollution, and temperature extremes. For example, increasing temperature extremes affect subjective well-being, but less so when nations are able to provide resources to buffer their citizens against this impact (Zhang, Zhang, & Chen, 2017).

The second is that spending time in nature is itself highly conducive to subjective well-being. In an expansive study using experience sampling to gauge an individual's level of happiness on different days/times, MacKerron and Marouto (2013) find that people are happier when they are in natural environments than in urban environments. One factor explaining this effect may be the reduced noise within natural environments. Noise is widely known to affect subjective well-being, as it seems to be one of the factors of our daily lives that we can't adapt to.[4] Many advocate for including the degree of "noise nuisance" in our assessments of the environmental impact of industries such as air travel (e.g., Van Praag & Baarsma, 2005).

Within the context of environmental policies, happiness research presents a new framework from which to gauge the value of particular policies. For example, by understanding the degree to which air pollution affects subjective well-being, we can assess the value of efforts to curb air pollution in terms of this impact. This approach provides a way to quantify the amount of financial resources worth devoting to environmental policies in ways that offer a more robust understanding of their value than traditional economic valuation of those policies.

Bhutan: A Short Case Study

This chapter has explored the many ways in which happiness can be used to inform public policy and some of the important philosophical considerations at stake when happiness is used as such. By way of conclusion, let us consider the efforts one country has made to prioritize happiness as the central aim of its public policies.

Traditionally, the health of a country has been gauged by its gross domestic product, which is a measure of the values and goods produced within that country. In 2008, the prime minister of Bhutan, J. Y. Thinley, advocated for a turn toward embracing "gross national happiness" (GNH) to serve as the standard form by which to measure the country's health. In a speech to the United Nations, Thinley argues in favor of prioritizing GNH:

> Gross National Happiness is based on the belief that happiness is the single most important goal and purpose in life for every individual and that the end of development must be the promotion and enhancement of happiness. It must, therefore, we believe, be the responsibility of the State to create an enabling environment within which its citizens can pursue happiness. (quoted in Burns, 2011, p. 76)

Taking GNH to be the primary indicator of a nation's health involves seeing material development not as the end toward which we are striving but rather as one of many different *means* to advance happiness.

Within Bhutan, GNH is defined by four pillars:

- Sustainable and equitable socioeconomic development
- Environmental conservation
- Promotion of culture
- Good governance

Motivating each of these pillars are beliefs about what kinds of things will promote people's happiness and a commitment to allocating resources accordingly.

As reported by Burns (2011), within Bhutan the following policies have been made to support these pillars. Recognizing that healthy and educated people will be happy, GNH supports devoting over 30% of its budget to ensuring equitable and free access to education. Recognizing the impact overdevelopment has on the environment, and responding to incidents wherein the overdevelopment of areas surrounding Bhutan generated landslides that devastated neighboring villages, GNH mandates that 60% of total land be maintained under forest cover. Recognizing that materialistic values and cultures are associated with declines in happiness, GNH mandates the promotion and teaching of traditional values in schools. Recognizing that good governance promotes happiness of its citizens first and foremost, GNH mandates a government committed to democratic procedures.

It is difficult to assess the impact of these policies on the overall happiness of the Bhutanese. An analysis by Biswas-Diener et al. finds that the Bhutanese do tend to be happier than those within countries of similar geographical profiles and income levels but that their absolute levels of happiness tend to be moderately ranked (Biswas-Diener, Diener, & Lyubchik, 2015). Bhutan's approach to sustainable development in particular is one that many take as a model, and

Biswas-Diener et al. find that the Bhutanese enjoy higher levels of "environmental well-being" than any nation.

Conclusion

Promoting happiness can be an important aim of public policy, and there is much that public policies can do to promote the happiness of citizens. Policies that address climate change, that support health care, and that uphold other welfare programs can make dramatic improvements in the conditions of people's lives and are all justifiable by appeal to happiness. More controversial are policies that promote happiness by restricting one's freedoms, such as through the regulation of advertisement and the restriction of people's choices. The paternalistic nature of these policies stands in tension with Mill's arguments that the best way to promote individual happiness is by promoting individual freedom. Yet the more we learn about what does make people happy, the more we might think paternalistic measures are justifiable. The position of libertarian paternalism maintains that paternalistic measures are warranted to influence a person's choices and to encourage him to make choices that are more conducive to his happiness.

Chapter Summary

- Bentham provides a framework for how to evaluate laws based on their effectiveness in promoting the greatest happiness for the greatest number.
- J. S. Mill held that the best way for a government to promote happiness was by granting individuals as much freedom as possible to make their own decisions.
- Mill's prioritization of individual authority is challenged by contemporary psychological research on just how bad people are at making decisions that promote their happiness.
- Paternalism describes the practice of making decisions for an individual, on her behalf.
- Thaler and Sunstein defend a version of paternalism that strives to influence people to make choices conducive to their well-being while nonetheless preserving their freedom to choose. They call this "libertarian paternalism."
- Welfare states include programs designed to support and enhance the well-being of their citizens. These programs seem to also enhance their citizens' subjective well-being, and citizens of those with robust welfare systems report greater life satisfaction in comparison to those with less robust welfare systems.
- Considerations of happiness may justify measures such as public funding of community builders such as local festivals as well as the regulation of

advertising, designed to help influence people to develop preferences that are most conducive to happiness.

- Happiness research offers a new way to understand and justify the value of environmental policies designed to help mitigate the effects of climate change, reduce noise, and protect the natural world.
- Bhutan provides an interesting case study of a nation committed to the prioritization of happiness through its endorsement of gross national happiness.

End Notes

1 See especially Chapter 13.
2 Easterlin identifies Finland, Denmark, and Norway as "ultra-welfare" states.
3 See Chapter 9 in particular.
4 See Chapter 11.

References

Bentham, J. (1988). *An introduction to the principles of morals and legislation*. New York: Prometheus Books.

Biswas-Diener, R., Diener, E., & Lyubchik, N. (2015). Wellbeing in Bhutan. *International Journal of Wellbeing, 5*(2), 1–13.

Burns, G. W. (2011). Gross national happiness: A gift from Bhutan to the world. In R. Biswas-Diener (Ed.), *Positive psychology as social change* (pp. 73–87). Dordrecht: Springer Netherlands. https://doi.org/10.1007/978-90-481-9938-9_5

Clark, A. E. (2010). Work, jobs, and well-being across the millennium. In E. Deiner, D. Kahneman, and J. Helliwell (Eds.), *International Differences in Well-Being* (pp. 436–468). New York: Oxford University Press.

Di Tella, R., MacCulloch, R. J., & Oswald, A. J. (2001). Preferences over inflation and unemployment: Evidence from surveys of happiness. *The American Economic Review, 91*(1), 335–341.

Dolan, P. (2008). Developing methods that really do value the "Q" in the QALY. *Health Economics, Policy and Law, 3*(1), 69–77.

Easterlin, R. A. (2013). Happiness, growth, and public policy. *Economic Inquiry, 51*(1), 1–15.

Graham, C. (2008). Happiness and health: Lessons—and questions—for public policy. *Health Affairs, 27*(1), 72–87.

Haidt, J., Patrick Seder, J., & Kesebir, S. (2008). Hive psychology, happiness, and public policy. *The Journal of Legal Studies, 37*(S2), S133–S156.

Iyengar, S. S., & Lepper, M. R. (2000). When choice is demotivating: Can one desire too much of a good thing? *Journal of Personality and Social Psychology, 79*(6), 995–1006.

Kirkcaldy, B., Furnham, A., & Veenhoven, R. (2005). Health care and subjective well-being in nations. In A. Antoniou, C. Cooper (Eds.), *Research Companion to Organizational Health Psychology* (pp. 393–412). Cheltenham, UK: Edward Elgar Publishing Ltd.

Layard, R. (2006). Happiness and public policy: A challenge to the profession. *The Economic Journal, 116*(510), C24–C33.

MacKerron, G., & Mourato, S. (2013). Happiness is greater in natural environments. *Global Environmental Change, 23*(5), 992–1000.

Mill, J. S. (1989). *"On Liberty" and other writings* (Collini, S., Ed.). Cambridge: Cambridge University Press.

Mill, J. S. (2002). *Utilitarianism* (Sher, G., Ed.; 2nd ed.). Indianapolis, IN: Hackett Press.

Schwartz, B. (2009). *The paradox of choice: Why more is less, revised edition.* New York: HarperCollins.

Thaler, R. H., & Sunstein, C. R. (2003). Libertarian paternalism. *American Economic Review, 93*(2), 175–179.

Thaler, R. H., & Sunstein, C. R. (2009). *Nudge: Improving decisions about health, wealth, and happiness.* New York: Penguin.

Van Praag, B. M., & Baarsma, B. E. (2005). Using happiness surveys to value intangibles: The case of airport noise. *The Economic Journal, 115*(500), 224–246.

Veenhoven, R. R. (2004). "Happy life years: A measure of gross national happiness." In K. Ura & K. Galay (Eds.), *Gross national happiness and development* (pp. 287–318). Thimphu, Bhutan: The Centre for Bhutan Studies.

Zhang, X., Zhang, X., & Chen, X. (2017). Happiness in the air: How does a dirty sky affect mental health and subjective well-being? *Journal of Environmental Economics and Management, 85,* 81–94.

Suggested for Further Reading

For public policy and happiness:

Dolan, P., & White, M. P. (2007). How can measures of subjective well-being be used to inform public policy? *Perspectives on Psychological Science, 2*(1), 71–85.

Frey, B. S., & Stutzer, A. (2012). The use of happiness research for public policy. *Social Choice and Welfare, 38*(4), 659–674.

Haybron, D. M., & Tiberius, V. (2015). Well-being policy: What standard of well-being? *Journal of the American Philosophical Association, 1*(4), 712–733.

Layard, R. (2006). Happiness and public policy: A challenge to the profession. *The Economic Journal, 116*(510), C24–C33.

Nussbaum, M. C. (2012). Who is the happy warrior? Philosophy, happiness research, and public policy. *International Review of Economics, 59*(4), 335–361.

For utilitarianism as a framework for public policy:

Driver, Julia, "The History of Utilitarianism", *The Stanford Encyclopedia of Philosophy* (Winter 2014 Edition), Edward N. Zalta (ed.), URL = <https://plato.stanford.edu/archives/win2014/entries/utilitarianism-history/>.

Sen, A. (1979). Utilitarianism and welfarism. *The Journal of Philosophy, 76*(9), 463–489.

Veenhoven, R. (2004). Happiness as a public policy aim: The greatest happiness principle. *Positive Psychology in Practice,* 658–678.

For Mill's defense of liberty and individual authority:

Bogen, J., & Farrell, D. M. (1978). Freedom and happiness in Mill's defence of liberty. *The Philosophical Quarterly (1950–), 28*(113), 325–338.

Jacobson, D. (2000). Mill on liberty, speech, and the free society. *Philosophy & Public Affairs, 29*(3), 276–309.

Strasser, M. (1984). Mill and the utility of liberty. *The Philosophical Quarterly, 34*(134), 63–68.

For empirical challenges to individual authority:

Gilbert, D. T., & Ebert, J. E. (2002). Decisions and revisions: The affective forecasting of changeable outcomes. *Journal of Personality and Social Psychology, 82*(4), 503–514.

Kahneman, D. (2011). *Thinking, fast and slow.* New York: Macmillan.

Kahneman, D., & Tversky, A. (2013). Prospect theory: An analysis of decision under risk. In W. T. Ziemba and L. C. MacLean (Eds.), *Handbook of the fundamentals of financial decision making: Part I* (pp. 99–127). Hackensack, NJ: World Scientific.

Thaler, R. (1980). Toward a positive theory of consumer choice. *Journal of Economic Behavior & Organization, 1*(1), 39–60.

Wilson, T. D., & Gilbert, D. T. (2005). Affective forecasting: Knowing what to want. *Current Directions in Psychological Science, 14*(3), 131–134.

For libertarian paternalism:

Bovens, L. (2009). The ethics of nudge. In T. Grüne-Yanoff, S. O. Hansson (Eds.), *Preference change* (pp. 207–219). Dordrecht: Springer.

Hausman, D. M., & Welch, B. (2010). Debate: To nudge or not to nudge. *Journal of Political Philosophy, 18*(1), 123–136.

Sunstein, C. R. (2014). *Why nudge?: The politics of libertarian paternalism.* New Haven, CT: Yale University Press.

Thaler, R. H., & Sunstein, C. R. (2009). *Nudge: Improving decisions about health, wealth, and happiness.* New York: Penguin.

For health and happiness:

Borghesi, S., & Vercelli, A. (2012). Happiness and health: Two paradoxes. *Journal of Economic Surveys, 26*(2), 203–233.

Diener, E., & Chan, M. Y. (2011). Happy people live longer: Subjective well-being contributes to health and longevity. *Applied Psychology: Health and Well-Being, 3*(1), 1–43.

Graham, C. (2008). Happiness and health: Lessons—and questions—for public policy. *Health Affairs, 27*(1), 72–87.

Hausman, D. M. (2015). *Valuing health: Well-being, freedom, and suffering.* New York: Oxford University Press.

Kirkcaldy, B., Furnham, A., & Veenhoven, R. (2005). Health care and subjective well-being in nations. In C. Cooper and A. Antinou (Eds.), *Research Companion to Organizational Health Psychology,* (pp. 393–412). Cheltenham, UK: Edward Elgar Publishing.

For unemployment and happiness:

Clark, A. E., & Oswald, A. J. (1994). Unhappiness and unemployment. *The Economic Journal, 104*(424), 648–659.

Di Tella, R., MacCulloch, R. J., & Oswald, A. J. (2001). Preferences over inflation and unemployment: Evidence from surveys of happiness. *American Economic Review, 91*(1), 335–341.

Lucas, R. E., Clark, A. E., Georgellis, Y., & Diener, E. (2004). Unemployment alters the set point for life satisfaction. *Psychological Science, 15*(1), 8–13.

For climate change and happiness:

Luechinger, S. (2010). Life satisfaction and transboundary air pollution. *Economics Letters, 107*(1), 4–6.

Luechinger, S., & Raschky, P. A. (2009). Valuing flood disasters using the life satisfaction approach. *Journal of Public Economics, 93*(3–4), 620–633.

MacKerron, G., & Mourato, S. (2013). Happiness is greater in natural environments. *Global Environmental Change, 23*(5), 992–1000.

Welsch, H. (2006). Environment and happiness: Valuation of air pollution using life satisfaction data. *Ecological Economics, 58*(4), 801–813.

Zhang, X., Zhang, X., & Chen, X. (2017). Happiness in the air: How does a dirty sky affect mental health and subjective well-being? *Journal of Environmental Economics and Management, 85*, 81–94.

On gross national happiness:

Burns, G. W. (2011). Gross national happiness: A gift from Bhutan to the world. In R. Biswas-Diener (Ed.), *Positive psychology as social change* (pp. 73–87). Dordrecht: Springer Netherlands.

Di Tella, R., & MacCulloch, R. (2008). Gross national happiness as an answer to the Easterlin Paradox? *Journal of Development Economics, 86*(1), 22–42.

Veenhoven, R. R. (2004). "Happy life years: A measure of gross national happiness." In K. Ura & K. Galay (Eds.), *Gross national happiness and development* (pp. 287–318). Thimphu, Bhutan: The Centre for Bhutan Studies.

Conclusion

15

A BRIEF CONCLUSION

At the outset of this book, I suggested that while we all value happiness, most of us probably have a limited understanding of what happiness is. If you've made it through, I expect that by now you probably know a lot more about happiness.

On a theoretical level, we know that happiness is a subjective mental state and that theories of happiness seek to describe this mental state. While there is disagreement about how exactly to identify this mental state, we know that it likely involves feelings of pleasure and satisfaction. We've seen that pleasure may involve more than just sensations, and we've seen that while satisfying desires is important, when it comes to happiness an overall sense of life satisfaction may be more important. We know that how we think about happiness varies depending on whether we are thinking about it from a short-term ("feeling happy") or long-term ("being happy") perspective and that feelings of happiness may lack the depth we associate with being happy. We've also seen that while happiness depends on external circumstances, what might be most important is the mindset we take that informs our experience of those circumstances.

On a practical level, we know that there is much we can do to become happy and to help others become happy, although we also have learned that making dramatic changes to our overall happiness levels is difficult. We know that we should invest less in material possessions and more in relationships. We know that by training our minds to be more optimistic, and to care more about others, we can probably become happier. We know that it is possible to study happiness and that the more we can learn about the kinds of biases that inform self-report measures the better position we will be in to evaluate that research.

There's a lot more that I hope you've learned about happiness over the course of reading this book. But I wanted to conclude by raising one important question we have not addressed. This is the question of just how important happiness is and how much value we ought to grant it in our lives. We hit up against this question in our discussion of public policy, where the dynamics of resource allocation make it essential for governing bodies to decide just how much to invest in its citizens' happiness. As individuals, we are less pressed to priotize formally and certainly less pressed to appeal to good reasons for our priorities. Unfortunately, this leads many of us to go through life without ever thinking seriously and with rigor about what is important to us, what we will prioritize, and why.

How important is happiness? How do we gauge the importance of happiness in comparison to the other important things we care about, such as health, achievement, financial stability, and education? We've been assuming all along that happiness is an important prudential value, yet questions regarding the role happiness ought to play in our lives and the extent to which a good life prioritizes happiness are ones I won't attempt to answer here, for they are more properly the subject of well-being. I will encourage you to see this book as having given you important information that can structure your own reasoning about the good life. Coming to a better understanding of what happiness is, and of the many things it is correlated with, allows us to think more clearly about the role we are prepared to grant it within our own lives.

I write this conclusion while sheltering at home during the COVID-19 pandemic of 2020. Most day-to-day activities have been brought to a halt, and the economy is shut down. Every day during this period, people are choosing to prioritize their health and the health of others over *everything else*: Economic productivity, travel, education, sports, and so on. While this may be a forced choice for many, its effect is a blanket reestablishing of priorities. This runs the gamut from the small, wherein each of us must ask ourselves what really counts as essential, to the large, wherein we recognize that staying alive and healthy is more important than going to work, to church, or to the gym, and that we need to do this not just for ourselves but for others.

While we make these difficult choices, we are hearing more public discussion than ever before about the importance of happiness and the things we can do to choose happiness even while giving up so much else. We can stay connected to each other. We can take care of ourselves and our families, and we can be compassionate. We can choose to help those more vulnerable than ourselves. We can meditate, exercise, and be optimistic. We can have virtual dance parties and laugh. We can be grateful and express gratitude to those working for our benefit.

The key to all this is to make the choice to prioritize happiness and to work within our circumstances—whatever they might be—to find ways to do all these things. Dire situations can bring clarity to what counts and motivate us to pursue what counts. Yet we shouldn't wait for dire situations to strive for this kind of clarity or depend on them as sources of motivation. You have the tools to reflect on the importance of happiness, what is involved in happiness, and how you want to structure your life. Use them now. Use them repeatedly.

INDEX